HAPPY BIRTHDAY
JULY, 1984

Rick

Linda

Paul Todd

Lorrie D.

Carolyn Hull

Lisa Silbaugh

Jeanette Adams

Kathy Messick

James C. Ward Ward

Laura Ward

Marcia Fanzin

Donna Snyder

PHANTOM

A LEGEND IN ITS OWN TIME

Francis K. Mason

Motorbooks International
Publishers & Wholesalers Inc
Osceola, Wisconsin 54020, USA

Front endpaper *Evening view of US Navy F-4B-6-MCs of VF-74 aboard the carrier USS* Forrestal *in February 1962* (McDonnell Douglas, Neg No 7749)

Frontispiece *One of the last Phantoms built—a slatted F-4E* (McDonnell Douglas, Neg No 146-29, dated 27 September 1979).

Rear endpaper *The meaning of camouflage. A quartet of German RF-4Es of Aufklärungsgeschwader 52 merge with the landscape of the Rhineland* (McDonnell Douglas, Neg No 102905, dated March 1973).

First published in 1984

ISBN 0-85059-580-8

Sole distributors for the USA

Motorbooks International
Publishers & Wholesalers Inc
Osceola, Wisconsin 54020, USA

Printed in Great Britain.

Contents

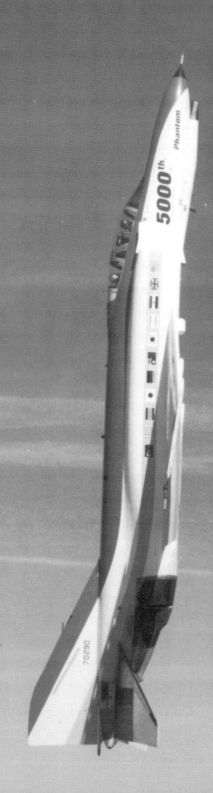

The 5,000th Phantom—see page 178 (McDonnell Douglas, Neg No 48-3, dated March 1978).

Introduction

In service with America's armed forces, accustomed to enjoying the fruits of world technological leadership, the McDonnell Phantom II fighter represented—for all its extraordinary angularity—an astonishing masterpiece of design ingenuity and commercial persistence. It moreover reversed the time-honoured, but hitherto apparently irreversible convention whereby naval air forces had had to rest content with deck-landing adaptations of aircraft primarily evolved for shore-based operation.

Designing the aircraft from the outset for shipboard use by the United States Navy, and beaten in early competitive evaluation by design tenders from elsewhere, the manufacturers persevered in the belief that they in fact possessed a potential world-beater, and succeeded in producing not only by far the most potent naval fighter in the world but one whose performance and punch came near to eclipsing the most sanguine *future* tactical requirements of the land-based United States Air Force.

That this phenomenon should occur during a period of relative peace in international affairs was also to some extent fortuitous, as previous experience had tended to support the theory that the greatest technological strides (and therefore those with least restraint placed upon them) came only to fruition during a state of war, or with the threat of such, and it enabled the United States Air Force to acquire a superlative and operationally flexible combat aeroplane in large numbers, at minimum realistic cost, in time to contribute a vital rôle in America's traumatic involvement in the Vietnam conflict.

The Phantom thus represented a watershed in naval aviation: it demonstrated in unequivocal manner that never again need the naval fighter be so compromised by deck-operating accoutrements that it would necessarily suffer at the mercy of land-based contemporaries. Graphic evidence of this has been demonstrated by the exploits of more recent naval aircraft such as the American F-14 Tomcat and the British Sea Harrier.

Acknowledgements

It is probably true that for nigh on twenty years the F-4 Phantom attracted more interest and attention the world over than any other contemporary military aeroplane, and it is therefore not surprising that it has been the subject of some previous works (of which I list a number in an Appendix for 'further reading'); yet I have detected instances wherein information has only fairly recently been made available, and have attempted to produce a narrative which I hope places this excellent aeroplane in a perspective better viewed with longer hindsight. I have obviously leaned heavily upon agencies and individuals in the United States, for which pride of place must go to McDonnell Douglas itself, for the company has made available a mass of material without which I could not have even started this book. I am aware that the Privacy Act in the United States precludes mention of all those who may wish their contributions to remain unaccredited; I am, however, particularly grateful to the following for their help and encouragement: Lieutenant Colonel Nick P. Apple, USAF, Air Force Office of Public Affairs, Arlington, Va; Commander Doyle J. Borchers II, USN, US Navy Fighter Squadron VF-1, US Navy; Lieutenant Andrew M. Bourland, USAF, HQ Tactical Training, US Air Force; Technical Sergeant Robert M. Burns, USAF, 23d Tactical Fighter Wing, US Air Force; Lieutenant-Colonel John H. Ditto, USMC, Marine Attack Squadron VMA-211, USMC; Lieutenant-Colonel Tod A. Eikenbery, USMC, Marine Attack Squadron VMA-231, USMC; Ensign M.T. Francis, USN, Navy Fighter Squadron VF-14, US Navy; Lieutenant R.C. Henty, USN, Navy Fighter Squadron VF-151, US Navy; Major-General John W. Huston, USAF, Office of Air Force History, Washington DC; Lieutenant Scott D. Inglis, USN, Navy Fighter Squadron VF-11, US Navy; Master Sergeant Robert A. Jarvis, USAF, 67th Tactical Reconnaissance Wing, US Air Force; Lee D. Livingston, Chief of Recognition Analysis Section, Randolph AFB, US Air Force; John D. McGrath, Director, External Relations, McDonnell Aircraft Company; Geoffrey Norris, McDonnell Douglas Corporation, European Operations; Lieutenant Rick Rogers, USN, Navy Fighter Squadron VF-161, US Navy; Lieutenant Michael S. Shelton, USN, Navy Fighter Squadron VF-1, US Navy; Richard Strecker, Navy Fighter Squadron VF-201, US Navy; Robert C. Sullivan, Historian, HQ Tactical Training, Luke AFB, US Air Force; Major Gerald R. Taff, USAF, 21st Tactical Fighter Wing, US Air Force; Ann Tilbury, Aviation Research, Woking, Surrey; Lieutenant Douglas C. Tippett, USMC, Marine Fighter Attack Squadron VMFA-451, US Marine Corps; Lieutenant Laura L. Tracy, USAF, 33d Tactical Fighter Wing, US Air Force; Richard Ward, Photo research, Canterbury, Kent; and Keith Wilson, Photo research, Baldock, Herts.

Chapter 1

Jets at sea

The background to naval aviation in the 1950s

The Korean War of 1950–3 proved to be a unique experience for the forces of the United Nations, involving as it did the very core of American military strength in a localised, as distinct from a world conflict. Only the ultimate resort to nuclear weapons was withheld. Moreover the very geography of the Korean peninsula imposed a unique character upon the war: bordered upon three sides by sea, the United Nations' territory was essentially regarded as an island, whereas that of North Korea—sustained throughout by neighbouring Communist China—was part of a continental land mass. And although the greater proportion of air operations over the front line was land-based, the peninsular nature of the long campaign, the dependence on over-sea supply routes and the extensive coastline emphasised the importance of UN maritime air superiority, the gaining and maintaining of which fell largely to the US Navy.

Despite efforts to evolve carrier-based jet aircraft by both American and British navies during the five years following the end of the Second World War, neither navy could claim to have travelled far beyond the first milestone of early squadron experience. Indeed only a small number of Sea Vampires with the British Fleet Air Arm had undertaken limited exercises at sea by mid-1950, and none was in the Far East.

The US Navy on the other hand had rapidly overhauled the British in the introduction of naval jet fighters, the first Navy Fighter Squadron, VF-5A (later VF-51) embarking in USS *Boxer* (CV-21, 36,380 tons) in March 1948 with the first North American FJ-1 Fury jet fighters. The design of this small 547 mph single-engine fighter had, in effect, represented an earlier stage in the development of the land-based XP-86 (to become the F-86 Sabre), and in view of the promise already being shown by the swept-wing prototype, the FJ-1's life was shortlived and VF-5A, though the first operational jet-equipped naval squadron at sea, remained the only FJ-1 squadron. Navy Fighter Squadron VF-17A, equipped with the McDonnell FD-1 (later re-designated FH-1) Phantom I fighters, completed carrier qualification with 16 aircraft aboard USS *Saipan* (CVL-48, 18,760 tons) in May 1948; with a top speed of only 479 mph the Phantom* was only built in small numbers and was to be quickly eclipsed by the next Navy jet, the Grumman F9F Panther.

Early design problems with the F9F provided all the evidence of American lag in jet engine development as it had originally been intended that this aeroplane would employ *four* of the diminutive 1,500 lb-thrust Westinghouse J30 turbojets, and when difficulties arose with the unwieldy installation of these engines in the wing roots the decision was taken to switch to a single, imported Rolls-Royce Nene turbojet, rated at 5,000 lb-thrust. In the event the early production version, the F9F-2 (of which 437 were built) was

Not, as will become clear, to be confused with the McDonnell F-4 Phantom II, the main subject of this book.

The US Navy's first Phantom, the McDonnell FH-1 of 1947–48; powered by two 1,600 lb-thrust Westinghouse J30 turbojets, it was the Navy's first operational jet to fly from a carrier (McDonnell Douglas, Neg No 8918, dated February 1948).

powered by the Pratt & Whitney J42 (a licence-built Nene), and it was this aircraft that first arrived off the Korean coast in June 1950 aboard USS *Valley Forge* (CV-45, 36,380 tons).

Though possessing an unswept wing and a performance (top speed 576 mph, Mach 0.75) substantially below that of the transonic North American F-86A, then entering service with USAF fighter-interceptor squadrons, the F9F Panther proved to be a well-liked aeroplane, rugged and hard-hitting as well as adaptable, and it was not long before a Panther pilot became the first in the US Navy to destroy an enemy jet, shooting down a MiG-15 on November 9 1950 over Korea. Later versions were powered by the American 6,250 lb-thrust Pratt & Whitney J48 engine and total production—which included camera-equipped reconnaissance versions—of the F9F-5 reached 655 aircraft.

It was now firmly believed that significant speed performance advances could only be achieved in aircraft using swept wings of substantially reduced thickness/chord ratio (although this facile belief was soon to be confused by the Mach 2 Lockheed F-104 Starfighter), and in this respect America had advanced far beyond Britain in the post-war years, particularly by the development of the F-86. The Supermarine Attacker, which joined the Fleet Air Arm in 1952 with an unswept wing, impressed everyone by its sheer mediocrity.

The US Navy on the other hand now introduced two swept-wing shipboard fighters, the Grumman F9F-6 Cougar (a continuation of the Panther design) and the North American FJ2/4 Fury (a direct development of the F-86 Sabre), and as these two aircraft dominated the naval scene for the next half-decade, a more detailed account of their design and operational concepts is necessary in order to understand the philosophies underlying the evolution of future requirements.

The Grumman F9F-6/8 Cougar

Development of the Cougar was a direct result of the worsening war situation in Korea, and was initiated by the letting of a study contract on March 2 1951 to produce three prototypes adapted from the current F9F-5 Panther production line. Only seven months elapsed before Grumman test pilot Fred Rowley flew the first prototype from Bethpage on September 20; early the next year production aircraft were already being evaluated at the Naval Air Test Center, Patuxent River, Maryland, and Cougars joined their first operational Navy squadron, VF-32, on the Atlantic coast before the end of 1952. They did not, however, reach combat service over Korea simply because the newly-introduced F-86E and F-86F had found the measure of enemy jets in the war theatre.

Being a relatively straightforward 'aerodynamic' development of the Panther, the Cougar introduced no radical change in combat tactic concept. Experience over Korea had been limited to gun-firing passes in fleeting periods of air combat, the criteria for success—as for generations past—being superior altitude, superior manoeuvrability, steadiness of gun platform and, above all, superior training and weapon aiming. So far as the F-86 was concerned most of the design criteria had been satisfied—after introduction of a slatted wing—although the F-86 always remained marginally slower than the MiG-15, and it soon became obvious that the 0.5-inch gun armament was far from adequate. The latter shortcoming had already been obviated in the US Navy whose Panther had included a battery of four 20 mm guns. The Cougar retained this armament together with the standard AN/APG 30 radar ranging gun sighting system and, in combat at firmly subsonic manoeuvring speeds, this proved no more than adequate at the time.

While the Cougar possessed a top speed of around 0.93 and was transonic in a shallow dive (a performance roughly the same as the RAF's land-based Hunter which entered service two years later), its range capabilities were outstanding, an important feature in a carrier-based fighter. Using only its internal fuel capacity of 919 US gallons (to which 300 gallons could be added in drop tanks) its normal range was 1,320 miles at 495 mph. A flight refuelling probe was soon introduced so that the Cougar's endurance came to be limited only by that of the pilot.

Perhaps not surprisingly, having regard to its origins of adaptation—particularly in the mating of a swept wing to an existing design—handling of the Cougar left a lot to be desired, stick force per g being too high, and directional stability and control very poor until introduction of a yaw damper. Stalling characteristics were also particularly bad, the accelerated stall being accompanied by a sharp pitch-up and instant wing drop. In due course a number of aerodynamic expedients—the well-practised remedies of the 1950s, wing fences, extended wing leading edges and lengthened wing root fillets—improved the handling of later F9F-6s, '-7s and '-8s, apart from reducing the effective thickness/chord ratio and hence marginally increasing the critical Mach number.

It was, however, in the obvious limitations of gun-only air combat that greatest thought was being given during the Korean War era. While argument still raged (as it had during the Second World War) between the proponents of 'lots of little guns spewing lots of little bullets' and those of fewer, bigger guns, it was soon seen to beg the question of bringing the gunsight to bear at all in the fleeting moments of high-speed combat, in which gun bearing visibility by pilot or radar would be measured in split seconds.

The North American FJ-2/4 Fury

After discontinuation of the straight-winged FJ-1, US Navy interest in a swept-wing naval development of the F-86 waned in the belief that the Sabre's high landing speed and poor low-speed handling precluded it from carrier operation and, although a small number of FJ-2s—which were in effect navalised, four 20 mm gunned F-86Es with arrester hook, catapult points and lengthened nosewheel leg—was ordered and completed, and first flown on February 14 1952, they were not deemed as suitable for carrier operation as the Cougar, even after introduction of a slatted and fenced wing, and most aircraft were delivered to the US Marine Corps.

To overcome such disagreeable phenomena in the FJ-2 as an abrupt roll-and-yaw immediately before stall, which occurred without feel warning, extended wing leading edges with small fences were flown on test aircraft and introduced to good effect in the FJ-3 which, with a 7,800 lb-thrust Wright J65 (British Sapphire engine built under licence), was first flown on July 3 1953 and entered production that year.

Whereas FJ-2s only equipped Marine Squadrons VMF-122, -232 and -312 of the US Atlantic Fleet, and VMF-235, -334 and -451 of the Pacific Fleet, the FJ-3 and sub-variants, of which 538 were completed, flew with VC-3, VA-172, VF-12, -33. -73, -84 and -173, VMF-122 and -334 of the Atlantic Fleet, and VF-21, -24, -51, -91, -121, -142, -143, - -154, -191 and -211, and VMF-235 of the Pacific Fleet. FJ-3s of VF-21 were the first combat-ready jet fighters to embark in the first of America's very large attack carriers, USS *Forrestal* (CVA-59, 75,900 tons), on January 4 1956.

Last of the Fury jet fighters was the FJ-4 with extensively redesigned structure to include increased wing area of reduced thickness/chord ratio, increased internal fuel and a Mach 0.88 maximum level speed. Numerous other alterations were progressively incorporated, not least of which were much enhanced store-carrying ability in the FJ-4B, whose service with the US Navy and Marine Corps was confined to Attack Squadrons VA-55, -56, -63, -116, -126, -146, -151, -192 and -212, and VMA-212, -214 and -223, all of the Pacific Fleet. 372 FJ-4s were built, bringing the total North American Fury production to 1,112 between 1952 and 1958, compared with 1,985 Cougars delivered by Grumman over much the same period (the last Cougar, an F9F-8T two-seat trainer was retired by Navy Training Squadron VT-4 in February 1974!)

The missile era opens

The earlier comments upon the difficulties experienced in high-speed gun-only combat during the Korean War serve to highlight what had become increasingly obvious in the course of normal combat training in more peaceful skies, and although the 'gun lobby' had persisted in advocating faster-firing guns (particularly in Britain where the excellent 30 mm Aden gun was introduced into service in the mid-1950s), an alternative form of semi-active air-to-air weapon, that is a weapon whose accuracy for kill no longer depended upon instant line-of-flight discharge and line-of-sight trajectory, was being studied.

The answer lay in a rocket-propelled missile which, once discharged, either flew or coasted along a radar beam towards its target or was guided there by a self-contained radar or infra-red heat-seeking system—the latter assuming the target to be a heat-discharging jet aeroplane. In Britain the early Fairey Fireflash was an example of the beam-riding missile, while the de Havilland Firestreak was infra-red seeking; the latter entered service in the late 1950s.

In America numerous companies had, since the mid-1940s, been pursuing similar ideas, and in 1949 work started at the US Naval Ordnance Test Station, China Lake, California, on what was, over the next 30 years, to become one of the most deadly efficient—yet simplest of all short-range air-to-air missiles, the Philco Sidewinder★.

The Sidewinder comprised a 6-inch diameter body containing an NPP solid-propellant

---

★*Originally termed the NOTS AAM-N-7 by the US Navy and GAR-7 by the USAF, the Sidewinder 1A was re-designated the AIM-9B by both Services, and the Sidewinder 1C the AIM-9C and D. For the sake of clarity the 'AIM' designation will be used throughout this book.*

Above *The prototype McDonnell XF2D-1 Banshee, production versions of which served as fighter-bombers in the Korean War of 1950–53* (McDonnell Douglas, Neg No 7094, dated May 1947).

Below *The McDonnell Banshee equipped with wing-tip tanks* (McDonnell Douglas, Neg No 13592, dated May 1949).

rocket, with a 10 lb high explosive warhead and a Philco infra-red homing head whose signals actuated cruciform control surfaces at the front of the missile; 21-inch span cruciform stabilisers were located at the rear. So simple was the guidance system that the missile contained no more than a couple of dozen moving parts.

Owing to early limitations in target acquisition and control manoeuvres the early Sidewinders' use was limited to a fairly narrow 'heat cone' behind the target aircraft. The firing procedure was also extremely simple, the pilot engaging in a stern attack and activating the missile heads; an audio signal in the pilot's headphones indicated acquisition and lock-on, and a missile would be fired when in range. The weapon had an active range of about two miles, its motor accelerating it to about Mach 2.5 before burnout.

The first test firing at Inyokern, China Lake, was carried out on September 3 1952, and the first fully-active, successful air launch on September 11 the following year. Within the next seven years no fewer than 40,000 missiles were to be delivered to the USAF, US Navy and Marine Corps, and 18 foreign air forces; indeed their baptism of fire was to be accomplished in service with the F-86 Sabres of the Chinese Nationalist Air Force against Chinese MiG-15s over the Formosa Straits during September 1958.

The Sidewinder entered the US Navy's inventory late in 1955 and first equipped an F9F-8 Cougar squadron in July 1956 when VA-146 joined the Atlantic Fleet with the missiles, followed a month later by similarly-armed FJ-3s with VF-111 aboard USS *Bon Homme Richard* (CV-31, later CVA-31, 36,380 tons) in the Pacific. Both Cougar and Fury were capable of mounting up to four Sidewinders—while retaining their close-range 20 mm guns.

Other US naval fighters of the 1950s

The Cougar and Fury constituted about 80 per cent of the jet fighters which served with the US Navy and Marine Corps during the period 1953–8. Having been developed exclusively from the post-war intermediate generation of sub-sonic fighters, their procurement in large numbers had been a relatively inexpensive expedient and tended to overshadow the introduction of progressively more sophisticated aircraft whose development was more closely integrated with developments in weaponry and air combat, while their cost inevitably limited the extent of production by comparison.

If the Cougar and Fury represented the culmination of the first generation of American jet naval fighters, the McDonnell F3H Demon, Douglas F4D Skyray and LTV F-8 Crusader presaged the second, with the Vought F7U-3M Cutlass providing a transient adaptation. Of these, two merit more than passing mention: the Demon on account of its obvious influence upon the later Phantom II, and the Crusader, whose design was officially preferred to that of a Demon development and was fairly farsighted and ingenious, even if its operational requirement was not.

Early trials with the North American FJ-1 Fury had enabled long term plans to be laid for the development of more advanced concepts, made possible by the modernisation programmes being undertaken in the *Essex* Class attack carriers; Programme 27A, initiated in 1948, involved the strengthening of the flight deck, removal of twin 5-inch guns to increase deck space, increasing the aviation fuel capacity and generally tidying up the deck environs; Programme 27C, started in 1951–2, was similar but also included the introduction of heavier duty arrester gear and steam catapults (a British invention), substituting a deck-edge elevator on the starboard quarter for the inboard No 3 elevator, and enclosing the forward hangar deck to allow increased operational capability in rough weather.

The McDonnell F3H Demon

First aircraft ordered specifically for operation from the modified *Essex* carrier was the McDonnell F3H, an entirely new design intended to use the Westinghouse J40 turbojet. The first of the two XF3H-1 prototypes flew on August 7 1951, and one year later the US Navy ordered 150 F3H-1 Demons, to be powered by the J40-WE-22. In the meantime however the Service requirement was changed to include a somewhat ill-defined 'limited all-weather general purpose' rôle, a change that was to increase the F3H's all-up weight from 22,000 to 29,000 lb, in turn resulting in a switch from the J40-WE-22 to -24 engine. The latter failed (by a wide margin) to achieve its intended thrust rating with the result that, after 56 F3H-1s had been completed with 7,200 lb-thrust -24 engines, production was halted and some of the newly-built aircraft grounded. A costly re-design was undertaken and re-appeared in June 1955 as the F3H-2 with the 9,500 lb-thrust Allison J71-A-2 with re-heat.

The 231 F3H-2s featured a fixed armament of four 20 mm Colt cannon and carried

Representing a vital link in the development of the later Phantom II, the McDonnell F3H-2M Demon remained in front-line service with the US Navy until 1965 (McDonnell Douglas, Neg No 71041, dated June 1956).

Hughes APG-51 radar, and were employed as strike aircraft with a variety of weapons and drop tanks carried under the wings. Two other limited all-weather fighter versions were delivered to the US Navy, the F3H-2M (95 built) armed with four Raytheon Sparrow III air-to-air missiles (see Chapter 2) and 125 F3H-2N with four Philco AIM-9C Sidewinder missiles.

Production of the F3H-2M and -2N ran out in November 1959 and the last F3H-2M (designated the F-3B Demon by then) disappeared from front line service in 1965, its place being taken by a more illustrious stablemate, the McDonnell F-4B.

There is no doubt but that the confusion surrounding the Demon, with its blurred requirements and constant revision of Service demands—not to mention the traumas invoked by the implications of a fundamental engine change—brought about a process of thought rationalisation in McDonnell during 1952–3. That is not to suggest that either the company or the Bureau of Aeronautics merited responsibility for the setbacks, simply that technical and military developments at this time were undergoing fundamental change at an unprecedented rate. And it was in a spirit of collaboration with the Service that the company itself embarked on rational study of the problems of military requirement definition in that atmosphere of change—with a view to formulating a design tender which itself might eventually come to be accepted as a definitive replacement for the Demon.

At all events, in spite of its functional compromise, the Demon provided the design basis at which McDonnell's future proposal could start.

The Vought F8U (F-8) Crusader

Combat experience over Korea, extrapolated with possible confrontation with the Soviet Union, resulted in the US Navy issuing a requirement for a supersonic air-superiority fighter in 1952. Emphasis was placed on high level-flight speed with dependence continuing primarily upon a built-in gun armament with strictly limited all-weather operational capability. No fewer than eight design proposals were tendered, including one by McDonnell for an initial design advance from the F3H Demon which, as just recorded, had been experiencing considerable difficulty with the Westinghouse J40 engine. It was, however, the Chance Vought (later Ling-Temco-Vought) design which was selected for further development in 1953, and this aircraft was flown in prototype form as the XF8U-1 (later XF-8A) on March 25 1955. Subsequently 1,217 production aircraft, named the F-8 Crusader, joined the US Navy with production stretching well into the 1960s.

Equating high performance with modest deck landing demands was ingeniously accomplished in the Crusader by incorporating a variable-incidence swept wing; by mechanically increasing the wing incidence relative to the fuselage datum the landing speed could be limited without the pilot being severely handicapped by exaggerated nose-up attitude. The transient nature of weapon philosophy at this time was demonstrated by the retention of a four 20 mm Colt gun armament, supplemented by a built-in battery of 32 2-inch air-to-air unguided, folding fin projectiles; provision was made to mount a pair of Sidewinders on the sides of the centre fuselage.

Although much later the F-8 underwent considerable re-engineering to allow four Sidewinders to be carried alternative to a 5,000-lb bomb load, the aircraft must be recognised more as the pinnacle of a past generation rather than heralding the new. It was after all conceived as a dedicated, single-engine air superiority fighter, with no more than limited all-weather interception capability, handicapped by pilot-only accommodation. And it must therefore be against this aircraft that the McDonnell F-4 Phantom II is measured to appreciate exactly what a dramatic advance it represented.

Chapter 2

Genesis

A new Phantom appears

The war in Korea had been over for about three months when McDonnell submitted its proposals for a new naval all-weather, general-purpose, long-range single-seat fighter to the US Navy Bureau of Aeronautics. No requirement for such an aircraft existed at the time and many of the aerodynamic implications broke entirely new ground, although the performance estimates produced at that time were not only relatively modest but highly speculative in their dependence upon a level of powerplant criteria not yet fully understood—in particular high efficiency intake design. This proposal was referred to in company records as the F3H-G/H, reflecting a progressive advance from the F3H Demon. Central theme of the new concept was, by proposing multi-rôle capability, that the new aircraft would be able to perform a number of tasks normally undertaken by different specialist aircraft embarked in a single carrier—for example, air interception,

Original mock-up of the AH-1, seen here in May 1954, showing the single-seat, flat-wing and tailplane configuration (McDonnell Douglas, Neg No 43697).

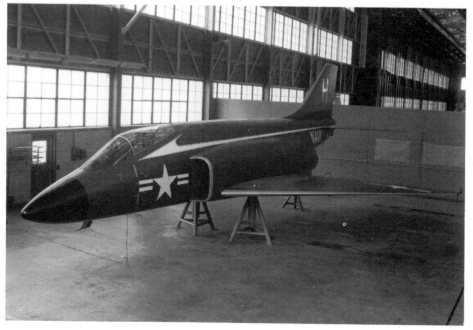

surface strike, electronic countermeasures and reconnaissance—thereby either reducing the number of aircraft required to be embarked in any carrier or, conversely, allowing an increase in the strength available on board to carry out dedicated tasks.

Mention should be made here of the various US Navy carriers in commission in 1953. The backbone of the American carrier force was provided by the 'attack carrier' (CVA) of which 24 had been completed since 1942; these 36,380-ton ships of the so-called *Essex* Class had 872–888 ft flight decks and had undergone modernisation at the time of the Korean War to be able to accommodate a reduced complement of early naval jet aircraft; their designed complement of 110 aircraft related to propeller-driven aircraft, a number substantially reduced by the operation of jet aircraft on account of long take-off run requirements and jet blast restrictions. Three other, much larger carriers, also classified as 'attack carriers' in 1952 were the 55,000-ton *Midway* Class ships whose deck length of 968 ft and three elevators were wholly adequate to operate a mixed complement of up to 137 aircraft. Under construction were four yet larger attack carriers, the 76,000-ton *Forrestal* Class ships with 1,039 ft flight decks, four elevators and a planned complement of up to 90 jet aircraft; it was this carrier class for which the F8U Crusader had been planned.

It may be seen that while the older and smaller carriers still constituted the bulk of the carrier force of the US Navy, the concept of a very high performance aircraft—with all its connotations of specialist equipment maintenance, large deck requirements and so on—was one which would demand considerable appraisal if worldwide flexibility of the Navy's fleets was to be sustained. The corollary of McDonnell's proposal was that by standardising with a multi-purpose high performance aircraft, maintenance complexity and spare part inventories would be *reduced*.

The multi-rôle capability of the F3H-G/H proposal was to be achieved by use of no fewer than seven interchangeable nose sections, each containing the specialised equipment and its associated cockpit controls and instrumentation. These configurations included:

1 Single-seat 'jet attack' with four 20 mm Colt guns, two external store mountings and provision to substitute 56 2-inch FFAR projectiles or in-flight refuelling probe for the guns.

2 Single-seat photographic reconnaissance with multi-camera and photo-flash equipment for day or night operation.

3 Single-seat electronic countermeasures with provision to detect, locate and eliminate hostile radio and radar by means of transmitters or chaff, or destruction by FFAR projectiles.

4 Two-seat conversion (without airframe profile change) for flight or electronic training, air strike co-ordination and electronic countermeasures during search and strike operations.

The concept of task module interchange was entirely new when proposed by McDonnell in 1953, yet the studies conducted by the company suggested that complete nose change could be accomplished by four men in no more than eight hours using the normal facilities available in a carrier at sea. Another innovation was the provision of no fewer than nine external store attachments, of which four were located under each wing and one on the aircraft's centreline.

To accomplish this multi-purpose high performance aircraft it was acknowledged from the outset that twin-engine configuration would be mandatory (whereas almost all previous high performance US Navy aircraft had featured single powerplant—only the McDonnell FH-1 and F2H, and Vought F7U Cutlass being twin-jet aircraft), and an

The revised mock-up of the F4H with provision for J79 engines and four Sparrow missiles; note the two-seat layout, but survival at this stage of the flat wing (McDonnell Douglas, Neg No 62637, dated December 1955).

alternative design tender, employing a single engine and known as the F3H-E2, was abandoned.

Thus to achieve the necessary compactness demanded by deck and elevator restrictions the resulting aircraft would certainly gross up at a very high weight, the initial figure of 45,000 lb being quoted by the design team. This compared with around 31,000 lb for the F-8 Crusader, F7U Cutlass and F3H Demon, and around 22,000 lb for the F9F Cougar and FJ-4 Fury. With maximum speed performance aimed at about Mach 1.5, McDonnell envisaged using a pair of afterburning 8,000 lb-thrust Wright J65 turbojets installed side-by-side in the centre fuselage, being fed by large lateral air intakes abaft the cockpit and exhausting under the tail.

For ten months, while the Navy Bureau of Aeronautics studied the implications of the G3H-G/H proposals, developments in aviation were taking place worldwide which were to have a profound effect on the shape of and attitude towards American air operational requirements. To begin with, it was known that the MiG-17 had achieved widespread service in the Soviet Union, probably outnumbering Western fighters of similar performance by as many as five to one. Intelligence was also filtering through to the West that a new twin-engine Soviet fighter (later identified as the MiG-19) had flown in September 1953 and that its performance was likely to be in the region of Mach 1.5. Such a rate of evolution was disturbing and certainly came as something of an unpleasant surprise to the military authorities in the West. It was immediately clear that the traditional technological processes in the Soviet Union—always suspected as being almost wholly dependent upon covert but wholly justifiable plagiarism of foreign achievements— had been largely superseded by a new-found independence of thought. Moreover the huge momentum in industrial output of military equipment, gained in the dark years of Soviet peril in the Second World War, had been sustained while that in the West had been allowed to decay in the interests of economic revival.

It was therefore with minds now tuned to a real threat of Soviet military superiority (and all that might presage in Europe, the Middle East and the Far East), rather than to total dependence upon the nuclear deterrent, that American strategic planning lengthened its outlook in 1955. This was the year in which the Boeing B-52 Stratofortress entered service with Strategic Air Command.

McDonnell, at the same time, not unaware of this significant shift in defence attitudes, kept its ear to the ground at the Bureau of Aeronautics and in the Office of the Chief of Naval Operations (CNO), as well as maintaining close liaison with Navy Operations Staffs, garnering information and balancing it to reflect the best design features in the company's new project. It was for instance aware that a new class of super carrier was being planned with revised and enlarged angled deck, as well as much higher capacity catapults—features that would tend to alleviate critical deck performance demands.

Early in 1954 a mock-up of the new project, now termed the AH-1, was completed at Saint Louis, and appeared as a long sleek single-seat aircraft with low-set swept wing with constant but small dihedral, and a sharply anhedralled single-piece tailplane. Armament provision was still for four 20 mm guns together with radar and associated fire control system; there were also now 11 store positions capable of mounting any weapon then in service with or scheduled for the US Navy.

Frequent inspections of the mock-up by members of the Bureau of Aeronautics continued throughout the year and on November 18 the company received a letter of intent from the Bureau initiating the construction of two prototypes. Almost immediately McDonnell was instructed to delete the gun armament altogether and concentrate armament studies on the inclusion of four Sparrow air-to-air missiles, these being semi-recessed into the undersides of the fuselage. And on December 14 the BuAer recommended replacing the Wright J65 engines by General Electric J79-GE-2 turbojets, then expected to deliver some 15,000 lb-thrust with re-heat. Almost overnight the US Navy had laid plans to acquire its first Mach 2 combat aircraft.

While still anxious to exploit the multi-rôle concept of the FH-1, the US Navy remained sceptical of its ability to excel in both the interception and strike rôles, particularly as these would be performed with the single-seat nose configuration. Indeed the whole system of nose interchangeability met with scepticism by the Operations Staffs who argued that the habitual and progressive updating of electronic equipment would impose a nightmare of plumbing and wiring interconnection during nose change. In answer to this it was pointed out that the introduction of system modules (with their proposed *in situ* circuitry testing equipment) would considerably reduce unserviceability. It was, however, argued that although alternative single- and two-seat nose configurations might not involve aero-dynamic complications, optimum location of equipment in a single-seat nose could well be compromised by two-seat constriction, a compromise that might be exacerbated in the interests of overall aircraft centre of gravity limitations. It was also stated that the provision of a second crew member, while mandatory in certain operational rôles—particularly in all-weather operation—need never be superfluous in any others, and in due course this seemingly nebulous hypothesis won the day. Accordingly the CNO decided on June 7 1955 simultaneously to abandon all thoughts of nose interchangeability and opt only for the two-seat configuration as standard, and to abstract the all-weather attack rôle from the task spectrum. (An entirely independent design competition was immediately initiated to select an aircraft for this rôle, resulting in the highly sophisticated North American General Purpose Attack Weapon, or NAGPAW, later to become the A-5 Vigilante.)

On June 23 McDonnell was instructed to go ahead with the two-seat, twin-J79 aircraft under the new designation XF4H-1, final confirmation of project definition being set out in a letter from CNO on July 19. Six weeks later a contract was let by the Bureau of Aeronautics to purchase an initial batch of five aircraft for Research, Development, Test and Evaluation (RDT&E).

The Raytheon (Sperry) AAM-N-6 Sparrow III

As already mentioned a decision had already been taken to arm the F4H with four Sparrow air-to-air missiles in preference to an in-built fixed gun armament. The weapon had originated as long ago as 1945 as the Sperry Gyroscope Company's 'Hot Shot' project for the Bureau of Aeronautics, had been test fired as the AAM-N-1 two years later, and first flown as the AAM-N-2 in 1951. By 1955 several thousand Sparrow Is had been issued to the US Navy, having been put into production by Sperry at the Naval Industrial Reserve Aircraft Factory at Bristol, Tennessee.

The Sparrow I was a beam-riding weapon which was stabilised immediately after launch by limited inertial elements. Much larger and heavier than the Sidewinder, with an overall length of 12 ft 6 in, a launch weight of 295 lb and a range of about five miles, the Sparrow I was strictly a first generation 'guided missile', and was taken out of production in 1956 by which time work was well advanced on what was effectively a completely new weapon, although designated the Sparrow III.

It was as the outcome of excellent test firing results by this missile that it was selected as the US Navy's standard long range air combat weapon in 1955 and the following year Raytheon, parent company of the semi-active radar homing head, negotiated to assume management of the Bristol plant, taking over from Sperry in 1957.

Marginally shorter (at 12 ft 0 in) than the Sparrow I, the Sparrow III (AAM-N-6) was powered by an Aerojet-General solid-propellant motor and achieved a burnout speed of between Mach 2.5 and 3.0 and a range of around seven miles. Launch weight was 350 lb and its 60 lb warhead gave it an extremely good near-miss lethality.

Capable of all-weather use (at medium and high altitude) and promising to be effective against approaching—though not head-on—targets, it was clearly dependent upon long-range target acquisition both by the carrier aircraft's radar and by its own radar head, a range which was well beyond the capabilities of the APQ-50 radar hitherto scheduled for McDonnell's F4H-1, and thus it was in 1956 that the Bureau of Aeronautics instructed the company to change to the Westinghouse APQ-72 air intercept and missile fire control radar and semi-automatic navigation equipment—itself still only in the development stage. While the six associated modules could be accommodated within the existing structural contours of the F4H-1, the 24-inch diameter scanner required relofting of the nose profile to match the enlarged radome, while still keeping the overall aircraft length—fixed by carrier deck/elevator parameters. As already stated, McDonnell proposed to mount the Sparrows semi-recessed into the underside of the fuselage rather than on underwing pylons; the missiles were to be ejected downwards by explosive charges, their rocket motors igniting roughly a half-second later.

The F4H-1 takes shape

At the time the wooden mock-ups had been produced in 1953 and 1954 no more than project design scheming had been attempted as any attempt to start detailed investigation would be effort wasted until some degree of agreement had been reached on the matter of powerplant, crew, armament and equipment parameters. The premature finalisation of the F3H was still fresh in McDonnell minds.

It was not until July 1955 that a detailed target specification for the aircraft, now

Above *The near-complete first prototype F4H-1 on its way to the paint shop in the Saint Louis plant* (McDonnell Douglas, Neg No 154639, dated April 1958).

Above right *Resplendent in pale grey and white paint scheme, the first F4H-1, 142259, in the final assembly shop prior to its first flight; in the background are numerous production F3H Demons and F-101 Voodoos* (McDonnell Douglas, Neg No 154800, dated April 1958).

defined as the F4H-1F fleet defense fighter, was prepared. Initial tunnel testing was confirming the benefits of angling down, first by 15 degrees and later by 23 degrees, the low-set tailplane to eliminate pitch-up—a phenomenon being widely encountered by many transonic and supersonic aircraft at that time. System rigs were being used to develop advanced boundary layer control by blowing hot air, bled from the engine compressors, along the leading edge flaps as well as ahead of the broad-chord trailing edge flaps.

The change to J79 engine imposed the greatest research effort. The much increased mass flow through the intakes demanded enlarged intakes and ducts as well as considerable accuracy in duct lofting which, to achieve exact consistency through production, was reproduced by chemically-milled skins attached to closely-spaced ribs, and included intake lips machined from the solid. To remove the boundary layer from the airflow entering the ducts, some 12,500 minute perforations were made in the splitter plate— itself distanced from the fuselage side by about 2 ins to avoid airflow distortion.

Further intake airflow control, matching throttle demands and airflow Mach number, was incorporated within the ducts. For maximum throttle setting, for instance at take-off when forward speed is low, large auxiliary doors were included in the bottom of the ducts, opened by rams and balanced against hydraulic springs, thereby being able to blow open if the throttle was closed rapidly or in the event of compressor stall at high indicated air speed.

The intakes themselves broke new ground, being variable to match engine demands and

the differing shock wave characteristics over a very large range of Mach numbers. Unfortunately full-scale supersonic duct-flow characteristics could not be reproduced under test conditions at this time and the intake ramp angle range was arbitrarily decided on as being between five and ten degrees.

Considerable development was undertaken of the aerodynamic surfaces, whose radical appearance always gave the impression of drastic, last-minute redesign to counter some unforeseen shortcoming in stability or control. Such was not the case and the final configuration was decided long before metal was cut. The most unusual feature was the marked dihedral (12 degrees) given to the outboard, folding wing sections to enhance stability; these outer sections were also of ten per cent greater chord, thus providing a 'dog-tooth' on the leading edge, designed to avoid pitch-up during flight manoeuvres; and the combined, single-piece 'slab' tailplane—henceforth referred to as the stabilator—was angled down so as to clear the turbulent wing wake at high angles of attack and to contribute a correcting moment for the rolling effect in yaw of the outer wings. The very large, low aspect ratio fin was fitted with a conventional rudder.

Lateral flight control was to be achieved by full power-assisted ailerons located inboard of the outer wing sections together with spoilers immediately ahead of them; these functioned in the normal sense except that the relevant spoiler extended upwards rather than the aileron. Thus to roll to the right, the right spoiler extended as the left aileron moved down, and *vice versa*. Approach speeds were reduced by delaying airflow separation over the drooping leading edge flaps and inboard trailing edge flaps by blowing hot air from the engine compressors over the surfaces to energise the local boundary layer.

The landing gear (of which the mainwheels retracted inwards into the wings and the nosewheel retracted aft into the fuselage directly below the front cockpit) was stressed for a load factor of 33,000 lb at a 22 ft/second rate of descent—substantially higher figures than ever before. Low profile, high pressure tyres were made possible by the US Navy's recently-strengthened flight decks.

The decision to adopt the two-seat configuration as standard resulted in the deletion of a 125-gallon fuel tank from this location (ie, the position now occupied by the rear crew member) and an increase in the capacity of the large external centreline fuel tank from 375 to 500 gallons. The accompanying movement aft of the aircraft centre of gravity was to some extent countered by the growing forward moment engendered by ever-increasing electronic equipment in the nose.

★   ★   ★

From the foregoing it can be seen that almost every aspect of the F4H-1 posed the risk of failure on account of so many radical features, the development and testing of which was bound to involve enormous financial investment. Accordingly the US Navy Bureau of Aeronautics decided on the prodigal step of seeking insurance against costly failure by the F4H-1 to meet its design and performance criteria by ordering, in 1956, an advanced development of the LTV F-8 Crusader for competitive evaluation of the respective prototypes.

Obviously such a 'competition' could never have been fully realistic as the F-8 was still a single-seat, single-jet fighter, but it was, however, thought possible in some quarters—particularly by LTV—that with significant changes in the original 'multi-rôle' concept, the inferred design compromise might well have placed it at a severe disadvantage. In due course the 'new' XF8U-3 Crusader III, though demonstrating a considerable improvement over the standard in-service version, also proved so innovatory as to suggest research and development funding on a par with that of the McDonnell aircraft, yet still retaining the apparently increasing anathema of single seat and single engine. More prosaically, however, it might be said that the existence of a potential competitor served to deprive McDonnell of a comfortable monopoly; though a costly expedient, it certainly ensured that the US Navy could expect to get the best aircraft available.

As the first prototype neared completion it became clear at once just what new ground was being covered by the new aircraft. Despite its size and weight it was obvious that it was the highest density operational aircraft ever produced for shipboard operation; it was also the first in which chemical milling was employed in structural components and the first with extensive integrated structure. Titanium, hitherto little used on account of a lack of experience in manufacturing techniques, was now in use in numerous structural components subject to high temperatures.

At last the prototype was completed and after ground running of the J79-GE-3 engines early in May, which served to confirm system functioning, these were replaced by flight-cleared J79-GE-2s, and on May 27, with McDonnell test pilot Robert C. Little at the controls, the first F4H-1, BuAer No *142259*, made its first flight from Lambert Field, Saint Louis, and went on to Edwards Air Force Base to continue its contractors' trials immediately afterwards.

Then it was required to undergo competitive evaluation against the first of five LTV F8U-3s to be produced, and it was as the result of its outstanding performance in these that, on December 17 1958, McDonnell received from the BuAer an initial contract for 23 development aircraft (including *142259* and *142260*, both of which had by then flown) and 24 production F4H-1 aircraft under FY 1959 fiscal funding.

The first prototype returned to Saint Louis in October 1958 at about the time the second aircraft made its maiden flight and together these two embarked on a comprehensive programme of flight trials to measure powerplant performance, investigate the behaviour of the engine intakes throughout the flight envelope and to confirm the design criteria of the various airframe systems.

Chapter 3

Research and records

The pressures to succeed

The year 1959 was one of unease for military strategists and politicians alike. It was also a crucial year for the McDonnell F4H-1 naval fighter, and as has been demonstrated so often in the past half-century international, indeed worldwide political trends have imposed pressures upon the military to modify or accelerate plans for the deployment of strength. Of course, whether such pressure has been justified can only be judged with hindsight as events unfold, and East-West relations since the end of the World War have been constantly soured by suspicion and intrigue on the largest possible scale.

While it is certainly true that no major armed conflict was in progress anywhere in the world in 1959, it is equally true that the 'Cold War' was approaching a nadir. The festering unrest in the Middle East had been exacerbated by the Suez Crisis which served to crystallise the fundamental allegiances (fostered by the supply of military equipment) to East and West and, by failure to recognise the wider implications of its failure to support Britain and France during the crisis, the United States—and in particular the US Navy—found itself shouldering a lone responsibility for peacekeeping in that theatre.

The first F4H-1, 142259, during taxying trials at Saint Louis on May 22 1958; Sparrow mock-ups are fitted but main landing gear fairings and D-doors have been removed (McDonnell Douglas, Neg No 156123).

Top *At the conclusion of the first flight Robert C. Little lands 142259 at Saint Louis on May 27 1958; note the reinstatement of the landing gear fairings* (McDonnell Douglas, Neg No 156626).

Above *Often described as a 'roll-out' picture, this photograph was in fact taken on June 5; confusion has arisen owing to the temporary removal of the landing gear fairings, although the D-doors remain in place* (via Richard Ward).

Below *Airborne during one of its early test flights in June 1958, Robert Little poses the F4H-1 '259 over the Mississippi River* (McDonnell Douglas, Neg No 1034).

Already the Soviet Union was adopting a politically (rather than an economically) motivated imperial stance—as was, to a lesser extent, the United States—as the widely-condemned European empires were dismantled, leaving behind economic vacuums and political unrest.

The global influence of the Soviet Union, sustained by a fast increasing maritime strength and proliferating worldwide influence, focused American attention on the traditional rôle of the US Navy in its two main tasks, those of ensuring free passage of shipping and of maintaining its ability to bring sufficient force to sustain peace in theatres in which its interests were threatened. To perform these tasks the US Navy comprised a number of fleets in which the large attack carrier was the principal fighting unit.

As already remarked, the United States was painfully conscious that the Soviet Union was now not only capable of outstanding advances in military technology but that, under Khrushchev in the mid-1950s, had accelerated the development and introduction of greatly improved military equipment. Already a big new naval programme—preliminarily based on large destroyers and ocean-going submarines—had been initiated, while in the air new aircraft, at least capable of matching American in-service equipment, were known to be in service or about to reach service status.

As long ago as 1956 a new supersonic aircraft, the E-66, had been displayed in public and this aircraft, now identified as the MiG-21, had entered service with squadrons of the Soviet Air Force early in 1958. (Later in 1959 an aircraft of this type was to establish a new World Absolute Speed Record of 1,484 mph.) The Mach 1.6 Sukhoi Su-7B—also identified in 1956—was on the point of entering operational service, while the Tu-22 strategic twin-jet supersonic bomber, of which American Intelligence was as yet only vaguely aware, was less than two years from service with the V-VS.

At the same time the process of introducing new American aircraft into service had not been without its troubles, shortcomings which are now asscribed to inadequate funding for research—despite the political motivation of the early 1950s; indeed it has also been suggested that the total research funding in aeronautics was in fact adequate but that in order to investigate too many avenues of advance the resources were spread too thinly for adequate progress in the mainstream. The so-called 'Century-series' of USAF fighters,

Second F4H-1, 142260, with high-visibility orange-red outer-wing panels, stabilator and fin (McDonnell Douglas, Neg No 1728, dated March 1959).

although theoretically far in advance of all other Western aircraft in the late 1950s, were accelerated through their development stages with the result that their introduction into service was erratic and dogged by limitations while remedies were hurriedly sought. And with the unwillingness by European nations, particularly Britain and France, to countenance appropriations for defence and military research adequate even to defend their own backyards, defence against the Soviet Union in Europe and the North Atlantic fell squarely upon the NATO Alliance—of which the United States was by far the most powerful component.

These were the influences at work in the wider sphere of military planning as the US Navy looked forward to the 1960s. Already its first three big carriers, the USS *Forrestal, Saratoga* and *Ranger,* were in commission, and the USS *Independence* was nearing completion, while two others, the USS *Kitty Hawk* and *Constellation* were well advanced. Moreover the first attack carrier with nuclear propulsion, USS *Enterprise,* had been laid down.

Although there was no reason to believe that the F4H-1 would not be capable of operating from the older, smaller *Essex* Class attack carrier, however, because of its size, ordnance and fuel capacities, maintenance and personnel requirements, it was the *Midway* and *Forrestal* Class on which sights were set for the aircraft's deployment some three years hence. In the meantime the McDonnell F3H-2 Demon, LTV F8U-2 Crusader and Grumman F9F-8 Cougar would constitute the US Navy's principal fighter equipment.

The first of the development batch of F4H-1s, BuAer No *143388,* was flown in December 1958, and was joined the following month by *'389.* These two aircraft remained for much of the next two years at Saint Louis, the former to develop flight systems and equipment, the latter to develop compatibility of the primary missile (Sparrow) system with the airframe. The third aircraft's first flight was delayed some months pending progress with the missile compatibility trials on *'389,* and was eventually assigned to Raytheon in June 1959 for preliminary missile firing tests. *'391* was flown in March and with ballast installed in place of much of the operational equipment was assigned to flight trials in preparation for the carrier suitability programme scheduled later that year.

The fifth development aircraft, *143392,* was in all respects prepared and equipped up to the initial standard of the preliminary production (Block 2b and 3c) aircraft. It first flew in May 1959 and underwent performance and specific fuel consumption measurement trials and handling in simulated deck conditions, before joining the first prototype in a number of flying demonstrations before senior US Navy officers and staffs.

The next batch of 11 development aircraft, F4H-1-MC-2 (Block 2b), *145307–145317,* all flew between June and December 1959. Most were fully equipped with Westinghouse APQ-72 fire control radar (with 24-inch diameter nose scanner), although for performance measurements a long nose boom was mounted on a metal nose fairing which replaced the radome. Aircraft *'307, '308, '310* and *'311* underwent engine development and performance trials under General Electric direction at Edwards Air Force Base early in 1960; *'313* and *'317* were employed on weapons trials with both Sparrow and Sidewinder missiles at the Navy Missile Centre; and *'314, '315* and *'316* were assigned for handling by US Navy pilots at Patuxent River.

A new feature had appeared on the Block 2b aircraft which was to create a characteristic drooped nose appearance; this was the new AAA-4 infra-red seeker whose radome was added directly below that of the APQ-72. However, acquisition range requirements stated by Raytheon now brought about enlargement of the main scanner dish diameter to 32 ins, necessitating relofting of the whole nose profile which, to avoid airflow separation

Top *Fourth development aircraft (sixth F4H-1 built), 143391, undergoing land catapult trials prior to the carrier suitability programme; note that the Sparrow missiles have their fins omitted to avoid damage from the catapult strop* (McDonnell Douglas, Neg No 186916, dated February 1960).

Above *Development F4H-1-MC-2, 145310, airborne from Saint Louis with a demonstration load of 24 531-lb Mk-82 GP bombs, but no Sparrow missiles* (McDonnell Douglas, Neg No 207632, dated April 1961).

forward of the engine intakes, resulted in slight angling-down of the nose forward of the front cockpit bulkhead frame—thereby further exaggerating the drooped nose. This change was incorporated in Block 3c (*146817–146821*) together with an alteration to the cockpit canopy profile; in the first 18 aircraft this profile had been flush with the upper line of the fuselage—considered essential for minimum supersonic drag. However, in the interests of visibility, access and space for the rear cockpit occupant the entire cockpit contour was raised and curved, a change that gave no appreciable drag rise nor airflow instability.

As each new stage in these early trials was successfully passed the company was coming to recognise the extraordinary stride forward being taken by its new aeroplane, and it was therefore appropriate that, as part of the celebrations to commemorate McDonnell Aircraft Company's 20th Anniversary, the occasion was chosen on July 3 1959 to bestow a name upon the F4H-1, and during a ceremony on the company's flight ramp at Saint Louis the name Phantom II was formally announced*.

It should be explained that two categories of trials with the Phantom were being conducted, the first under the aegis of the contractors (of which McDonnell was of course the prime party, but also included Raytheon, General Electric and Westinghouse, as well as others responsible for components, systems and equipment) to meet the requirements stipulated, the second by the US Navy in collaboration with the Bureau of Aeronautics. Allocation of development aircraft (all of which were the property of the US Government)

*The actual date of the company's incorporation was July 6 1939.

was the result of the manufacturers' forecast requirements as well as those of the Service test establishments. For instance McDonnell's Flight Test Division had originally stated that it would require the use of eight aircraft for a total of 35 months to accomplish all foreseeable tests prior to clearance up to fleet delivery. The US Navy settled for 12 aircraft over a period of 30 months. The remaining three aircraft in the original development order for 23 F4H-1s would be assigned as the need arose. During 1958 the two prototypes had flown a total of 187 hours in the course of 208 flights; in 1959 563 hours were flown by a total of 18 aircraft in 606 flights. Compared to normal Service utilisation these totals may appear very small in view of the urgency of the Phantom's future rôle, yet it should be remembered that considerable engineering effort is required during the trial stage between flights, correcting and modifying systems and equipment—all of which must be prepared by painstaking design before flight, and equally painstakingly analysed afterwards. The 1959 figures therefore represent only about three flights in every fortnight by each of the development aircraft, and an average flight duration of about 50 minutes. Added to the carefully orchestrated programme of trials and progressive evaluation by contractors and customer alike, there was also the necessary flight familiarisation by increasing numbers of pilots, each of whom was responsible for a particular area of investigation and evaluation.

The final batch of five development aircraft, F4H-1-MC-3 (Block 3c), *146817–146821*, joined the test programme in 1960, a year in which 1,044 flights were made, totalling 870 flying hours. However, as a result of preliminary work done with *'391*, the first important milestone had been reached in October 1959 when the Phantom was cleared for carrier suitability trials, and in February 1960 this aircraft started trials at sea aboard USS *Independence* (CVA-62), with catapult launches, arrested landings, procedural on-deck handling and elevator compatibility investigation. In May that year *'391* was joined by the first Block 3b aircraft, *'817*, in the carrier suitability programme, by which time the Phantom was declared ready for the crucial Board of Inspection and Survey (BIS) trials scheduled to begin at Patuxent River, Maryland, in July.

Left *One of the earliest Phantoms to wear US Navy unit markings was 143390 (a Block 1a aircraft) which flew with Navy Test Squadron VX-5 as XE-14; the tail stripe was green with white borders* (McDonnell Douglas, Neg No 5382, dated March 1961).

Above *A Block 3c aircraft, 146817, with enlarged radar and raised canopy, in flight with six Sparrow IIIs, two of them mounted on the inboard wing pylons; this armament was seldom used in service* (via Richard Ward).

The BIS trials

The purpose of the BIS trial programme is, as its title suggests, to evaluate the aircraft against progressive requirements issued to its manufacturers throughout the design and development stages. Experience has shown that few aircraft reach this stage that do not ultimately enter service with the US Navy, such is the tremendous cost of new aircraft procurement; implicit in this has been that most aircraft measure up fairly well to the requirements, perhaps falling marginally but acceptably short in some respects but averaging out as being acceptable overall.

Six Phantoms were assigned to the BIS trials: *'313, '314, '315* and *'316* from Block 2b, and *'818* and *'819* from Block 3c. Conducted under stringent conditions entirely by US Navy and Marine Corps pilots and crew members (including maintenance personnel), the trials lasted five months inclusive of all areas of evaluation. During those five months enthusiasm for the new fighter grew among the experienced Service personnel as one by one the multitude of targets were met and surpassed, so much so that on conclusion of the evaluation it was found that the cumulative percentage by which the Phantom had exceeded the stipulated criteria was some 75 per cent—a figure never previously approached.

The world records

Attempts to establish new world records (in speed, distance, climb, altitude and from point to point) are made for a number of purposes. National pride is often a byproduct but seldom the motivation. Occasionally inter-Service rivalry may play a part, but in the end authority must be sanctioned at a high administrative level, principally on account of the costs involved. It is at such a level that the true benefit of gaining records is balanced: propaganda value (technological, military and political) and financial return—after all there are few better sales gimmicks than possession of a clutch of world records. Against these attributes may have to be set security considerations, for it may be in a nation's better interests *not* to disclose an aircraft's ultimate capabilities.

It is difficult even now to assess the Soviet Union's true motives for setting up the Absolute Speed Record on October 31 1959 with the E-66 aircraft, unless it was a subtle exercise in deadpan sabre-rattling. After all the Soviets were particularly careful not to explain any relationship between the E-66 and the MiG-21, and certainly no Western observer was present at the event. Therefore with any thought of export sales excluded from the motivation it must be assumed that the record was captured (from an American Lockheed F-104A Starfighter) solely for national propaganda. Equally likely, its recapture by a USAF Convair F-106A only 15 days later was to reassure national pride in assumed American superiority.

Although the capture of numerous performance records by the Phantom spanned a period of 28 months from December 1959, it is convenient to describe the entire series here; however, it should be seen that the later records were established by production and in-service aircraft so that reference to them here is out of chronological sequence.

The proposal to establish new records with the Phantom was almost certainly motivated more by inter-Service rivalry than any other consideration—after all, America had regained the speed record, and certainly the manufacturers could not hope to export Phantoms for some years on the strength of performance records when no significant production order for the US Navy had yet been placed! It was simply that not since 1953 had a Navy fighter held the World Absolute Speed Record, and the new Phantom presented the Service with an excellent opportunity to re-establish its prestige.

It was, however, the World Absolute Altitude Record, then held by the Soviet Union's E-66 at 94,658 ft, which first attracted the Navy. This record, not to be confused with the *sustained* altitude record, is normally achieved by means of a zoom trajectory (or energy climb) in which the aircraft is not strictly lift-sustained but employs its surplus energy to follow a pull-up and weightless 'push-over' with speed falling off far below its normal point of stall.

After meticulous calculations to relate kinetic energy to engine performance and stick movement, it was decided to carry out 'Project Top Flight' on December 6 1959, during the last stage of the programme leading up to the carrier suitability trials. Flying solo in the first prototype F4H-1, *142259*, equipped with a sealed barograph, Commander Lawrence E. Flint, USN, took off from Edwards Air Force Base with reduced fuel load and climbed to 50,000 ft; at that height Flint opened the throttles to maximum power, accelerating to well over Mach 2.0 before pulling back on the stick to enter a ballistic zoom with the nose pointing almost vertically up. As the Phantom approached 70,000 ft the J79 engines flamed out in the near vacuum of the stratosphere, and as the airspeed thereafter quickly dwindled the pilot gradually eased forward on the control column until at the top of the weightless trajectory the true airspeed had fallen to around 45 knots. Then the nose dipped sharply and the aircraft simply fell out of the sky; carefully re-lighting the engines as he regained the troposphere, Flint landed after a flight of 40 minutes. When examined by the National Aeronautics Association observer, the barograph had recorded a maximum altitude attained of 98,557 ft.

A US Marine Corps pilot was the next to fly a Phantom on a record-breaking attempt, this time to establish a new 500 km closed circuit speed record. The regulations for this record make considerable demands on the pilot, particularly in the accuracy of flying the three sides of a triangle and in care taken not to lose height between the entry and exit of the course, for obviously this would disqualify the attempt. As no altitude is stipulated at which the record may be flown it was decided to fly a radar supervised course between 40,000 and 50,000 ft over the Mojave desert, using and jettisoning centreline and wing drop tanks before entering the measured course.

Top *Suitably inscribed 'Project Top Flight' for its Absolute Altitude Record attempt, the first F4H-1, 142259, is seen here with two forward Sparrow missiles fitted* (McDonnell Douglas, Neg No 203626).
Above *Another view of the Project Top Flight Phantom* (McDonnell Douglas, Neg No 2403).

On September 5 1960 Lieutenant-Colonel Thomas H. Miller, USMC, took off in an F4H-1 at Edwards with full centreline and wing drop tanks at an all-up weight of 49,500 lb, climbing to 38,000 ft without using afterburners. At this height, some 200 miles from the entry gate to the measured course, Miller dropped his wing tanks and turned towards the gate; at a distance of 150 miles he lit the afterburners to accelerate but, owing to overflying a populated area, was unable to drop the big centreline tank until he was only about 30 miles from the entry point. As it was he had only reached Mach 1.6 as he turned tightly into the first leg at 42,500 ft. By the time he was nearing the end of this leg his speed had built up to Mach 2.04 at 50,000 ft; turning on to the second leg was a precise balance between the tightest turn and the least drag and speed loss. At the second turn his speed was Mach 2.05 and his height 49,000 ft, and on the final leg he deliberately lost a further 3,000 ft as he accelerated to Mach 2.10, returning a net altitude increase of 4,000 ft and a time elapsed of 15 minutes 19.2 seconds—a record speed over the measured 500 km of 1,216.76 mph. Owing to the turn radii extending outside the actual corners of the course, Miller's true distance flown was 538 km, so his true speed was around 1,305 mph. His afterburners had remained lit throughout the measured course as well as the run-up acceleration, a total of 25 minutes 30 seconds—probably the longest 'wet' run by any Navy fighter to date.

An even more demanding record is the 100 km closed circuit. Once more no altitude is stipulated, as is no height loss; theoretically the course is set up as a 12-sided figure but with sides of around 9 km it would be impractical to attempt to fly individual legs in a Phantom. Instead the aircraft would be flown in a constant circular turn, accurately pulling constant g round the imaginary figure.

This time Commander J.F. Davis, USN, took off from Edwards on September 25 1960, adopting much the same climb technique as Miller, and levelling out at 46,000 ft before selecting full afterburners. Reaching a point tangential to the circular course, Davis rolled 70 degrees and pulled a 3 g turn to the left, turning through the full 360 degrees without loss of height. The turn was completed in 2 minutes 40.9 seconds, representing a mean

The Sageburner aircraft of VF-101 Detachment A, 145307, streaks low over Stallion Sight valley (McDonnell Douglas, Neg No 237096, dated August 1961).

speed of 1,390.24 mph over the statutory 100 km. Once again Davis had had to fly marginally outside the '12-sided' figure, but so accurately had he judged his turn that it was calculated that his actual distance covered was 104.9 km (and therefore the actual speed was 1,459 mph)—an astonishing speed for an aircraft pulling a sustained 3 g turn.

Transcontinental record flights have always held a fascination for the American people, linking as they do the 'new' West with the 'old' East. The year 1961 marked the 50th Anniversary of the foundation of US Navy aviation and it was decided to detach five F4H-1Fs (from production Blocks 4d and 5e) from VF-121, at that time working up to combat status at Miramar, California, to Ontario Field, Los Angeles, for an attempt on the West-East Transcontinental Speed Record.

Three crews were selected: Commander J.S. Lake, aircraft commander, Lieutenant E.A. Cowart, RIO*; Commander L.S. Lamoreaux, aircraft commander, Lieutenant T.J. Johnston, RIO, Lieutenant R.F. Gordon, aircraft commander, Lieutenant (jg) B.R. Young, RIO, and two others were to act as back-up crews. All five pilots took off from Ontario Field at intervals on May 24 1961 and climbed to 38,000 ft, setting course for New York and going into afterburner for a supersonic sprint at 50,000 ft for about 30 minutes. Each pilot then reduced to subsonic speed and descended to 35,000 ft to take on more fuel from North American AJ-1 Savage tankers over New Mexico. Between supersonic legs, two further refuelling rendezvous were made over Missouri and Ohio before the aircraft finally arrived over Floyd Bennett Field, New York. Commander Lake established a new record at 3 hours 5 minutes, but this was beaten in turn by Commander Lamoreaux in 2 hours 50 minutes and then by Lieutenant Gordon in 2 hours 48 minutes (the back-up aircraft not being required to complete the record flight). Gordon's achievement—which won for him and his RIO the coveted Bendix Trophy—represented a mean speed of 869 mph (estimated Mach 1.32) for the 2,445.9-mile flight.

If the transcontinental speed record was of particular significance for the American people, the Phantom still had to capture the Blue Riband of all flying records, the Absolute Speed Record over 3 km at low level (a maximum height of 100 m or 328 ft). Despite its traditional prestige (dating from an age before even supercharged piston engines) the record itself during the past 30 years has held little technical or operational significance owing to the enormous piloting and measuring difficulties, and the colossal stresses set up by turbulence close to the ground—not to mention the inconvenience of supersonic boom over a large area. In truth the record was already beginning to be considered as nearing the practical limit, having stood since October 29 1955 when Lieutenant-Colonel Frank K. Everest, USAF, flew a North American YF-100A Super Sabre at 755.15 mph (roughly Mach 0.98) over Salton Sea, California.

The practical difficulties of judging height at about or above the speed of sound—to the constant accompaniment of buffeting from thermals close to the ground—could not be alleviated to any significant extent by a radar altimeter, and of course terrain-following radar linked to the auto-pilot was still more than six years in the future.

Dubbed Project Sageburner the record attempt was to be made over a 3 km speed course set out over a desert valley at Stallion Sight which forms part of the huge White Sands Missile Range in New Mexico. The regulations laid down that at no time during the whole record flight was the aircraft permitted to exceed an altitude of 500 m (1,640 ft) thereby preventing it from gaining any significant dive advantage—and required it to fly two runs in each direction, thereby cancelling any possible wind advantage.

The aircraft (duly inscribed 'Sageburner') chosen for the flight was the first F4H-1-MC-2, *145307* (with flush canopy and infra-red seeker under the nose), then being used to work

Radar Intercept Officer.

Two views of Skyburner Phantom F4H-1F, 142260, *with centreline and wing drop tanks; Colonel Robinson's name is inscribed below the port canopy quarterlight* (McDonnell Douglas, Neg Nos 5430 and 7098, dated November 1961).

up Navy Squadron VF-101 (Detachment A) of the Atlantic Fleet, the pilot being Lieutenant Huntington Hardisty and his RIO Lieutenant Earl H. DeEsh, both USN.

Taking off from Holloman Air Force Base on August 28 1961, Hardisty made for a point some 60 miles south of the course with full afterburner, accelerating all the time before pulling round on to the heading of the measured section. The first run was flown on a northerly heading before turning to the right to start a wide circle to bring the aircraft back on a reciprocal course, after which the entire cycle was repeated to complete the four runs. Throughout the measured runs Hardisty was able to fly to such close tolerances that he remained between 125 and 175 ft above the desert sand. His mean speed was computed at 902.769 mph, or Mach 1.25 in the hot dry conditions prevailing. Such was the magnitude of his achievement that the record has remained intact for over 20 years.

In recognition of the obvious hazards attendant on these enormous speeds being attempted at the absolute limit of human judgement, the FAI had introduced new regulations governing absolute speed records at high altitude. However, although the measured course was increased to 15/25 km (9.5 and 15.5 miles) and the number of runs reduced to one in each direction, the altitude tolerance of 100 m remained in being. The record speed had been established by the British test pilot Peter Twiss at 1,132 mph in the Fairey Delta 2 research aircraft on March 10 1956, but significant improvements by other aircraft had been technically invalidated owing to infringements of the altitude tolerance*.

Once more it was the turn of the US Marine Corps to make a record attempt, this time named Project Skyburner, and the aircraft assigned to Lieutenant-Colonel Robert B. Robinson, USMC, was the second prototype F4H-1, *142260*; apart from the inclusion of water/alcohol injection into the intake ducts, the aircraft had remained unmodified since the final stages of the prototype's development trials of the J79 engines.

On November 22 1961 Robinson took off from Edwards in Skyburner loaded with centreline and wing drop tanks, climbing to 33,000 ft before selecting afterburners and accelerating to maximum speed, jettisoning the tanks (once again these could not be released at the optimum moment owing to populated areas below) and entering the lead-in 'window' at Mach 1.3 and 45,000 ft which positioned the aircraft for the measured course. As he entered the timed section the Machmeter read 2.45, increasing to 2.57 on exit. Cancelling afterburner, Robinson turned slightly left and flew about 100 miles before pulling round to the right and re-selecting afterburners for the run-up to the timed section again. Not handicapped by drop tanks this time, the Phantom entered the section at Mach 2.52 and finished at 2.62. Its mean speed over the two runs was 1,606.51 mph (Mach 2.59)—a new absolute record.

The final series of records captured by the Phantom were those of sustained altitude and of climb performance (time to height). These flights, under the name Project High Jump, were made in two series, using standard F4H-1-8-MC (redesignated F4B-8-MC) aircraft, among them Bu No *148423*, the climbs to 3,000, 6,000, 9,000, 12,000 and 15,000 m being flown from Brunswick Naval Air Station (NAS), Maine, and those to 20,000, 25,000 and 30,000 m from Point Mugu NAS, California.

As all times to altitude for record purposes are measured from a 'standing start' on the runway, the essence of the flight procedure is obviously to spend as little time on the ground as possible, thereafter to convert the aircraft's kinetic energy into potential energy (ie, altitude) by assuming the optimum climbing attitude as quickly as possible; to do so

---

* *Namely 1,207.6 mph by Major Adrian Drew, USAF, in an F-101A on December 12 1957, 1,404.09 mph by Captain Walter W. Irvin, USAF, in an F-104A on May 16 1958, 1,483.83 mph by Colonel Georgiy Mosolov V-VW in a Type E-66 on October 31 1959, and 1,525.95 mph by Major Joseph W. Rogers, USAF, in an F-106A on December 15 1959.*

the pilot must accelerate quickly and then pull the nose up at predetermined g so as to assume the optimum inverted trajectory into the climb. So powerful were the J79 engines, with full afterburners lit, that the Phantom's wheelbrakes were unable to hold the aircraft at rest without either the tyres being forced round their rims or the whole aircraft drifting forward on locked tyres; it was therefore necessary to start the timing from rest before the engines were opened up to full power—with a small penalty in time. To achieve maximum acceleration all take-offs were carried out without use of flaps.

The lesser altitude climbs were made first, Lieutenant-Commander John W. Young USN (some years afterwards to become famous as one of America's astronauts) taking off solo on February 21 1962 from Brunswick and reaching 3,000 m (9,843 ft) in 34.52 seconds from 'wheels rolling'. Because each altitude record demanded slightly different climb angles it was not sufficient to aim at a single high altitude and simply record the times to the intermediate heights, and each record was therefore undertaken on separate flights, each pilot being briefed on his individual climb profile. Later on the same day it was the turn of Commander David M. Longton, USN, to attack the 6,000 m (19,684 ft) record, and he returned a time of 48.78 seconds. On March 1 Lieutenant-Colonel William C. McGraw, USMC, made two flights, taking the record for 9,000 m (29,528 ft) at 61.62 seconds and for 12,000 m (39,370 ft) at 77.15 seconds. (As far as can be discovered this was the first time in history that two major performance records had ever been established by one man on two separate flights in a single day). Last of the Brunswick-based record flights was also flown on March 1, this time by Lieutenant-Commander Del W. Nordberg, USN, who reached 15,000 m (49,213 ft) in 114.54 seconds.

The technique adopted for the climbs to higher altitudes was completely different owing to the decay in kinetic energy generated in the initial acceleration; it thus was necessary to level out at an intermediate altitude to allow the aircraft to accelerate once more before pulling up into a new climb profile. On March 31 Lieutenant-Commander F. Taylor Brown, USN, took off from Point Mugu NAS to attack the 20,000 m (65,613 ft) record, returning a time of 178.5 seconds. The next record, once again flown by Lieutenant-Commander John W. Young, USN, was a time of 230.4 seconds to 25,000 m (82,017 ft), achieved on April 3.

The last time-to-height record was flown by Lieutenant-Commander Del W. Nordberg, USN—also making his second record flight—whose target of 30,000 m (98,420 ft) demanded a zoom climb and 'push-over' trajectory reminiscent of the Top Flight altitude record of December 6 1959. Nordberg passed the target height in 371.43 seconds, and at the top of his trajectory exceeded 100,000 ft.

One other record had fallen to a Phantom in the meantime when on December 5 1961 the sustained altitude record—which demanded that the aircraft flew a distance of 25 km without loss of height—was established by an F4H-1 which sustained a mean height of 66,443.6 ft for the required distance at a speed of Mach 2.2 (about 1,452 mph).

Not unnaturally most of the Phantom's records have been broken during the past 20 years. Their significance lay in the fact that so many records—reflecting various facets of performance—were established by a single type of aircraft, and a naval aircraft at that, by extraordinarily wide margins, and in some cases from research or prototype aircraft. Moreover no single type of aircraft ever succeeded in bettering all the Phantom's records.

Opposite *Dramatic photograph of the Project High Jump Phantom 149449 being flown by Lieutenant-Commander John W. Young, USN, on April 3 1962* (McDonnell Douglas, Neg No 8498).

Chapter 4

To sea

The Phantom joins the fleet

There can be no argument that the world records gained by the Phantom were in most respects superfluous. They had been achieved by line pilots of the US Navy and Marine Corps in aircraft representative of the operational versions now about to join line squadrons of the Atlantic and Pacific Fleets. However, nothing demonstrates an aircraft's flight envelope more convincingly to new pilots than world records broadcast to the world at large.

The first US Navy fighter squadron selected to receive the Phantom was VF-101 based at Miramar, California, its first F4H-1, *148256* from Block 4d, arriving on December 29 1960. Designated Pacific Fleet Fighter Replacement Training Squadron, VF-101 received about 24 similar aircraft during the following eight weeks and set about training an initial complement of some 46 pilots and RIOs, some of whom left later to join other squadrons scheduled to fly the Phantom. A number of VF-101 personnel (both air- and groundcrews) was assigned to Oceana NAS in June 1961 to provide the nucleus of a counterpart Atlantic Fleet Replacement Squadron, although new aircraft were not delivered until August.

Forming the Navy's Combat Readiness Air Wing (Replacement Air Group), VF-101 was joined by the second Squadron, VF-121, the former moving to Key West NAS (with tail codes AD) and the latter taking its place at Miramar NAS (with tail codes NJ).

Hitherto all Service flying training had been carried out using the F4H-1 powered by the J79-GE-2 (or -2a) rated at 10,350 lb-thrust military (dry) rating and 16,150 lb-thrust with afterburner. On March 25 1961 a new production version of the F4H-1 was flown at Lambert Field with J79-GE-8 engines rated at 10,900 lb-thrust dry rating and 17,000 lb-thrust with afterburner. To differentiate between the two Phantom versions it was now decided to designate all J79-2 (and -2a)-powered aircraft, ie, the 47 aircraft in Blocks 1a to 5e, as F4H-1Fs, and all -8 powered aircraft as F4H-1s.

The full-standard F4H-1 incorporated a flight refuelling probe, which retracted into a long compartment on the right of the cockpit, General Electric ASA-32 autopilot, Eclipse-Pioneer dead-reckoning navigation computer, AIResearch air data computer, Lear AJB-3 bombing system, Raytheon radio altimeter and ACF infra-red detector. To accommodate the requirements of the new engines, whose mass flow had increased from 165 lb/sec to 170 lb/sec, the intakes were slightly enlarged and their ramp geometry changed (10 degrees for the fixed ramp and 14 degrees for the variable ramp). Fuel capacity was standardised at 1,665 Imp gallons (2,000 US gallons) contained in six-bladder tanks in the fuselage and integral wing box tanks, to which a 500 Imp gallon (600 US gallon) centreline and two 308 Imp gallon (370 US gallon) underwing drop tanks could be added. This total of 2,781 Imp gallons (3,340 US gallons) bestowed a normal

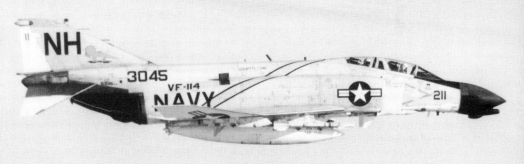

Top *Preparing to launch an F-4B-28-MC, 153915/NJ-113 of Navy Fighter Squadron VF-121* (McDonnell Douglas, Neg No 270-9, dated March 1967).

Above *An F-4B-27-MC, 153045/NH-211, of VF-114 flying from the USS* Kitty Hawk, *CVA-63, over the Gulf of Tonkin armed with the typical CAP mission mix of Sparrows and Sidewinders* (US Navy, Neg No 1130690, dated March 1968).

Below *153018/NH-205, an F-4B-26-MC of VF-114 assigned to Lieutenant-Commander Wayne Miller and Lieutenant George Stock; note the fin leading edge antenna which was introduced in Navy Phantoms early in the Vietnam conflict* (US Navy, Neg No 1130691, dated March 1968).

Above *First F4H-1 Block 11k aircraft, 149451, in the markings of the Pacific Missile Test Centre (pale blue strip across vertical tail), seen in storage at the Davis Monthan AFB in October 1978* (Starliner Aviation Press, Neg No CS555).

Above right *One of the first Marine Corps Phantoms was this Block 11k F4H-1 (almost immediately redesignated F-4B-11-MC), 149457/VW-1 of Marine Corps All-Weather Fighter Attack Squadron VMF(AW)-314 in flight over its base at El Toro, California* (US Marine Corps, Neg No A146370, dated December 1962).

Right *149453/VW-2 of VMF(AW)-314, like the aircraft above, an F-4B-11-MC* (McDonnell Aircraft, dated July 24 1962, via John W.R. Taylor).

ferry range of about 1,530 nautical miles. Initial external ordnance load was originally cleared up to 13,000 lb, but later increased to 16,000 lb.

The first operational Phantom Squadron to be activated with F4H-1s was Navy Fighter Squadron VF-74 of the Atlantic Fleet, and VF-114 of the Pacific Fleet, followed soon after by VF-102, also of the Atlantic Fleet.

As further squadrons were activated and re-equipped, VF-74 initially engaged in carrier qualification trials aboard the USS *Saratoga* (CVA-60), and in August 1962 became the first Phantom squadron to be operationally deployed at sea, joining USS *Forrestal* (CVA-59) alongside F-8 Crusaders for a commission in the Mediterranean. Within a few days VF-102 had embarked in USS *Enterprise* (CVAN-65) and joined the Fleet in the Mediterranean. In September that year VF-114 was embarked in USS *Kitty Hawk* (CVA-63) for a cruise in the Western Pacific. At that time it was normal practice in the US Navy for each Carrier Air Wing at sea to comprise two interceptor squadrons, the majority of such squadrons remaining being based ashore in the United States and 'rotated' in turn for commission at sea.

In June 1962 the F4H-1 started delivery to the US Marine Corps as an attack aircraft, Marine Corps Fighter Attack Squadron VMFA-314 receiving its first F4H-1s from Block 11k. This squadron was almost immediately re-classified an all-weather unit (VMF(AW)-314), and was followed by the Marine Attack Training Squadron VMFAT-122.

F-4B-28-MC, 153070/GD-9, of Navy Squadron VAQ-33 at Davis Monthan AFB in October 1978 (Starliner Aviation Press, Neg No CS569).

The change in American aircraft nomenclature

As will have been appreciated in the narrative thus far, the systems of designating American Service aircraft, although logical no doubt at the time they were conceived, had become so involved and confusing—particularly in the US Navy by 1962—that the decision was taken to adopt a uniform style of nomenclature for all Service aircraft, moving closer to that previously used by the USAF. However, whereas all US Navy and Marine Corps aircraft already in service were to be re-designated, only future aircraft of the USAF would conform to the new system. Reference to the aircraft's parent company in the basic designation would be omitted, and only included as a suffix when defining the aircraft's full production Block.

The production Block system (sometimes referred to as the Modification Block) remained as before, that usually employed by USAF aircraft differing slightly by definition and often between manufacturer and manufacturer.

Thus in September 1962 the so-called simplified nomenclature came into effect whereby all categories (by operational rôle) re-commenced at No 1, preceded by a basic rôle prefix, and followed by sub-variant number, and—in the full designation style—the Block number and letter(s) denoting the manufacturer.

The new nomenclature came into being shortly after the Phantom had been selected for use by the United States Air Force (see the following chapter) as the F-110, but this was now altered to become the F-4 for both US Navy and US Air Force. The F4H-1F (ie, the original 47 research and development Phantoms) were now re-designated—yet again—the F4A, and the F4H-1 became the F-4B. Generically the Phantom is usually referred to as the 'F-4', ie, the fourth fighter in the new designation system. Henceforth reference will only be made using the revised nomenclature.

Deployment of the navy Phantom continues

By the end of 1962 F-4Bs were deployed with three squadrons of the US Navy, namely VF-74, VF-102 and VF-114, as well as VMF(AW)-314 and VMFAT-122 of the US Marine Corps.

An F-4B-16-MC of VF-32 flying from USS John F. Kennedy *(CVA-67) in the Mediterranean launches a Beech HAST target drone* (US Navy, Neg No 1147255, dated December 9 1970).

At this time McDonnell was also at work developing the more sophisticated F-4J for the Navy (of which more in Chapter 7), but was required to bring forward an interim version; this, the F-4G*, was taken from the standard F-4B production line and equipped with an approach power compensation system, for use in a new automatic carrier landing mode, and the RCA AN/ASW-21 two-way digital data-link facility; both these features were standard in the F-4J. To accommodate the new system components, No 1 (front) fuselage fuel cell was reduced in size and a new racking compartment inserted between it and the rear cockpit.

No prototype F-4G as such was produced, although the first aircraft completed, and flown (BuAer No *150481*) on March 20 1963, was employed on prolonged trials to develop the Navy's data-link systems. Eleven further F-4Gs were completed from production Block 14n during the next three months and these were delivered to VF-96 at Miramar in mid-1963, this squadron being in effect a trials unit charged with working up the data link system.

VF-96, however, did not become operational with its F-4Gs and early in 1964 the aircraft were re-allocated to VF-121 pending re-assignment to VF-213 which was at that time running down with F-3C Demons. VF-213 had been notified that it would shortly be re-assigned to Carrier Air Wing 11 with F-4Gs and that its designation would be changed to VF-116 on September 1 1964.

The Phantoms duly arrived and were accordingly re-painted in VF-116 markings, but almost immediately the squadron re-designation was rescinded and VF-116 reverted to VF-213. Conversion and pre-deployment training were followed by transfer to USS *Kitty Hawk* (CVA-63) in October 1965 by the F-4Gs and two F-4Bs.

In 1966 some of the aircraft saw limited service in the Vietnam theatre, though none is thought to have been in combat, and in March five of them were given a camouflage paint scheme while disembarked at Clark Air Base in the Philippines as part of the US Navy's

---

* *Not to be confused with the US Air Force's F-4G 'Wild Weasel', which was to enter service nine years later.*

Above left *One of the 12 F-4Gs (previously F-4B-14-MC), 150642. This aircraft is shown landing aboard USS* Kitty Hawk *in the experimental Navy camouflage scheme applied at Clark AB in the Philippines* (McDonnell Douglas, Neg No 38097, dated July 1966).

Left and below left *Two views of early F-4Bs of VF-41. The upper photograph shows AG-102 and AG-105 each carrying 24 531-lb bombs; below is an F-4B-10-MC with centreline drop tank* (via Richard Ward, dated October 8 1962).

This page *F-4B-16 and -23 of VF-11 'The Red Rippers', flying from USS* Forrestal *(CVA-59) in the Atlantic* (US Navy, Neg Nos K 49472 and K51921, dated May 7 and June 24 1963).

1972 photographs of VF-11 F-4Bs (151469 and 153024) at Andrews NAS, Maryland; note the revised style of 'The Red Rippers' badge and extended air refuelling probes. Aircraft AA-111 also features the forward fin antenna (via Richard Ward, dated May 1972).

investigation of low visibility schemes. Another aircraft was damaged beyond repair while being re-embarked at Cubi Point.

USS *Kitty Hawk*'s Far East commission ended in June and the ten F-4Gs were delivered to the North Island and Cherry Point re-work facilities for conversion back to F-4B standard. (Six of them subsequently underwent further up-dating to F-4Ns under Project Bee Line, one became a QF-4N drone and three others were lost in accidents before the conversion programme started.)

Marine Corps reconnaissance

Committed to its tasks associated with support of amphibious and airborne assault, the US Marine Corps was tasked from the outset with strike and reconnaissance duties with its Phantoms, and it was for the latter that the McDonnell RF-4B (originally the F4H-1P under the old designation system) was developed.

Originally conceived in 1962 (largely as the result of USAF initiative for a reconnaissance version of the F-4C, described in the following chapter), the first RF-4B (BuAer No

Two F-4B-26-MC Phantoms of VF-51, disembarked from the carrier USS Coral Sea. *When previously assigned to VF-144 the aircraft shown in the upper photograph had destroyed a MiG-17 over Vietnam in April 1967. The tail feathers of the stylised eagle marking on the lower aircraft were painted in the element colours of Air Wing Fifteen (CVW-15)* (via Dr René J. Francillon).

151975) made its maiden flight on March 12 1965. Like the standard F-4B it was powered by J79-GE-8 engines and retained the Navy's 30 × 7.7-inch mainwheels. The nose was lengthened to accommodate a much enhanced array of sensors and other electronics, including APQ-99 forward-looking radar, APQ-102 sideways-looking radar, AAS-18 infra-red detector, ASN-56 inertial navigation system, ARC-105 HF transceiver (fitted in the rear fuselage) and LA-313A optical viewfinder; an HF shunt aerial was incorporated in the tailfin.

Not being given an air combat capability, the RF-4B had no missile control system, and flying controls were omitted from the rear cockpit. For night reconnaissance missions photo-flash ejectors were fitted in either side of the rear fuselage and—unlike the USAF's RF-4C—the RF-4B retained the in-flight refuelling probe on the starboard side of the front fuselage. Film-reconnaissance cameras included a forward-oblique unit and side-oblique components in rotatable mounts in the forward fuselage.

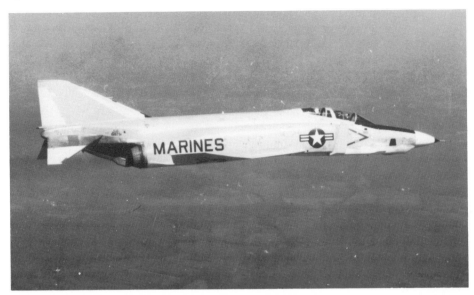

Above *A pre-delivery photograph of the first production RF-4B-20, 151975, for the US Marine Corps* (via Richard Ward, dated March 12 1965).

Below *Third production RF-4B-20, 151977/TN-26, of Marine Reconnaissance Squadron VMCJ-3; the fin marking is a green arrow head* (McDonnell Douglas, Neg No 31326, dated October 1965).

Opposite page *Two views of RF-4B-25, 153098/TN-8, of VMCJ-3 at Andrews NAS on March 27 1971* (Top, Dr Joseph G. Handelman, and bottom, Dr René J. Francillon).

Top *An F-4B-26-MC, 153019/NL-201 of VF-111 at Miramar NAS in 1970 with fin-tip antenna; this aircraft, flown by Lieutenant Garry Weigand and Bill Freckleton, shot down a MiG-17 over Vietnam on March 6 1972* (Duane A. Kasulka).

Above *F-4B-13-MC, 150472/NL-206 of VF-111* (via Dr René J. Francillon).

Below *Weatherbeaten F-4B-12-MC, 150412/DC-16, of Marine Corps Fighter Attack Squadron VMFA-122* (via Richard Ward).

Rocket launcher-equipped F-4B-24-MC, 152327/DW-3 of VMFA-251 at Beaufort MCAS, South Carolina, in May 1970 (James T. Brady via Roland P. Gill).

Only 46 RF-4Bs were produced, in three batches of nine, 27 and ten aircraft respectively, and these were in fact the longest-serving of all Phantoms, some remaining in service with the Marines until the early 1980s. The first deliveries were made to Marine composite-reconnaissance squadron VMCJ-3 at El Toro MCAS, California, in May 1965, followed by VMCJ-1 at Iwakuni and VMCJ-2 at Cherry Point.

Towards the end of the 1970s all surviving RF-4Bs (ten had been lost in accidents between 1966 and 1975) underwent a programme of updating to extend their lives in service under a major SLEP (Service Life Extension Programme). Known as Project Sure (Sensor Update Refurbishment Effort), this involved the addition of Honeywell AN/AAD-5 infra-red linescan sensors, substitution of the APQ-102 by AN/APD-10 sideways-looking radar, and the ASN-56 by AN/ASN-92 carrier-borne inertial navigation system, and inclusion of the AN/ASW-25 automatic carrier landing system. First of the re-worked RF-4Bs was completed at North Island in 1977, and the last in 1981, each conversion being carried out at a unit cost of around $4.5 m.

In the mid-1970s, when the Navy's and Marine Corps' reconnaissance and ECM facilities were audited for maximum effort-effectiveness, all RF-4Bs were re-assigned to a single Marine Corps fighter-reconnaissance squadron, VMFP-3, at El Toro, this squadron providing temporary detachments overseas when required.

*   *   *

In due course and prior to introduction into service of the Navy's F-4J (see Chapter 7), the F-4B eventually equipped Navy Fighter Squadrons VF-11, -14, -22L1 (Naval Air Reserve), -32, -41, -51, -92, -96, -102, -111, -114, -121, -161 and -213, as well as the Fleet Replacement Aviation Maintenance Personnel (FRAMP) division of VF-121; with the Marine Corps it served with VMFA-314, -323 and -542, VMFAT-101 and VMF(AW)-314.

Above *F-4B-17-MC of VMFA-312 with air refuelling probe extended* (via Richard Ward).

Below *Line-up of VMFA-312's F-4Bs at Beaufort MCAS in May 1970* (James T. Brady via Roland P. Gill).

Above right *Also seen at Beaufort in May 1970 was this F-4J-31-MC of VMFA-333,* 153848/DN-16 (James T. Brady).

Right *F-4J-37 and -41 of Marine Fighter Attack Training Squadron VMFAT-101* (McDonnell Douglas, Neg No 117784, dated November 1977).

Phantoms of Navy Test and Evaluation Squadron VX-4

Above *Phantom F-4B-14-MC/ XF-3, without fin-tip antenna and with white fuselage walkway, launches from a carrier (McDonnell Douglas, Neg No 44172, dated March 20 1967).* **Below** *The same aircraft, with fin-tip antenna and mid-grey walkway, in flight over Point Mugu NAS, California (US Navy, Neg No KN19050, dated May 14 1970).* **Left** *F-4B-14-MC, 150492/XF-2, with additional dorsal antenna and rocket launcher. Both 150487 and*

150492 *had previously served with the US Navy as F-4Gs* (via Richard Ward). **Above** *Spectacular overall black scheme featured by F-4J-29-MC/XF-1 which retained the medium blue fuselage and wing tip flashes with white stars but sported a white rabbit motif on the fin* (via Richard Ward). **Right** *Side-winder-equipped F-4J-34-MC, 155570/XF-8 in standard VX-4 colour scheme* (via Richard Ward). **Below** *F-4J-29-MC, 153783, re-assigned as XF-9 with rabbit motif replaced by unit codes, seen at Moffett Field NAS, California, in October 1969* (via Richard Ward).

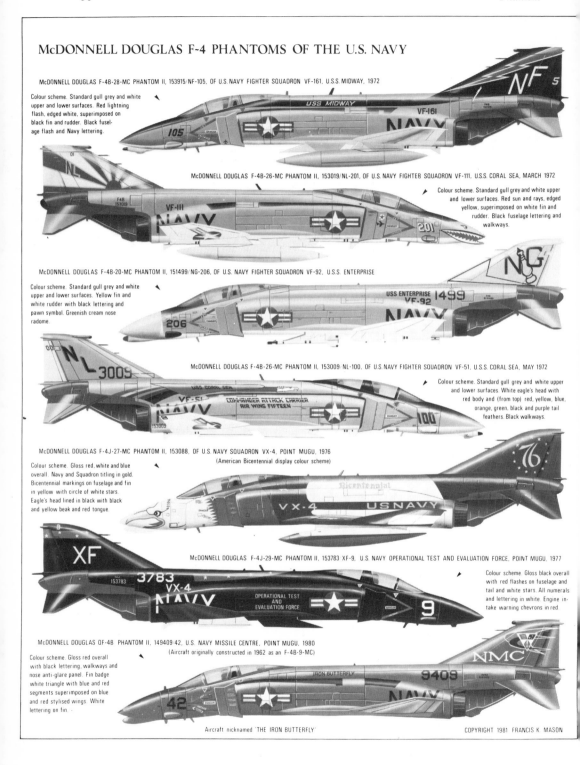

McDONNELL DOUGLAS F-4 PHANTOMS OF THE U.S. NAVY

McDONNELL DOUGLAS F-4B-28-MC PHANTOM II, 153915/NF-105, OF U.S.NAVY FIGHTER SQUADRON VF-161, U.S.S. MIDWAY, 1972

Colour scheme. Standard gull grey and white upper and lower surfaces. Red lightning flash, edged white, superimposed on black fin and rudder. Black fuselage flash and Navy lettering.

McDONNELL DOUGLAS F-4B-26-MC PHANTOM II, 153019/NL-201, OF U.S.NAVY FIGHTER SQUADRON VF-111, U.S.S. CORAL SEA, MARCH 1972

Colour scheme. Standard gull grey and white upper and lower surfaces. Red sun and rays, edged yellow, superimposed on white fin and rudder. Black fuselage lettering and walkways.

McDONNELL DOUGLAS F-4B-20-MC PHANTOM II, 151499/NG-206, OF U.S. NAVY FIGHTER SQUADRON VF-92, U.S.S. ENTERPRISE

Colour scheme. Standard gull grey and white upper and lower surfaces. Yellow fin and white rudder with black lettering and pawn symbol. Greenish cream nose radome.

McDONNELL DOUGLAS F-4B-26-MC PHANTOM II, 153009/NL-100, OF U.S.NAVY FIGHTER SQUADRON VF-51, U.S.S. CORAL SEA, MAY 1972

Colour scheme. Standard gull grey and white upper and lower surfaces. White eagle's head with red body and (from top) red, yellow, blue, orange, green, black and purple tail feathers. Black walkways.

McDONNELL DOUGLAS F-4J-27-MC PHANTOM II, 153088, OF U.S. NAVY SQUADRON VX-4, POINT MUGU, 1976
(American Bicentennial display colour scheme)

Colour scheme. Gloss red, white and blue overall. Navy and Squadron titling in gold. Bicentennial markings on fuselage and fin in yellow with circle of white stars. Eagle's head lined in black with black and yellow beak and red tongue.

McDONNELL DOUGLAS F-4J-29-MC PHANTOM II, 153783/XF-9, U.S. NAVY OPERATIONAL TEST AND EVALUATION FORCE, POINT MUGU, 1977

Colour scheme. Gloss black overall with red flashes on fuselage and tail and white stars. All numerals and lettering in white. Engine intake warning chevrons in red.

McDONNELL DOUGLAS QF-4B PHANTOM II, 149409/42, U.S. NAVY MISSILE CENTRE, POINT MUGU, 1980
(Aircraft originally constructed in 1962 as an F-4B-9-MC)

Colour scheme. Gloss red overall with black lettering, walkways and nose anti-glare panel. Fin badge white triangle with blue and red segments superimposed on blue and red stylised wings. White lettering on fin.

Aircraft nicknamed 'THE IRON BUTTERFLY'   COPYRIGHT 1981 FRANCIS K MASON

Chapter 5

Phantoms for the Air Force

The USAF adopts the F-4

At the end of the 1950s the tactical fighter and fighter-bomber rôles in the United States Air Force were still almost exclusively performed by the 'century-series' of aircraft: the North American F-100 Super Sabre fighter-bomber whose production ended in October 1959; the McDonnell F-101 Voodoo whose employment came to be centred on the WS-217A long-range interceptor and tactical reconnaissance rôles; the Convair F-102A Delta Dagger interceptor; the F-104C Starfighter dual rôle interceptor/ground attack fighter; the Republic F-105B and D tactical strike fighter; and the Convair F-106A and B Delta Dart interceptors which, like the F-102 were deployed in the United States by Air Defense Command.

These aircraft had constituted a formidable array of tactical supersonic combat weapons systems; the F-100 in particular, though possessed of the least advanced performance, gained a fine reputation for rugged reliability and ability to withstand battle damage. However, in parallel with the introduction of these aircraft from five different aircraft manufacturers and two engine companies had come a large range of specialist weapons and navigation systems (each virtually tailored to a particular aircraft type) such that, owing to the lack of standardisation-with-amortisation, unit costs were already beginning to cause concern in the Department of Defense—then also faced with funding heavy production programmes involving the Boeing B-52 Stratofortress strategic bomber and the Convair B-58 Hustler supersonic bomber (an aircraft of spectacularly high unit cost).

In 1960, while the US Navy was already beginning to consider the performance parameters of a fleet fighter ultimately to replace the Phantom, the US Air Force's Tactical Air Command put forward a strike fighter requirement for an aircraft intended to replace the F-105 Thunderchief. The following year, urged by Defense Secetary Robert McNamara, the Department of Defense ruled for a merging of the two Services' requirements, calling for a variable-geometry aircraft, the TFX which, with maximum airframe and powerplant commonality, would be capable of performing both rôles. The Navy's favourite project, the F6D Missileer, was abandoned and the General Dynamics design—later to become the F-111A for the USAF and F-111B for the US Navy—was selected.

In much the same way that the British Ministry of Defence was becoming wholly absorbed in the TSR-2 strike project at roughly the same time (and for the same motives), the TFX became a dominant fixation at the US Department of Defense. However, because the first such aircraft was not due to fly until 1964, and would not enter service until the late 1960s, the Defense Department accepted that an interim aircraft would be required quickly and, profoundly impressed when an early Navy Phantom lifted no less than 22,000 lb of ordnance during a demonstration in 1962, switched its attention to the F-4B as likely USAF equipment. On closer examination (the USAF had never previously

Above *Inscribed 'F-110A' in line with the then-current USAF fighter designation and with the badge of Tactical Air Command, this Navy F-4B was loaned to the USAF for demonstration purposes and crew familiarisation; the 'buzz number' FJ-405 may have been spurious* (McDonnell Douglas, Neg No 7521, dated January 1962).

Below *Bearing the tail code DM of Davis-Monthan AFB, Arizona, this F-4C-15-MC, 63-7415, seen at Williams AFB in 1964, served with the 4453d Combat Crew Training Wing, replacing the F-4Bs loaned by the US Navy* (Bryan Baker, via Master Sergeant David W. Menard).

even considered a Navy fighter for its own first-line duties), it was seen that the F-4B possessed better radar than any in-service USAF fighter, could carry a much greater weapon/fuel load, returned lower maintenance hours per flying hour and better service-ability; and its demonstrated performance was as good as or better than the best 'century-series' fighters in almost every respect. However, the similarity with the situation in Britain then disappeared for, when the TSR-2 was strangled at birth by a newly-elected Socialist government, the British Services had no fall-back, whereas while the TFX suffered delay for the USAF and cancellation for the US Navy the Phantom continued not only to perform its 'interim' allotted tasks but to perform them more efficiently and at lower cost than any other comparable fighter for ten years with both US Navy and US Air Force. It was, moreover, ironic that both the Royal Air Force and Royal Navy opted to fly the Phantom when the Hawker P 1154 was also cancelled (as described more fully in Chapter 9).

Initially 12 F-4Bs were taken from the Block 14n production batch and given USAF BuAer Nos (*62-12167* to *62-12178*). Some underwent an initial evaluation at Edwards AFB in 1962*, and all (together with 18 further aircraft from subsequent Blocks) were eventually delivered to the 4453d Combat Crew Training Wing before being handed back to the US Navy after deliveries of the USAF's own F-4Cs had started.

During 1962 an appraisal of the equipment required by the USAF's F-4C, in the tactical strike rôle, was undertaken against a background of economic stringencies which emphasised minimum alteration of the Navy's basic airframe, a policy which, bearing in mind the major shift in combat mission, could have compromised the USAF's Phantom from the outset. However, such was the range of equipment and flight subsystems available—the 'state of the art' in the then-new jargon on the day—that the Air Force was able to put forward a realistic equipment specification with confidence that it would at relatively low cost be made compatible with the F-4's airframe and performance envelope.

The F-4C (or F-110A as it was styled for a short time prior to the Department of Defense's standardisation of Service nomenclature) featured a number of essential air-frame changes as well as a switch to the J79-GE-15 engine; this featured a self-contained cartridge/pneumatic starter mounted on the lower wheel case—replacing the Navy's turbine-impingement system that used an external air supply; the engine-driven alternators, each of 20 kVA, were enclosed within a bullet-fairing on the front of the compressor face instead of being mounted on the engine-driven waist gearboxes.

The Navy's low-section wheels gave too small a footprint and were of too high a pressure for TAC's asphalt runways, so the tyres were broadened from 7.7 ins to 11.5 ins, and the rims widened to match them; this in turn allowed an anti-skid braking system to be included but necessitated bulging the underwing roots to enclose the retracted gear. The Navy's air refuelling probe was discarded in favour of a dorsal 'receptacle' type of connection to match the USAF KC-135 flying boom refuelling system.

At the outset it was the USAF's policy to crew the F-4C with two rated pilots, the front cockpit occupant being termed the Aircraft Commander (AC) and the rear occupant simply Pilot. Later on, when the USAF adopted many of the Navy F-4 training policies, the rear crew member was no longer necessarily a rated pilot and was normally termed the Weapon System Operator (WSO, or, as dubbed in the Service, the 'Wizzo'). The F-4C also featured enhanced dual controls in the rear cockpit, and the instrument panel of this cockpit was lowered by about 3 ins to improve the rear pilot's forward field of vision. The Navy's arrester gear was retained.

---

* *The first F-4Bs to wear USAF markings were, in fact, a pair of aircraft, 149405 and 149406, lent by the US Navy, for crew training and evaluation.*

Above *F-4C-20-MC, 63-7617, of the USAF's Tactical Air Command on delivery to Eglin AFB, Florida, in November 1964* (Master Sergeant David W. Menard).

Left *Fourth production F-4C-15-MC, 63-7410, with the Air Force Flight Test Centre, Air Force Systems Command, Edwards AFB, in October 1978; despite its 15-year age the aircraft never acquired a camouflage scheme* (Starliner Aviation Press, Neg No CS502).

Below *Another long-serving Phantom, an F-4C-18-MC, 63-7497, in the markings of the 58th Tactical Training Wing at Luke AFB, Arizona, during 1978* (Starliner Aviation Press, Neg No CS504).

The main aircraft radar was changed to the AN/APQ-100 with plan position (mapping) displays in both cockpits; the navigation computer was replaced by a Litton ASN-46 long-range inertial navigation system; provision was made to carry GAM-83B Bullpup air-to-surface missiles on the wing pylons, the associated AJB-7 bombing system and LADD timer being added between front and rear cockpits. The AAA-4 infra-red seeker was retained under the nose.

★   ★   ★

The first US Air Force McDonnell F-4C (BuAer No *62-12199*)—effectively a pre-production systems feasibility aircraft—made its first flight on May 27 1963, five years to the day after the original Navy F4H Phantom prototype's first flight. The aircraft was followed by two similar aircraft before production got underway with an initial batch of 36 Block 15 and 16 aircraft, most of which replaced the F-4Bs with the 4453d CCTW at McDill AFB. The second and third pre-production F-4Cs, *62-12200* and *62-12201*, became the prototype YRF-4C reconnaissance aircraft shortly afterwards, and '*200* the YF-4E later still; in 1979 '*200* was delivered for display at the Air Force Museum, Wright Patterson AFB, Ohio; '*201* was put on display at the Technical Training Center, Chanute AFB, Illinois. Of the original production Blocks 15 and 16 aircraft, no fewer than 28 were still flying 16 years later, the majority of them with Fighter Interceptor Squadrons of the Air National Guard. A total of 583 F-4Cs was built at Saint Louis in the 36 months up to May 1966, by which date production had switched entirely to the F-4D.

The first F-4Cs to reach an operational unit of the USAF were delivered to the four squadrons of the 12th Tactical Fighter Wing, also at McDill, the majority of their crews having received conversion training with the 4453d CCTW. The 12th TFW was followed by the 8th TFW (the 'Wolfpack'), the 35th TFW and the 366th TFW (the 'Gunfighters') during the following three years, these four Wings later deploying a total of ten Tactical Fighter Squadrons in Vietnam and Thailand during the period 1965–67 (see Chapter 7).

During the 15 years in which the F-4C served with the US Air Force it flew with the 8th, 12th, 18th, 35th, 52d, 58th, 81st, 366th and 401st Tactical Fighter Wings, the 57th Fighter Weapons Wing, the 58th Tactical Training Wing (and Tactical Fighter Training Wing), as well as the Air National Guard Squadrons of Arkansas, Illinois, Indiana, Louisiana, Hawaii, Michigan, Mississippi, Missouri and Texas. Numerous examples were flown on weapons and systems clearance trials at the Armament Development Test Center and Air Force Flight Test Center of the Air Force Systems Command at Eglin AFB, Florida, and Edwards AFB, California, respectively. As described in later chapters a number of F-4Cs were modified during the second half of the Vietnam War for suppression of surface-to-air missile radars as the F-4G 'Wild Weasel', and 36 aircraft of the 81st TFW were handed over to the Spanish Air Force in 1972.

The reconnaissance RF-4C

No doubt encouraged by the relative ease with which the F-4C proved compatible with Air Force requirements, the Department of Defense sanctioned an investigation into the possibility of replacing the McDonnell RF-101C Voodoo with a reconnaissance version of the F-4C and, in May 1962, McDonnell received a letter contract for a feasibility study. By November that year a mock-up had been completed and gained preliminary approval by the Air Force.

Opposite page *An early RF-4C with an unusual demonstration payload of 11 820-lb M-117 GP bombs* (McDonnell Douglas, Neg No 31802, dated November 1965).

Above *An RF-4C-22-MC, 64-1050/JM of the 4416th Tactical Electronic Warfare Squadron, 363d Tactical Reconnaissance Wing, Shaw AFB, South Carolina; in the late 1970s this aircraft flew with the 173d TRS, Nebraska Air National Guard* (via Richard Ward).

Below *A 67th Tactical Reconnaissance Wing RF-4C-27-MC*, 65-0921 (Norman Taylor, via Master Sergeant David W. Menard).

In the event the RF-4C proved to represent a much more radical breakaway from the basic F-4B than the F-4C; however, the much improved cost-effectiveness promised by the two USAF Phantom versions unquestionably blunted the McNamara philosophy of maximum commonality, with the result that the Air Force (as well as the Navy shortly afterwards) obtained a relatively sophisticated tactical reconnaissance aircraft without opposition from the Defense Department.

With all air-to-air and conventional air-to-ground (ie, missile and bomb) weapon systems deleted, the RF-4C was conceived as a photo and multiple-sensor reconnaissance aircraft with a nuclear weapon delivery capability, thereby combining the tactical rôles of both the F-101C and RF-101C, which equipped a total of six squadrons of the USAF at that time.

The 17,000 lb-thrust J79-GE-15 engines of the F-4C were retained, as were the larger mainwheels and dorsal air refuelling receptacle; however, almost all the tactical strike electronics were replaced by specialist reconnaissance systems.

The nose was lengthened to accommodate AN/APQ-99 radar; the AN/ASQ-19 communications-navigation-identification system was replaced by an AN/ASQ-88B CNI; an AN/ASN-56 inertial navigator was fitted, as were AN/APQ-102 sideways-looking radar mapping set, AN/ASQ-90 data display set, AN/ALR-17 countermeasures receiving set, AAS-18 infra-red detector, ARC-105 HF transceiver and AN/APR-25 homing and warning systems. A basic fit of film cameras in three positions, front, centre and rear, was available: a KS-87 forward-framing camera with 6-inch lens, a KA-56 low-altitude pan camera with 3-inch lens and a KA-55 high-altitude pan camera with 12-inch lens, the latter in a stabilised mount; the centre KA-56 low-altitude camera could be replaced by a fan of three with 6-inch lenses in the oblique units and a 3-inch lens in the vertical. The full range of alternative film cameras (as shown in Appendix B) covered high and low level, day and night photographic missions, the latter in conjunction with photoflash ejectors in the aircraft's rear fuselage.

In addition to the AN/ALR-17 ECM receiving set mounted internally, AN/ALQ-71, -72 and -87 ECM pods could be carried externally. In the nuclear strike rôle the MK-28 (EX or RE), MK-43 or MK-57 weapons could be carried on the centreline attachment, usually in company with a pair of underwing drop tanks; for training purposes in the delivery of these nuclear weapons an SUU-21/A practice bomb dispenser could be carried on the centreline. Maximum take-off weight of the RF-4C was 58,000 lb, a limit imposed by airframe and undercarriage stressing rather than by engine power.

★   ★   ★

As already mentioned, the second and third pre-production USAF-funded F-4Cs (*62-12200* and *62-12201*) were modified to become the prototype YRF-4Cs, although their nose profile was no more than an aerodynamic mock-up. First flight in this configuration and with only a very limited reconnaissance equipment fit was made on August 8 1963, and delivery to Edwards AFB took place later that month.

It was not until April the following year that the first production RF-4C (*63-7740*) was completed, the first of 503 aircraft built to Specific Operational Requirement (SOR) 196, and flown on May 18. However, a reconnaissance commitment over Cuba in October 1962 had focused attention on some deficiencies in USAF equipment resulting in changes to SOR-196 and improvement of some camera mounts (in particular the gyro-stabilising of the high-level vertical camera) and blurr-elimination by image-motion compensation in the low-level obliques. Thus the early Service deliveries were of aircraft lacking fully operational systems, a situation not entirely rectified until mid-1965.

RF-4Cs were hurriedly delivered to South-East Asia in October 1965 when the war in Vietnam began deteriorating, and within two years four tactical reconniassance squadrons

Background photograph *This RF-4C-31-MC, 66-0438, seen here in 1967, later served with the 15th Tactical Reconnaissance Squadron, 18th Tactical Reconnaissance Wing at Kadena AB, Okinawa* (McDonnell Douglas, Neg No 49509).

Inset *Another RF-4C-31-MC, 66-0444/BB, of the 4th TRS, 75th TRW, at Bergstrom AFB, Texas* (via Dr René J. Francillon).

Sharkmouth marking on an RF-4C of the 32d Tactical Reconnaissance Squadron, 10th Tactical Reconnaissance Wing, at RAF Alconbury, England (via Richard Ward).

(including those of the 432d TRW) were deployed, eventually replacing the RF-101 Voodoo. Meanwhile in USAFE the RF-4C had equipped the 10th TRW at Alconbury in the UK, and went on to fly with the 26th, 67th, 75th and 363d TRWs in the late 1960s and 1970s. They also flew with the tactical reconnaissance squadrons of the Air National Guard, namely the 106th TRS, 117th TRW (Alabama); 153d TRS, 186th TRG (Mississippi); 160th TRS, 187th TRG (Alabama); 165th TRS, 13th TRW (Kentucky); 173d TRS, 155th TRG (Nebraska); 179th TRS, 148th TRG (Minnesota); 190th TRS, 124th TRG (Idaho); and the 192d TRS, 152d TRG (Utah).

Progressive modification of the RF-4C has taken place over the years to upgrade its efficiency in the presence of advancing technology, although the facility to eject an in-flight pre-processed film cassette (for instance over a field command post) was deleted from production Block 44 onwards as being too unreliable. Introduced during the 1970s was a Westinghouse ALQ-101 jammer, frequently carried in a centreline pod, as was the range of AIL AN/ALQ ELINT (electronic intelligence) airborne receiver and recorder systems.

The RF-4C, for all its relative age, still epitomises the extraordinary capability of modern reconnaissance from the air. The infra-red detection system, for example, can detect concealed targets simply by their heat signatures. Infra-red pictures of an airfield can even disclose where and what aircraft *have previously been* dispersed on it simply by reproducing the contrast in ground temperature caused by their shadows from the sun. Underground installations can be detected by their contrast in heat dissipation from that of their surroundings. It is even possible to determine how long an aircraft has been parked on an airfield by the relative heat of its airframe compared with that of its neighbours.

By employing the doppler shift principle in the long-established moving-target indicator mode, it is possible for the sideways-looking radar to detect (and measure) the movement of targets, even when moving at walking pace at right angles to the flight path of the aircraft, which itself may be flying at more than 700 mph low over the ground.

The absence of a self-protection missile or gun armament in the RF-4C has been questioned (the Sparrow recesses are faired over), but is justified by the time-honoured reasoning that a reconnaissance pilot might be tempted to engage in air combat rather than escape with his vital intelligence—the raison d'être of the entire reconnaissance philosophy.

McDONNELL DOUGLAS F-4 PHANTOMS OF THE U.S. AIR FORCE

McDONNELL DOUGLAS F-4C PHANTOM II, 63-666, OF THE 171ST FIGHTER INTERCEPTOR SQUADRON, MICHIGAN AIR NATIONAL GUARD, U.S.A.F.

Colour scheme. Natural metal overall. Black
and yellow checks on rudder and splitter
plates. Yellow 'arrow heads' on fin.

McDONNELL DOUGLAS F-4E PHANTOM II, 67-362, 58TH TACTICAL FIGHTER SQUADRON, U.S.A.F., VIETNAM, 1972.
(As flown by Capt. Richard S. Ritchie, 555th Tactical Fighter Squadron, 8th July 1972.

Colour scheme. Dark and mid green and mid sand
brown upper surfaces, and pale grey lower
surfaces. Blue fin tip and canopy sills.

McDONNELL DOUGLAS F-4G PHANTOM II, 69-579, (WILD WEASEL II) 81ST TACTICAL FIGHTER SQUADRON, U.S.A.F., SPANGDAHLEM, GERMANY, 1976.
(Aircraft originally constructed in 1971 as F-4E)

Colour scheme. Dark and mid green and mid sand
brown upper surfaces, and pale grey lower
surfaces. Green and yellow fin-tip
fairing.

McDONNELL DOUGLAS F-4 PHANTOMS OF THE U.S. MARINE CORPS

McDONNELL DOUGLAS F-4B-9-MC PHANTOM II, 149421/SB-00, OF U.S. MARINE CORPS FIGHTER ATTACK TRAINING SQUADRON VMFAT-101

Colour scheme. Standard gull grey and white upper
and lower surfaces. Green panels and bars on
white fin and rudder. Grey walkways
white nose radome.

McDONNELL DOUGLAS F-4J-33-MC PHANTOM II, 155519/DR-11, OF U.S. MARINE CORPS FIGHTER ATTACK SQUADRON, VMFA-312, 1970.

Colour scheme. Standard gull grey and white upper and
lower surfaces. Red and yellow vertical surfaces
with red and yellow check bands on tail and
fuselage. White nose radome.

McDONNELL DOUGLAS F-4N PHANTOM II, 152295/EC-05, OF U.S. MARINE CORPS FIGHTER ATTACK SQUADRGN, VMFA-531, 1978.

Colour scheme. Standard gull grey and white upper
and lower surfaces. Blue fin with grey skull,
white stars and letters, and yellow
flash. White rudder and grey
walkways.

McDONNELL DOUGLAS RF-4B-26-MC PHANTOM II, 153103 RF-20, OF U.S. MARINE CORPS RECONNAISSANCE SQUADRON VMFP-3, 1980.

Colour scheme. Dull mid grey overall with
mid blue-grey, dark reddish grey and
black insignia. Blue-grey walkways
and anti-glare panel

Chapter 6

The Phantom is blooded

The F-4's operations over Vietnam

America's involvement in Vietnam and the war of 1964–73 proved to be the most frustrating and politically debilitating chapter in that nation's 20th century history. Dedicated to resisting the advances of insidious Communist influences within her own spheres of influence overseas, America had in May 1957 assumed from the French the responsibility of training the Vietnamese Air Force (VNAF), and members of the US Military Assistance Advisory Group (MAAG), which had been established as long ago as 1950, undertook the task of up-grading that poorly equipped air force. The task was compromised from the outset owing to the South Vietnamese government's refusal to hold unification elections (called for by the 1954 Geneva Protocols) on the grounds that North Vietnam's totalitarian (communist) government would prevent a democratic choice of unified state—a view, it must be said, shared by the Eisenhower administration.

By 1959 the number of MAAG personnel in Vietnam (popularly referred to as advisors, but regarded by the communists as mercenaries) had doubled to 658. The following year

Seen early in the Vietnam War this bomb-laden F-4C-22-MC, 64-0711, displays a weather-worn paint finish that belies its age. A dozen years later this same aircraft was serving with the 199th Fighter Interceptor Squadron, Hawaii Air National Guard (US Air Force, Neg No 101357).

the VNAF's aged Grumman F8F Bearcats were replaced by Douglas AD-6 Skyraiders. Against a background of increasing attacks by communist infiltrators, both American and South Vietnamese efforts in counter-insurgency measures were re-doubled during the Kennedy administration, a phase which culminated late in 1961 with a show of strength when Viet Cong guerrillas cut numerous principal roads in South Vietnam, prompting President Diem to declare a state of emergency.

Thereafter military operations steadily escallated as Soviet and communist Chinese war materiel flooded into North Vietnam, and southwards along the newly-operated Ho Chi Minh Trail. America, reluctant to engage in active warfare, responded first by supplying Army Piasecki H-21 Workhorse helicopters by sea to the South and later by providing pilots to fly them (but not in action). However, it was not long before outright hostile action broke out against the Americans: on May 2 1964 the aircraft transport ship USNS *Card* (ex-CVE-11) was sunk by a Viet Cong underwater demolition team as she was disembarking helicopters in Saigon; on August 2 that year the American destroyer, USS *Maddox* (DD-731) was attacked in international waters in the Gulf of Tonkin by three Soviet-built P-4 torpedo boats, and two nights later the destroyer USS *Turner Joy* (DD-951) was attacked by five other torpedo boats. In response, as President Johnson announced that American forces were making a 'measured response' to these unprovoked attacks, US Navy A-1 and A-4 strike aircraft from the carriers USS *Ticonderoga* (CVA-14) and *Constellation* (CVA-64) carried out highly successful raids on Hon Gai and the North Vietnamese patrol boat base at Loc Chao. One A-1 and one A-4 were shot down.

There was no formal declaration of war by America, simply a progressive drift towards greater military involvement, involving local setbacks followed by retaliation. On Christmas Eve 1964 Viet Cong infiltrators attacked a hotel in Saigon used by American officers, and on February 7 1965 a Viet Cong mortar attack on Pleiku Air Base killed eight American personnel. In retaliation the US Navy mounted a series of heavy air strikes in Operation Flaming Dart, involving aircraft from the carriers USS *Ranger* (CVA-61), *Hancock* (CVA-19) and *Coral Sea* (CVA-43) of Task Force 77 on station in the Gulf of Tonkin; their targets were Viet Cong barracks and harbour facilities at Dong Hoi and the Vit Thuu military installations. Mortar attacks then followed on American installations, resulting in numerous casualties and provoked counter-retaliation in Operation Flaming Dart II with attacks by the US Navy, US Air Force and VNAF against Viet Cong barracks at Chanh Hoa and Vit Thu Luu. A new phase in the war opened on March 7 1965 when 3,500 US Marines landed at Da Nang for combat against the Viet Cong. By July that year there were 75,000 American combat troops in Vietnam—a figure that was to grow to 510,000 by 1968.

It should be explained that at this stage in the war North Vietnamese air power was minimal, and probably comprised no more than about 50 ten-year-old MiG-15bis fighters, whose pilots kept well out of the way of American aircraft. The Vietnamese People's Air Force (VPAF) was, however, beginning to receive a steadily increasing flow of F-4s (the Chinese designation given to the 'licence'-built Soviet MiG-17*) and it was to be this aircraft that was to cause the Americans most problems during the 1960s, as will be seen in due course.

⋆   ⋆   ⋆

It is beyond the scope of this book to describe the enormous range of American air operations during the war in Vietnam, save to outline the scope of such operations as they

---

⋆ For purposes of clarity and uniformity Soviet fighter designations are used throughout this book, namely MiG-15, MiG-17, MiG-19 and MiG-21, although in many cases, not determined in official sources, the VPAF certainly flew the Chinese communist variants.

As a bomb- and Sidewinder-armed A-7A Corsair II prepares to launch, a VF-21 F-4B-26-MC, 153014/
NE-103, makes ready to follow from the deck of the carrier USS Ranger *in the Gulf of Tonkin during*
December 1967 (US Navy, Neg No K42954).

involved or provoked actions by the US Navy, US Marine Corps and US Air Force
Phantoms. Suffice it therefore to state that all manner of air operations had been flown by
the USAF over Vietnam since 1962—counter-insurgency *training* with Douglas RB-26
Invaders, transportation with Douglas SC-47s and Vertol H-21 Shawnee helicopters, air
reconnaissance by four McDonnell RF-101C Voodoos, and jungle defoliation (Operation
Ranch Hand) by Fairchild C-123 Providers—but none had involved air combat with the
VPAF. On the other hand, however, the North Vietnamese had begun to deploy very
substantial flak defences around military targets and key communications centres in the
north, and it had been to these defences that the first US Navy aircraft had fallen.

The first Navy Phantoms to arrive in the Vietnam theatre were the F-4Bs of Rear-
Admiral H.L. Miller's flagship USS *Ranger*, and these were employed in flying CAP
(Combat Air Patrols) in the vicinity of the air strikes which were mounted with growing
frequency from February 1965 onwards. On April 3, during a successful attack by 50
strike aircraft from *Coral Sea* and *Hancock* on a road bridge 65 miles south of Hanoi, a
number of MiG-17s made a single firing pass as they flew through the American
formation but without doing any damage. The next day two USAF Republic F-105s were
shot down by MiG-17s over North Vietnam. On the 9th four F-4Bs from *Ranger* were
flying a CAP south of Hainan island during a 72-aircraft strike south of Hanoi when four
MiG-17s approached and began a series of in-close gun-firing attacks. Not being armed
with guns, the Navy pilots sought to use their superior speed to open out the fight so as to
gain lock-on with their missiles. Eventually one Sidewinder was seen to explode close to a
MiG-17, and it was claimed as probably destroyed. One Phantom failed to return to its

Two F-4B-26-MC Phantoms, 153011/NH-104 and 153017/NH-107, of VF-213 airborne over North Vietnam from the USS Kitty Hawk at sea in the Gulf of Tonkin on January 23 1968; each carries a centreline drop tank, ten MK-82 bombs, two Sparrow and two Sidewinder missiles. Note the newly-introduced fin-tip antennae (US Navy, Neg Nos 1129908 and 1129909).

Above *An F-4B-26-MC, 153006/NE-401 of VF-154, flown by Lieutenant J. Quaintance from the USS Ranger (CVA-61), releases its load of 18 560-lb MK-81 Snakeye retarded bombs over a North Vietnamese artillery battery in support of the 3d US Marine Division in February 1968 (US Navy, Neg No 1117963).*

Below *Performing a strictly fighter-reconnaissance (or photo-chase) rôle over Vietnam, this F-4C-23-MC, 64-0742, was armed with four AIM-7D Sparrow missiles and carried two camera pods on the inboard wing pylons; each of these pods accommodated two 16 mm Miliken movie cameras and a single 70 mm still camera. A camera-documentation operator occupies the rear cockpit on strike missions to record on-the-spot cover of the attack (US Air Force, Neg No 95422).*

carrier, but at the time American authorities stated that it probably ran out of fuel (air refuelling facilities were not yet generally available). Hanoi radio, however, claimed that it was shot down by a Sidewinder from another Phantom. USS *Midway*'s Phantoms flew their first armed night reconnaissance mission over Vietnam on April 15, and all returned safely.

Up to this point both the US Air Force and US Navy had been suffering growing losses—largely from flak but also from batteries of surface-to-air missiles (SAM-2s), large numbers of which were now being supplied by the Soviet Union. North Vietnamese radar cover over the Gulf of Tonkin was now so complete that VPAF fighter controllers were able to watch the CAPs by US Navy F-4Bs and judge accurately if and when to intercept land strikes with their MiG-17s.

On June 17 the Navy pilots were to draw blood. On that day two F-4Bs of Navy Squadron VF-21 from USS *Midway*, flown by Commander Louis C. Page (Lieutenant John C. Smith, RIO) and Lieutenant Jack D. Batson (Lieutenant-Commander Robert B. Doremus, RIO) encountered four MiG-17s over the Gulf of Tonkin. Page spotted the enemy aircraft approaching on his radar at about 35 miles and alerted Batson as the two sections closed head-on at a speed of about 1,100 knots. Obtaining missile acquisition at a range of about ten miles, both pilots fired a single Sparrow and both scored hits, the MiGs erupting in sheets of flame; the other two MiG-17s broke away and made off.

Apart from confirming the deadly efficiency of the Sparrow missile (significantly in the head-on arc)—these were the first kills by American pilots using heat-seeking missiles, although Chinese Nationalist pilots flying F-86 Sabres had scored with Sidewinders over the Straits of Formosa some six years earlier—the combat on the 17th brought about profound analysis of the tactics of American fighters, in particular the F-4 Phantom.

To begin with, the war was still being fought under stringent limitations imposed by Washington. Air strikes were being conducted only against 'interdiction' targets, with strict instructions that weapons could only be used in conditions that ensured maximum accuracy and that, if such accuracy could not be guaranteed, weapon loads should be brought back, and not jettisoned even over the sea, no matter how they might restrict aircraft performance. In air combat American pilots had been forbidden to open fire unless and until they had been fired on, and only then having made positive identification of an enemy aircraft. It was thought likely that Soviet and Chinese 'instructors' were at work in North Vietnam, and the US government had no wish to provoke any sort of incident with other powers, however deliberately such an incident might be misconstrued. Strictly speaking therefore, according to the limitations in being, the action of June 17 should not have taken place, as the Sparrow missiles were obviously fired before visual identification of the MiG-17s could possibly have been made. The absurdity of the limitations in the split-second decisions of air combat was accordingly brought home to the American authorities who had clearly framed them in the context of close-in gun-only combat and, if previous inconclusive combats had failed to disclose the anachronism, the destruction of the MiG-17s by Sparrows at long-range brought about a swift removal of the 'identification first' restriction.

It was, however, an initial analysis of the F-4B/MiG-17 confrontation that concentrated minds in the US Navy and Air Force and began to sow seeds of doubt as to the correctness of their overall concept of fighter armament and combat tactics.

As has already been shown, neither the Navy's F-4B nor the Air Force's F-4C possessed any in-built fixed gun armament, whereas the opposing MiG-17s as yet possessed no air-to-air missiles—depending solely upon a heavy gun armament. Moreover the CAP missions being flown by the F-4Bs at high subsonic speeds (to prolong mission endurance) placed the Navy fighters at a considerable disadvantage if jumped by MiG-17 pilots whose tactics were confined to single gun-firing passes. By diving away at supersonic speed the enemy pilots were relatively safe as the F-4Bs went into afterburner and accelerated too late.

These tactics in turn disclosed a fundamental divergence by the F-4B's combat potential from that of fighters of lower power and performance, such as the MiG-17, and this disparity did not necessarily favour the American fighter. The huge reserve of power provided by the twin J79s represented surplus *energy*, energy which could be translated into combat in the vertical plane, into lightning climbs and zooms which no MiG-17 pilot could hope to match. And it was in such combat manoeuvring that American F-4 pilots, in mock combat against other F-4s, had concentrated their training for three years. The communist MiG pilots, being confined to combat at strictly limited altitude bands by power limitations, were content to engage in combat in the horizontal plane. For the first time in the history of air combat, superior altitude did not necessarily favour the higher aircraft, particularly as heat seeking missiles such as the Sparrow and Sidewinder were unreliable when discharged against a target below the launching fighter on account of ground returns 'confusing' the heat-seeking missile head.

While these matters were being digested, and the 'identification first' limitation waived, it was the turn of the US Air Force to destroy a pair of MiG-17s. Now warned to avoid close-in fighting, American pilots were careful to avoid combat with MiGs unless a missile launch could be made with positive acquisition in the horizontal plane at medium or long range. On July 10 two F-4Cs of the 45th Tactical Fighter Squadron, 2d Air Divison, flown by Captain Kenneth E. Holcombe (Captain Arthur C. Clark, rear cockpit) and Captain Thomas S. Roberts (Captain Ronald C. Anderson, rear cockpit)*, destroyed two MiG-17s over North Vietnam. However, while American aircraft continued to carry out operations in the north for the remainder of 1965, air combat between opposing fighters was scarce, and only two further enemy jets fell—one to an F-4B of Navy Fighter Squadron VF-151 and the other to an A-1H of Navy Attack Squadron VA-25. On the other hand the Americans continued to lose fairly heavily to enemy flak and SAMs.

It was not long before American Intelligence learned that not only were the Viet Cong's surface-to-air missile defences being massively strengthened but that the much more modern MiG-21 was arriving at bases in the North (a build-up considerably assisted by a unilateral bombing ceasefire ordered by President Johnson between Christmas 1965 and the end of January 1966). In some respects this new arrival was greeted with relief by the American air forces for—being missile-armed—the new fighter would tend to engage in combat at longer range and therefore even the odds for superior American missile fire control, and it was at this time that the mixed complement of long-range Sparrow and medium-range Sidewinder became widely adopted by the F-4Bs of the US Navy. However, during 1966 the MiG-17s continued to deploy in defence principally along the seaboard of North Vietnam with the result that no MiG-21s were destroyed by the US Navy F-4Bs that year, F-8 Crusaders (of VF-211 and VF-162) with gun armament claiming four MiG-17s, and an F-4B of VF-161 from USS *Constellation* (CVA-64) shooting down another on July 13 that year.

Flying from their bases in Thailand, where Udorn was the principal F-4C base, the USAF encountered increasing numbers of MiG-21s as they launched strikes along the Hong River ('Thud Ridge'), north of Hanoi itself. Carefully husbanding their limited numbers of the new fighter, the Viet Cong were able to track the incoming raiders on radar and position the MiG-21s to carry out single missile passes from dead astern (the

---

* *At this time the US Air Force (unlike the US Navy) employed rated pilots in both crew positions of the F-4C, the occupant of the front cockpit being termed the 'aircraft commander'.*

With a load of eight 750-lb bombs, four Sparrows and two underwing drop tanks, an F-4C-21-MC, 63-7687, flies over Vietnam late in 1965 (US Air Force, Neg No 95369).

dreaded six o'clock). Their early Atoll air-to-air missiles could only acquire lock-on in the heat zone immediately behind the target. As the American F-100s and F-105s flew at medium or low altitude and at subsonic speed, the MiG-21s would make a supersonic sprint from astern, release their missiles and turn away without any possible reaction by the American pilots. To counter these tactics it was necessary to assign the F-4Cs to 'MIGCAP' missions designed to counter any enemy fighters approaching the raiding formations (which now included small numbers of B-52 heavy bombers). Five MiG-21s were destroyed by USAF F-4Cs, all of them aircraft of the 480th Tactical Fighter Squadron (originally of the 35th Tactical Fighter Wing and later of the 366th Tactical Fighter Wing). Twelve MiG-17s were shot down in the same period, seven by F-4Cs and five by F-105Ds.

The pattern of air combat in 1967 changed perceptibly as the US Navy stepped up its efforts to mine coastal waters in the north, partly to prevent the movement of commando-style infiltrators to the south by sea. The deep water ports were, however, not mined for fear of sinking Soviet or Chinese merchantmen, although they were known to be delivering large quantities of war materiel to the Viet Cong! These mining sorties were usually carried out by Grumman A-6 Intruders, invariably covered by F-4Bs flying CAPs. Overland the F-105s continued their frequent strikes over 'Thud Ridge' and also made some extremely hazardous attacks on the extensive SAM sites in the north. The MiG-17 continued to oppose the Navy fighters but the success of the F-8's gun armament was further exphasised as aircraft of VF-24 shot down five MiG-17s, VF-211 a further four and VF-162 one; compared to these successes F-4Bs of VF-114 destroyed two MiG-17s and VF-142 one. However, it was on August 10 1967 that VF-142's Phantoms encountered and shot down two MiG-21s.

On this occasion Lieutenant Guy Freeborn (Lieutenant Bob Elliot, RIO) and Lieutenant-Commander Bob Davis (Lieutenant-Commander Swede Elie, RIO) took off from USS *Constellation* to cover a Navy strike on Phu Ly. Carrying centreline and wing drop tanks, four Sparrows and four Sidewinders apiece, the Phantoms rendezvoused with a KA-3B tanker and topped up with fuel before setting course for Nam Dinh at 16,000 ft.

The Phantom pilots had a grandstand view of the strike going in below them and, although they heard a number of warnings of MiG attacks, they spotted no enemy fighter.

Air refuelling from KC-135A tankers from Strategic Air Command became commonplace during operations by the US Air Force and Navy over Vietnam as a means of enabling tactical fighter-bombers, such as the Phantom, to deliver worthwhile bombloads against targets in the North (US Air Force).

As they completed a patrol run to the south Freeborn spotted two MiG-21s breaking through the overcast 6,000 ft above in a perfect position for a 6 o'clock attack. However, it was clear that the enemy pilots had not spotted the Phantoms, and Freeborn and Davis pulled a tight 360-degree turn, finishing astern of the MiGs. Davis fired a Sparrow but it failed to launch as Freeborn decided on a Sidewinder attack, and fired one which exploded close to one of the enemy fighters. Davis then fired a Sidewinder which also exploded near the second MiG; his second Sidewinder went 'ballistic', but his third and fourth both hit, and the MiG blew up in a great fireball. Freeborn went after the other enemy fighter and, after a second Sparrow hung up, fired a Sidewinder which evidently flew directly into the enemy's tailpipe before exploding. The wreckage of both MiGs was seen to hit the ground and neither enemy pilot ejected. Taking care to watch behind for further attacks the two Phantom crews flew out to sea to make a second tanker rendezvous before returning to the *Constellation* to celebrate the Navy's first MiG-21 kills.

If MiG-21 victories had been hard to come by for the Navy in 1967, no fewer than 17 fell to the USAF, 16 of them to F-4Cs and the other to an F-4D of the 433d TFS, 8th TFW, at the end of the year. 42 MiG-17s were also destroyed, more than half of them by F-105s.

Undoubtedly the best-known of the USAF's MiG-21 destroyers at this time was Colonel Robin Olds who commanded the 8th TFW 'Wolfpack' at Udorn in 1967. Olds was indeed a veteran fighter pilot, having achieved 'ace' status as long ago as the Second World War. His first victim over Vietnam was a MiG-21, shot down on January 2 1967 while flying with Lieutenant Charles C. Clifton; his next, also a MiG-21, fell on May 4 near Phuc Yen; and on May 20, with Lieutenant Steve Croker in the rear cockpit, he destroyed two MiG-17s—the first with a Sparrow and the second with a Sidewinder.

*   *   *

Early in 1968 the North Vietnamese launched a series of major attacks on bases and cities in the South, coinciding with the truce called to mark the Tet New Year; this so-called Tet Offensive was in due course repulsed, but only after a considerable build-up of American and SEATO forces, and in April the North Vietnamese retreated in the face of determined counter-attacks. At this point negotiations started to prepare for peace talks (which eventually commenced in Paris in 1969), and the United States called a halt in November to its bombing of targets in the North as a gesture of goodwill towards such talks.

It is therefore convenient at this point to record the deployment of Phantoms in Vietnam in 1968.

The 12th TFW, which had been at Cam Ranh Bay AB since November 1965 with four squadrons of F-4Cs, re-equipped with F-4Ds in 1968, and at the same time de-activated two of its squadrons. The 8th TFW was based at Ubon RTAFB, Thailand, from December 1965, and in 1968 started operating some F-4Ds alongside its F-4Cs. The 366th TFW had arrived at Phang Rang AB in March 1966 with three F-4C squadrons, but moved to Da Nang AB in October that year.

First of the reconnaissance RF-4C Phantoms (which had arrived in October 1965) were organised to equip the 460th TRW at Tan Son Nhut AB in February 1966 with two squadrons. Finally, the 432d TRW, which was activated in September 1966 at Udorn RTAFB, Thailand, with two squadrons of RF-4Cs, increased its establishment by adding two squadrons of F-4Ds in 1967–8.

Thus at the time of the bombing halt there were some 180 USAF F-4Cs, RF-4Cs and F-4Ds in South Vietnam and Thailand, of which about a quarter were RF-4Cs. At sea were some 60 F-4Bs of the US Navy.

Chapter 7

Vietnam interlude

Introduction of the F-4D, E and J

It has already been seen that the F-4 was not the ideal fighter in the context of the Vietnam War, although there can be little doubt but that it was probably the finest fighter in the world during the late 1960s. Colonel Robin Olds is said to have remarked that 'a fighter without a gun is an aeroplane without a wing'.

To overcome the absence of a fixed-gun armament a rapid-firing gun-pod, with a six-barrel Vulcan 20 mm gun (the so-called Gatling) had been developed and, mounted on the centreline attachment point, had been used to fairly good effect in a number of close-in combats (for instance Major James A. Harrgrove Jr and Captain James T. Craig Jr, flying F-4Cs of the 48th TFS, 366th TFW, had destroyed a pair of MiG-17s using the Vulcan

Scarcely visible are the sharkmouth markings of this F-4E-35-MC, 67-0315/JV belonging to the 469th Tactical Fighter Squadron, 388th Tactical Fighter Wing, based at Korat AB, Thailand. The detonator-extenders on the bombs were used to ensure maximum blast effect (via Richard Ward).

Above *The prototype YF-4E, 65-0713, seen here at the Air Force Flight Test Center, Edwards AFB in 1981. The normal experimental designation 'XF-4E' was avoided owing to an absence of appropriations available to support a new Defense Department project, cover being provided by normal Air Force funding. The aircraft, a converted F-4D, features the subdued formation light strips on fuselage and fin* (Starliner Aviation Press, Neg No BW1058).

Opposite page *From top to bottom: F-4D-28-MC, 65-0753/MC, of the 56th TFW, MacDill AFB, Florida, in October 1978; fin tip and drop tank nose caps are yellow (Neg No CS516). F-4C-24-MC, 64-0847/GA, modified as a 'Wild Weasel', of the 35th TFW, George AFB, California, in October 1978 carrying a pair of finless AGM-45 Shrike missiles (Neg No CS511). F-4D-29-MC, 66-7502/LN, of the 48th TFW, RAF Lakenheath, England; the fin tip is red (Neg No CS518). F-4D-32-MC, 66-8714/SP, of the 23d TFS, 52d TFW, based at Spangdahlem AB, West Germany, but seen at Greenham Common, England, during 1981; the aircraft carries a Pave Spike laser designator pod in the forward port Sparrow recess, and a LORAN 'towel rail' antenna on the fuselage (Neg No CS522. All photographs, Starliner Aviation Press).*

pod over Vietnam on May 14 1967). The installation was not, however, entirely satisfactory for, not only were some airspeed and g limitations imposed for a short time, the gun on the centreline prevented use of the tactically important 600 US gallon drop tank. (Rather later the M-61 SUU-16/A pod could be carried on the outboard wing pylons, but only for ground strike missions; and the much smaller 'minigun' of 7.62 mm calibre—of which no fewer than 15 could be carried on wing and centreline positions— was useless for air combat.) Nevertheless it was always a feature of the gun pod installation that mounting distortion during gun firing resulted in considerable shot dispersion, effectively cancelling all the efforts being made to achieve improved gun aiming systems.

At the beginning of the Vietnam War the standard USAF Phantom version was the F-4C, but in March 1964 the Air Force had been afforded funding to proceed with a new version, the F-4D, more suited to its own requirement—rather than those of a naval CAP fighter. To achieve greater accuracy in attacks against surface targets an ASQ-91 weapon release computer was installed in No 1 fuel tank bay, together with an ASG-22 lead-computing optical sight system; forward of these components was an improved ASG-63 inertial navigation system. A part-solid state APQ-109 radar was mounted in the nose, giving an air-to-ground ranging capability. In the course of development trials with early F-4Ds (as well as F-4Cs) a considerably increased range of external stores was cleared, and this Phantom was compatible from the outset with the Maverick AGM and Falcon AAM as well as the future generation of smart (laser-guided) bombs.

First flown in December 1965, the F-4D did not reach combat units in Vietnam until 1967, the first air victory being gained by Major Everett T. Raspberry Jr of the 555th TFS, 8th TFW, who shot down a MiG-17 on June 5 that year. In due course, the F-4D replaced all F-4Cs in Vietnam.

The US Navy had in fact planned its F-4B replacement earlier than the USAF, and development of the F-4J had started in 1963. In line with the Navy Phantom's primary task, the CAP mission remained paramount in the F-4J and this version represented an

answer to the problem of earlier aircraft radars' inability to detect and track targets flying at lower altitudes in the radar sea/ground responses. To achieve this the F-4J incorporated an AWG-10 pulse-doppler radar with look-down capability. An ASW-25 one-way data link for automatic carrier landing, miniaturised CNI, AWG-10 missile control system and AJB-7 bombing system were also included—together with 30-KVA generators to provide additional power, as in the F-4D.

Structural changes included the fixing of the inboard wing leading edges, drooping ailerons and stabilator with fixed inverted slat. An additional fuel cell (No 7) was included in the rear fuselage. The ailerons were arranged to droop 16½ degrees with landing gear down to reduce the landing approach speed, and to allow for greater recovery weight (38,000 lb) the undercarriage was re-stressed to allow a 23.3 ft/sec sink rate. At the same time the US Navy selected the same enlarged mainwheel tyres (30 × 11.5-inch) as had been adopted by the USAF in the F-4C. To cater for the much increased all-up weight, J79-GE-10s, of 17,900 lb-thrust with afterburners were fitted.

US Navy F-4Js also reached Vietnam in 1967, an aircraft of VF-96 probably destroying a MiG-21 on May 9. However, they never completely replaced the F-4B in the war theatre (indeed the last communist aircraft shot down by an American fighter over Vietnam, a MiG-17, was destroyed by an F-4B of VF-161 on January 12 1973).

Neither of these versions of the Phantom had, however, rectified the lack of fixed-gun armament, this finally being achieved in the USAF's F-4E, the most important of all versions. Yet, strangely, production F-4Es were already moving through the Saint Louis plant before the decision was taken to mount an 'internal' gun. The raison d'être of the F-4E was in fact a pulse-doppler radar, the APQ-109/CORDS.

The CORDS (coherent-on-receive doppler system) had not been tested when the first F-4D first flew and, in view of fairly widely-held misgivings, the USAF decided that if the system did not come up to demands the Service would take no further Phantoms after the D. However, the CORDS got the go-ahead on July 22 1966 and it was decided to fit it in the 35th F-4E, but problems delayed it until the 120th aircraft. Further setbacks eventually caused its cancellation altogether on January 3 1968.

In the meantime the Westinghouse APQ-120 had been adopted and it was the compactness and reliability of this radar which undoubtedly saved the Phantom in the USAF.

McDonnell Douglas F-4D-31-MC, 66-7712, of the 81st TFW seen at Bentwaters, England, in 1969 (Starliner Aviation Press, Neg No BW 1060).

Above *An F-4E of the 526th TFS, attached to the 26th TRW at Takhli AB, Thailand, April 15 1969* (US Air Force, Neg No 105422).

Below *This slatted F-4E-41-MC, 69-0248/GA, flew with the 35th TFW at George AFB until 1979; the yellow fin tip identified it as being employed on the training squadron for the German Luftwaffe. In 1979 the aircraft underwent modification to 'Advanced Wild Weasel'* (Starliner Aviation Press, Neg No CS532).

Above *An F-4E-36-MC, 67-0375/MC, of the 68th TFS, 347th TFW, landing at Moody AFB, Georgia* (Courtesy of the 68th TFS, USAF).

Above right *In spite of the somewhat confusing inscription on the nose, 153072 was in fact the second production McDonnell Douglas F-4J-26-MC, seen here in flight over Saint Louis in 1966* (via Richard Ward).

Right *Assigned to VF-121 this F-4J-29-MC, 153784/NJ-00, was flown by the Commander Readiness Attack Carrier Air Wing Twelve; the fin tip was red and the rudder segmented in the Wing element colours. The aircraft was photographed at Edwards AFB in May 1968* (Dr René J. Francillon).

With the considerably longer nose than on previous Phantoms, and with IR seeker omitted from beneath it, it was now possible to fit the six-barrel 20 mm rotary gun in its place, space for a magazine with 640 rounds being found aft of the radar. To balance the centre of gravity the No 7 fuel tank was included (as in the Navy's F-4J). Martin-Baker zero-zero rocket-assisted ejection seats were fitted as standard.

From 1972 F-4Es were fitted with new wing slats (a development that had been under-taken for the German F-4F, of which more elsewhere), but these were not available to combat units during the war in Vietnam.

The first F-4E was flown in June 1967 and the first combat evaluation aircraft arrived in Udorn RTAFB the following year. However, opportunities for air combat had by then temporarily receded, and it was not until May 23 1972 that F-4Es claimed enemy fighters when Lieutenant-Colonel Lyle L. Beckers and Captain James M. Beatty Jr of the 35th TFS, 366th TFW, shot down a MiG-19 and a MiG-21 respectively.

'Top Gun'

As previously remarked, air combat training with F-4s in the US Navy and the US Air Force prior to the Vietnam War had, not unnaturally, been designed around the entire combat flight envelope of the aircraft, and largely in view of the excellent climb performance (resulting from high thrust/weight) the tactics being employed were based on target acquisition capabilities of the missile fire control system—within the limitations of the rules of 'visual identification' imposed at the beginning of the war—with evasion and manoeuvring in the vertical plane. These tactics were not compatible with those of the communist MiG-17.

An analysis of Vietnam air combat was completed by Captain Frank W. Ault, USN, early in 1968 (coinciding with the bombing halt in South-East Asia) and as an outcome of

his recommendations it was decided to initiate a re-training commitment in air combat with three aims: to improve air combat capabilities among all US Navy fighter squadrons, to improve missile reliability and to create a nucleus of high-capability combat instructors.

Formally named the 'US Navy Post-Graduate Course in Fighter Weapons Tactics and Doctrine', the programme was taken over by part of Fighter Squadron VF-121, the F-4 replacement training squadron of the Pacific Fleet, which in effect became the Navy Fighter Weapons School at Miramar NAS. Despite the absence of a fixed gun in the Phantom, the new course was quickly dubbed 'Top Gun'.

At the outset the course lasted four weeks for each batch of eight line crews, starting in March 1969. One week was spent on air-to-ground weapons firing and three weeks on air combat, involving roughly 25 flying hours (plus 75 hours' ground instruction in theory of combat, briefing in enemy tactics and weapons, ECM, and other operational procedures). In due course the flying was increased to 35 hours and the overall programme extended to five weeks.

'Top Gun' instructors included successful crews fresh from Vietnam, including Commander Ronald McKeown and Lieutenant Willie Driscoll (Randy Cunningham's RIO), and each 'student' crew brought his own F-4 to Miramar from his squadron. Air combat training was undertaken against US Navy Douglas A-4E Skyhawks simulating the MiG-17 and Northrop T-38s simulating the MiG-21 (the power/weights and performance being in many respects much closer to these counterparts than that of the Phantom).

There is no doubt that 'Top Gun' brought about a transformation in the standard of air combat performance by US Navy F-4 crews. Of course the progressive improvement in the F-4 itself was to some extent responsible; nevertheless statistics quoted shortly after the end of American involvement in Vietnam showed that prior to 'Top Gun' the overall air combat kill-to-loss ratio by the US Navy was 3.7:1; afterwards it was 13:1.

Vietnam: the second phase

While the performance of the US Navy's fighter crews improved considerably during the second phase of the Vietnam War, that of the US Air Force—in terms of kill-to-loss ratio—declined. Yet no valid comparison exists for, while the tasks allotted to the F-4s and F-8s of the Navy were largely protective, those of the Air Force's F-4s and F-105s were almost entirely offensive and particularly hazardous—being carried out within Viet Cong radar cover and therefore capable of being confronted by superior numbers and from the best intercept position. Moreover the nature of the USAF's targets was such that heavy opposition from enemy SAM sites was the rule rather than the exception; and these sites had undergone continuous extension and strengthening during the bombing halt under the supervision of technicians from the Soviet Union. Little wonder therefore that the USAF's overall kill-to-loss ratio in air combat reduced from around 3:1 to 2:1—statistics which nevertheless reflected the USAF's superior equipment and training.

However, the nature and motivation of the Vietnam War underwent a profound change during the final phase. The first formal talks aimed at achieving peace had started in Paris during July 1969, and were accompanied by the commencement of an American withdrawal of forces from South Vietnam and Thailand, ostensibly to lend conscience to the peace talks but, in fact, accelerated by vociferous pacifist factions at home in the United States. In spite of this goodwill gesture by America—or, more likely, because of it—the North Vietnamese paused only momentarily before recommencing their infiltration into, and attacks on the South, and from December 1971 until January 1973 was fought an increasingly ferocious war in the air. For instance, when US Air Force B-52s resumed their bombing of Hanoi and Haiphong between December 18 and 27 1971, in response to attacks by the Viet Cong, no fewer than 15 of these huge bombers were lost.

To maintain air superiority over American and South Vietnamese forces in the South, as well as to protect the bases vital to American withdrawal, the Phantom strength was maintained right up to the end; indeed for a period of about six months in 1972 seven additional F-4D and E squadrons were assigned to Thailand from the United States, as follows: the 58th TFS, 33d TFW, from Eglin AFB, Florida, to Udorn RTAFB; the 307th and 308th TFS, 31st TFW, from Holmstead AFB, Florida, to Udorn RTAFB; and the 7th, 8th, 9th and 417th TFS, 49th TFW, from Holloman AFB, New Mexico, to Takhli RTAFB.

In addition to these squadrons, the 8th TFW was still based at Ubon RTAFB, and the 366th, now with three squadrons of F-4Es, moved from Da Nang in South Vietnam to Takhli RTAFB in June 1972. The 388th TFW, which had given up F-105s for F-4Es in May 1969, was based at Korat RTAFB with two squadrons. Two squadrons of the 12th TFW were deployed to Udorn with the 432d TRW in November 1971. At the height of

Above 155513 *was an F-4J-33-MC assigned to the Naval Air Test Center, Patuxent River NAS, Maryland* (Dr Joseph G. Handelman, dated April 21 1971).

Below *A pair of US Navy F-4Js perform an interesting variation of formation flying* (Author's collection).

Two contrasting studies of VF-31's F-4Js. **Upper photograph** *F-4J-35-MC,* 155833/AC-107, *flying from the carrier USS* Saratoga *(CVA-60) in the Mediterranean in 1969* (US Navy, Neg No K79837, dated December 1969). **Lower photograph** *F-4J-34-MC,* 155580/AC-107, *flying over VF-31's home station of Oceana NAS, Southern Virginia in July 1968. Note the Squadron's celebrated 'Felix the Cat' insignia on the fuselage* (US Navy, Neg No K54541, dated July 30 1968).

the air fighting in 1972 the USAF's inventory of Phantoms in the theatre had increased from 180 in 1968 to more than 250. Embarked at sea or on land bases were around 150 US Navy and Marine Corps F-4Bs and F-4Js of Fighter Squadrons VF-31, -51, -92, -96, -103, -111, -114, -142 and -161, and Marine Corps Fighter Attack Squadron VMFA-333.

By way of introducing the nature of this phase of the air war it is worth describing in some detail the combat successes of the most outstanding Navy Phantom pilot of the war, Lieutenant Randy Cunningham, a member of VF-96 embarked in the carrier USS *Constellation* (CVA-64). His own aircraft on each of the following occasions was an F-4J with 17,900 lb-thrust J79-GE-10s, slotted stabilator and APG-59 pulse-doppler radar.

On January 19 1972 Cunningham was pilot of one of two F-4Js assigned to a MIGCAP over Quang Lang airfield where a reconnaissance mission was being flown to record the presence of MiG-21s; in his rear cockpit was Lieutenant Willie Driscoll, and crewing the other Phantom were Lieutenants Brian Grant and Jerry Sullivan. Both aircraft were loaded with centreline and wing drop tanks, four Sparrows and four Sidewinders. On arrival over Quang Lang at about 15,000 ft the Phantom pilots decided to place themselves between the target and another MiG base at Bai Thuong to counter any threat to the reconnaissance aircraft. Unfortunately they found themselves directly between two SAM sites and although 18 missiles were fired at them (one passing within 100 ft of Grant's aircraft without exploding) neither aircraft was hit. While violently evading these SAMs Cunningham spotted two MiG-21s below him evidently flying out from Quang Lang at about 1,000 ft along a ravine. Diving down behind them Driscoll reported the Sparrows locked on to a target, but suspecting these missiles might not hold at such low level Cunningham fired a Sidewinder; either warned by his wingman or by tail radar, the leading enemy pilot selected afterburner, pulled up sharply and started turning. As Cunningham, also in afterburner and closing rapidly, was unable to match the MiG's turn there was a danger that he would overshoot until suddenly the enemy pilot reversed his turn at a range of about 3,000 ft presenting a perfect target. Cunningham's second Sidewinder found its target and blew the enemy's entire tail off. The second MiG-21 was already making off at top speed.

Cunningham's second victory was gained on May 8 1972, this time flying a MIGCAP during a strike near Dong Suong; again his radar intercept operator was Driscoll and Grant his No 2. After patrolling the target area for some minutes at 10,000 ft Cunningham was warned by a ground radar controller of an enemy aircraft 15 miles astern and closing. Selecting afterburner and pulling up into the vertical, he looked back to see a MiG-17 firing at Grant who promptly jettisoned his tanks, went into afterburner and pulled away, only to have an Atoll missile fired at him. This missile missed him (despite the increased heat source from his burners), and at that moment two more MiG-17s appeared overhead and went into a diving turn to get behind the Phantoms. Cunningham fired a Sidewinder but it couldn't 'make the corner'; it did, however, force the enemy pilots to break towards it, reversed in front of the Phantom and attempted to make a run for it. The Navy pilot squeezed off a second Sidewinder which flew straight into one of the MiGs and destroyed it. In evading the attacks by another MiG, Cunningham pulled a 12g turn, damaging his wing and flap panels, and after escaping from the danger area spotted a convoy of enemy vehicles below him; with no other weapon available he decided to try his luck with a Sidewinder, and succeeded in scoring a direct hit despite the target's very low heat source.

Cunningham's last three victories only two days later were all achieved in a single mission that must rank as one of the epics of air combat. Again flying with Grant as his No 2, Cunningham was this time part of a major strike against the Haiphong rail centre; his aircraft, BuAer No *155800*, was loaded with two Sparrows in the rear recesses, a

centreline tank, two Sidewinders on each inboard wing pylon and triple-ejector racks below them with six Rockeye bombs. As the strike approached the target the heavy gun and SAM defences opened up, hitting several A-6s, A-7s and F-4s; enemy MiGs from Bai Thuong, Kep, Phuc Yen and Yen Bai started to assemble on the seaward side of the target, awaiting the attackers outside the flak- and SAM-defended area.

Cunningham and Grant made their bombing attacks just as two SAMs were fired at them, but the missiles did not guide and shot past the F-4s. Pulling up, Grant spotted two MiG-17s closing from 7 o'clock and warned Cunningham. Obeying the old dogfight rule, Cunningham broke towards the attack and managed to get behind one of the enemy fighters, which he despatched with a Sidewinder. Meanwhile two further MiGs had latched on to Grant, so both Phantom pilots selected afterburner and escaped in a near-vertical pull-up to 15,000 ft.

At this height Cunningham looked down and saw eight MiG-17s, a pair of MiG-19s and a MiG-21 wheeling towards three F-4s, and decided to go to their assistance. One of the Phantoms, flown by Commander Dwight Timm, CO of VF-96, was in afterburner and was being boxed in by a pair of MiG-17s and the MiG-21. Cunningham, who was

Above left *F-4J-35-MC, 155807/NG-202, disembarked from USS* Constellation *(Dr Joseph G. Handelman).* **Left** *Bearing the distinctive markings of VF-142 and Miramar NAS codes, this F-4J-36-MC, 155846/NK-212, featured yellow tips of tip, stabilator, wings and Sidewinder rails; fin codes and fuselage flash were outlined in yellow, and the rudder carried four white and four yellow stripes* (Dr René J. Francillon). **Below left** *A VF-142 F-4J launches from the USS* Constellation *(CGA-64) in the Gulf of Tonkin during the Vietnam War* (US Navy, Neg No K82409, dated February 24 1960).

Two F-4Js of VF-33 seen at Miramar in 1970. **Below** *155781/AG-202, an F-4J-34-MC, and* **bottom** *155536/AG-205, an F-4J-33-MC* (Dr Joseph G. Handelman).

Above *Phantoms of VF-84 (an F-4J-32-MC, 153905/AE-218, and an F-4J-36-MC, 155854/AE-210) flying from the USS* Franklin D. Roosevelt *(CVA-42) over the Caribbean in August 1969. The aircraft markings included black fin with yellow tip, and white skull and crossbones, and black fuselage band outlined in yellow* (US Navy, Neg No K78955).

Opposite page *F-4Js of VF-102.* **Top** *F-4J-33-MC, 155552/AG-110, the markings comprised red rudder and wing tips with white diamonds, and red diamonds on the fuselage; fin codes were black on a red-outlined white diamond* (US Navy, Neg No 1145133, dated September 1970). **Centre** *F-4J-33-MC, 155568/AG-107, at Andrews AFB on April 27 1972* (Frank MacSorley). **Bottom** *The same aircraft lands aboard the carrier USS* America *(CVA-66) on October 22 1969* (US Navy, Neg No 1142916).

trailing the group at its 7 o'clock position, could not fire a Sidewinder for fear of it going for the Phantom, called Timm to pull to the right to force one of the MiGs across Cunningham's nose. As Timm turned, Driscoll warned of two MiG-19s diving down astern, followed by four MiG-21s. Cunningham just had time to loose off a Sidewinder which hit the MiG-17 as it was in a position to open fire on Timm; the enemy pilot was able to eject. (For this action Cunningham was nominated for the Congressional Medal of Honor.)

Now faced by at least nine MiG-17s, -19s and -21s, Cunningham decided to make good his escape and turned towards the coast in the east. Almost immediately he spotted a single MiG-17 approaching head-on, and this opened fire with 23 and 37 mm guns. Thinking he could evade the MiG by climbing, Cunningham hauled up into the vertical, but was astonished to find the MiG had also pulled up and was keeping station, almost cockpit to cockpit, just 30 ft away! As the Phantom bored on upwards the MiG dropped back and again opened fire, narrowly missing the F-4. Eventually forced to wing over, the Phantom was now 6 o'clock to the MiG, but unable to fire off a Sidewinder owing to ground interference. For several minutes the two pilots engaged in an old-fashioned dog-fight, the Phantom pilot gaining fleeting firing positions only to find that he was overshooting too fast. Although speeds fluctuated between 150 and 550 knots, Cunningham realised that his only chance of escaping the MiG's gunfire was to keep his speed high to allow energy climbs out of trouble; the difference this time was that the MiG pilot seemed willing and able to fight it out in the vertical as well as the horizontal.

At last Cunningham found himself in a vertical climb at only 150 knots with full afterburner; the MiG pilot tried to follow but pitched over first, followed now by the Phantom. Cunningham loosed off a Sidewinder more in desperation (as both aircraft were now diving vertically), and as he was about to fire his fourth missile the previous weapon

Navy Fighter Squadron VF-103 was deployed to the Mediterranean aboard the attack carrier USS Saratoga at the end of the 1960s. **Above** *F-4J-35-MC, 155826/AC-200 (US Navy, Neg No K78654 dated October 20 1969).* **Left** AC-206 *tucks up its wheels on take-off from Rota, Spain, on September 13 1970 (US Navy, Neg No 1-45742).*

evidently struck the MiG, which blew up and flew straight into the ground. (It was afterwards deduced that the enemy pilot was Colonel Toon, the leading North Vietnamese fighter ace.)

Cunningham's troubles were far from over. He was then attacked by four further MiG-17s and a MiG-21 and managed to evade them but, as he was about to cross the coast near Nam Dinh, a SAM exploded about 400 ft away, damaging the F-4's hydraulics and causing the aircraft to pitch up violently. Pushing forward to avoid stalling, Cunningham then started a series of slowly descending rolls, beginning at 27,000 and finishing at 17,000 ft, flying 15 miles out to sea in this manner before the back-up hydraulic system also ran out of pressure. The Phantom went into a spin, and although Cunningham deployed his drag chute nothing could now save the aircraft; both occupants ejected over the Gulf of Tonkin, being picked up by Marine Corps helicopters from USS *Okinawa* and returned to the *Constellation*. Cunningham and Driscoll were the only Navy crew to destroy five jet fighters over Vietnam, and the only one to shoot down three in a single mission.

Background photograph *Sidewinder-equipped F-4J-30-MC*, 153809/NE-206, *flying over the Sea of Japan* (US Navy, Neg No 1144001, dated January 10 1970).

Inset *F-4J-34-MC*, 155761/NK-107, *of VF-143, disembarked from USS* Enterprise*; fuselage flash, fin leading edge and tip are dark blue, whereas on 155773 in the background these are red* (Dr René J. Francillon).

The US Marine Corps tended to retain their F-4Bs well after the US Navy fighter squadrons had changed to the F-4J; by and large the older aircraft proved more suitable for the close-support rôle of the Marine Attack Squadrons. This F-4B-27-MC, 153036/VE-00, belonged to VMFA-115 based at Iwakuni MCAS, Japan (Public Affairs Office, 1st Marine Air Wing, USMC).

Two facts were emerging at this time—both forcefully demonstrated during the strike on Haiphong, and by Cunningham's fight in particular: the North Vietnamese air and SAM defences were now immeasurably stronger than at any time previously, and the enemy pilots were now not only more aggressive but much better trained; few would be of Colonel Toon's quality (at the time of his death he had 13 victories) but clearly many had received combat training in China or the Soviet Union.

During the last phase of the war, Navy and Marine Corps pilots (all in F-4Bs or F-4Js) destroyed 16 MiG-17s, two Mig-19s and eight MiG-21s, for the loss of two F-4s in combat; 11 F-4s were shot down by flak or SAMs, and about eight were destroyed in accidents. One of the MiG-21s was shot down by Major Tom Lassiter and Captain John Cummings, US Marine Corps, of VMFA-333 flying from the carrier USS *America* (CVA-66).

*   *   *

By comparison the USAF in the same period destroyed 43 MiG-21s and eight MiG-19s; of these, F-4D crews shot down 24 MiG-21s and four MiG-19s, and F-4Es shot down 17 MiG-21s and four MiG-19s (two MiG-21s were credited to B-52D gunners). One other MiG-21 was destroyed by a number of aircraft from different units.

As already remarked, however, the USAF undertook a very wide range of tactical missions deep into North Vietnam, whose flight paths lay across long tracts of enemy territory and exposed the aircraft to prolonged enemy action. As in the Korean War, 20 years previously, many of the targets were along enemy supply routes, particularly road and rail bridges. An example of these attacks was provided by those on the Thanh Hoa rail bridge. During the 'Rolling Thunder' bombing campaign of the first phase, no fewer than 700 sorties had been flown against it without causing significant damage, but with the loss of eight aircraft. On April 27 1972 five F-4Es, each loaded with two 2,000-lb 'smart' (ie, laser-guided) bombs, hit and destroyed the bridge.

A graphic illustration of the type of action being fought by USAF F-4 crews in 1972 was provided by the mission flown by Captains Sam White and Frank Bettine of the 4th Tactical Fighter Squadron, 366th Tactical Fighter Wing, flying from Takhli RTAFB on August 19 that year. Their aircraft was one of four assigned to fly MIGCAP for eight chaff-dropping F-4s which in turn covered a flight of anti-SAM radar F-105F 'Wild Weasels', the whole formation preceding a strike force of fighter-bombers and Skyraiders briefed to attack a target north-east of Hanoi, a return flight involving almost 1,500 miles. The target area would be covered by reporting radar aboard a US Navy cruiser in the Bay of Tonkin.

White's F-4E-42-MC (BuAer No *69-0291*) was loaded with three drop tanks, four Sidewinders, two Sparrows in the rear recesses and ECM pods in the forward recesses, as well as the standard 20 mm rotary gun in the nose. The MIGCAP F-4s made first for the coast of the Gulf of Tonkin where they topped up with fuel from a KC-135 tanker before turning north to join the chaff F-4s.

While the pre-strike anti-SAM operation was in progress the Navy radar reported the approach of MiGs from the direction of Hanoi; splitting into two pairs, the Phantom crews were drawing apart in the hope of 'scissoring' the enemy fighters when one of the WSOs called up a MiG-21 dead astern and closing fast. White and his No 2 pulled up into a roll to place themselves above and behind the enemy fighter; instead of putting his nose down to open the range in the ground clutter, the MiG pilot pulled into a barrel roll, presenting White with a perfect target. He fired off both Sparrows, the first of which caused the MiG-21 to explode, and the second detonated in the fireball; the enemy pilot either managed to eject or his seat fired in the explosion. On the flight home White again refuelled from a KC-135 over the sea before turning towards Takhli.

Like the US Navy the USAF produced one F-4 fighter 'ace' pilot, Captain Richard S. Ritchie of the 555th TFS, 432d TRW, flying F-4Ds, who destroyed MiG-21s on May 10 and 31, two on July 8 and another on August 28. However, Weapons Systems Operator Captain Charles B. DeBellevue, of the same squadron, was involved in the destruction of four MiG-21s and two MiG-19s, flying with various aircraft commanders, and Captain Jeffrey S. Feinstein, a WSO of the 13th TFS 432d TRW, was also flying with different pilots who destroyed five MiG-21s between April 16 and October 13 1972.

Total USAF Phantom losses (F-4C, RF-4C, F-4D and F-4E) amounted to 362 aircraft.

*　　　*　　　*

Summing up the Phantom's involvement in Vietnam, it was clearly the most advanced multi-purpose tactical aircraft on both sides, although it has to be said that it was not the ideal air superiority fighter in circumstances where enemy pilots of lower performance aircraft were able to close within gun range; the MiG-17 proved to be deadly in close combat until the appearance of the gun-armed F-4E. However, provided the Phantom's superior power and speed were employed wisely (that is to say, for instance, avoiding the use of afterburner when being closed by an Atoll-armed MiG in the rear hemisphere), to keep combat 'at arm's length', its weapons systems and missiles were far superior to those of the North Vietnamese fighters. The communists only introduced the short-range Atoll AAM partway through the war, and this proved much inferior to the AIL-9L Sidewinders of the American aircraft. Though thought less highly of by the Americans, the Sparrow was a useful weapon at longer ranges, but often suffered unlocking during the short delay before ejecting from its fuselage recess.

Phantoms of the US Navy's 'Blue Angels'

Official US Navy Phantom aerobatic team was the 'Blue Angels' whose early F-4Js sported a striking glossy dark blue paint scheme. **Above left** *The team performs a display at Moffett Field NAS, California, on August 9 1969* (US Navy, Neg No K76570). **Left** *The team leader's aircraft, an F-4J-26-MC (153075/1), flown by Commander Bill Wheat, USN, and Lieutenant Dick Schram, USN, seen at Elmendorf AFB, Alaska, on July 5 1969; this aircraft later crashed and was replaced by another -26, 153072* (John W.R. Taylor). **Below left** *The front pair of Sparrow missiles was not always carried during the team's displays* (US Navy, Neg No 1148177, dated June 1971). **Above** *The extraordinarily tight formation adopted by the 'Blue Angels' is well emphasised in this view of the four-aircraft team* (McDonnell Douglas, Neg No 508863, dated May 7 1969). **Below** *Close-up of a 'Blue Angels' F-4J on the flight line at Roosevelt Roads NAS, Puerto Rico, on March 20 1970* (US Navy, Neg No K82531).

Chapter 8

The new generation

Proliferation of electronics

The F-4E of the USAF remained numerically the most important aircraft in Tactical Air Command's inventory throughout the 1970s, at the end of which increasing deliveries of Fairchild A-10A Thunderbolt IIs, McDonnell Douglas F-15A Eagles and General Dynamics F-16A Fighting Falcons began to replace the Phantom. The war in Vietnam had clearly demonstrated the ability of the F-4 to undertake a wide range of specialist duties, not least that of SAM radar-suppression. Whereas this rôle was adopted primarily by F-105F and G 'Wild Weasels' (following earlier installations in two-seat F-100F Super Sabres), the first F-4C conversions arrived in Vietnam during 1972.

From the outset in Vietnam the Soviet-built SA-2 Guidline SAM was deployed in huge numbers, but early efforts to jam its radar using the USAF's EB-66 and Navy's EA-6B stand-off ECM aircraft proved only partly successful, and it was quickly realised that a combined ECM/strike aircraft was required which not only pinpointed and jammed the enemy missile radar but was capable of disabling, if not destroying, the SAM site. To be given any chance of survival in the presence of enemy fighters (which themselves might be fitted with some form of IFF/immunity equipment) this aircraft would have to possess high evasion performance; hence the selection of such aircraft as the F-100 and F-105, and ultimately the F-4.

Initially 34 F-4Cs and two F-4Ds underwent modification for radar suppression beginning in 1968, these aircraft perpetuating the codename 'Wild Weasels'. (They were referred to as EF-4Cs and EF-4Ds unofficially, though as the USAF has pointed out this nomenclature was inaccurate as the 'E' prefix denoted a passive ECM category, which the F-4 'Wild Weasel' certainly was not.) Basic operational equipment comprised Westinghouse ECM pods and a weapon-mix of AGM-45 Shrike and AGM-78 Standard anti-radiation missiles. The first dozen or so F-4C 'Wild Weasels' operated over Vietnam during 1972, and by 1974 two USAF squadrons (with the 18th and 52d TFWs) were fully equipped.

A much more extensively modified aircraft, known as the F-4G 'Advanced Wild Weasel', was produced during the late 1970s by modifying some 116 F-4Es when they returned for life-extension engineering in the United States. The major electronic subsystem is the McDonnell Douglas APR-38 radar warning and homing system, part of whose equipment is housed in a long cylindrical fairing on top of the aircraft's fin. Indeed, so extensive are the integral ECM systems that there are no fewer than 52 additional aerials distributed throughout the airframe; associated with the APR-38 is a Texas Instruments computer whose purpose is to accommodate varying future circumstances without demanding additional electronic hardware in an already densely packed aircraft. Aircraft from production Block 42 onwards were modified to F-4G

Above *The original F-4C prototype 62-12200 (which served in turn as the YRF-4C and YF-4E) was rebuilt with a Survivable Flight-Control System (SFCS, or fly-by-wire), employing command channels with full authority and no mechanical back-up; flown on April 29 1972 it was used as a basis for development of a fly-by-wire system in the General Dynamics F-16. The aircraft was later rebuilt as the F-4CCV (control-configured vehicle) with full-power canard foreplanes, direct-lift trailing edges and fly-by-wire; it was flown in this form on April 29 1974 (McDonnell Douglas, Neg No 1462-5, dated April 29 1972).*

Below *An F-4E-32-MC, 66-0318/WD, of the 414th Fighter Weapons Squadron, 57th Fighter Weapons Wing, normally based at Nellis AFB, Nevada, seen here landing at Saint Louis on February 19 1970; the fin markings were black and yellow checks (via Richard Ward).*

standard, and by 1979 equipped squadrons of the 3d, 35th, 50th, 86th and 347th TFW. Some aircraft have—like the F-4E—been equipped with LORAN.

Operation of the majority of suppression equipment is undertaken by the rear crew member, nicknamed the 'Bear', whose instrument panel extends right up to the canopy. He has three fundamental displays, namely a plan position indicator, a panoramic display and a homing indicator. The PPI is duplicated in the front cockpit and provides target/threat range and azimuth data; superimposed are data annotations assigned to 15 threat sources ('A' indicating anti-aircraft gun, '2' an SA-2, '3' an SA-3, and so on). The APR-38 also features automatic and blind weapon firing and delivery. In addition to the AGM-45 and -78 missiles already mentioned as being carried by the F-4C 'Wild Weasel', F-4Gs are also compatible with the electro-optically guided AGM-65 Maverick and, more recently, the AGM-88 HARM. An ALQ-119 ECM pod is usually mounted in one of the forward Sparrow recesses, only the rear recesses remaining equipped to load the AIM-7. The nose gun has been removed to make way for elements of the forward components of

Left *An excellent view of a late production F-4E during an early test flight with slatted wing, slatted stabilator and revised gun fairing* (McDonnell Douglas, Neg No 1331-10, dated February 11 1972).
Below left *A slatted F-4E with Target Identification System Electro-optical (TISEO) fairing on the port wing leading edge, often used in conjunction with the Maverick missile; for test flying from Saint Louis, McDonnell Douglas invariably mounted an EROS collision avoidance unit in the left front Sparrow recess; just visible beyond this (under the starboard wing) is the combat camera fairing* (McDonnell Douglas, Neg No 4265-1, dated July 1975).

Below *A late production RF-4E-63-MC, 75-0419, with revised (smooth contour) camera fairing under the nose; this version had the slatted stabilator but not the slatted wing. The aircraft shown here is painted in the USAF's low visibility grey overall scheme* (McDonnell Douglas, Neg No 26-6, dated March 1977).

the APR-38 (in a similar-shaped fairing); the F-15 type centreline fuel drop tank is normally standard on the F-4G as being cleared to 5g when full (compared with the F-4's centreline tank's 3g).

The F-4G will eventually be replaced in service with the USAF by the General Dynamics EF-111A.

The Navy's up-dating programme

The arrival of the US Navy's superlative F-14 Tomcat fighter in service shortly after the end of the Vietnam War did not offset the urgent need to upgrade the F-4B which still equipped the majority of Navy fighter squadrons and were being joined by the F-4J. Indeed, many of the old F-4Bs were re-built to 'J' standard when undergoing life extension programmes.

Left *The prototype 'Advanced Wild Weasel' F-4G, converted from an F-4E-43-MC (just visible are its previous 57th Fighter Weapons Wing markings). In-built ECM sensors are located in the fin tip, wing tips and chin fairing. The entire vertical tail and outer wings were painted orange-red for improved definition during spinning trials* (McDonnell Douglas, Neg No 116953-4, dated December 1975).

Below *Fine view of an elderly RF-4C-19-MC still serving with the 160th Tactical Reconnaissance Squadron, Alabama Air National Guard in March 1978; the following year it was moved to the Sheppard TTC* (McDonnell Douglas, Neg No 118012-21).

Opposite page *Advanced Wild Weasels.* **Top** *Bearing the 'Wild Weasel' badge and yellow fin tip that identified the 81st Tactical Fighter Squadron, this F-4G, 69-7588/SP (previously an F-4E-45-MC) of the 52d Tactical Fighter Wing at Spangdahlem, Germany, was flown at Alconbury, England, in May 1981. It carried an ALQ-119 ECM pod in the forward port Sparrow recess and two AGM-45A Shrike missiles* (Neg No CS545). **Centre** *F-4G, 69-7208/WW (previously one of the F-4Es loaned to the Royal Australian Air Force), an Advanced Wild Weasel of the 635th TFW at George AFB, California, in October 1978; it carries four advanced Sidewinders and two Shrikes* (Neg No CS541). **Bottom** *A 52d TFW F-4G, 69-0253/SP (previously an F-4E-42-MC) at Greenham Common, England, in July 1981. The inboard pylon stores are travel pods* (Neg No CS596. All photographs, Starliner Aviation Press).

Above *A late-standard, slatted F-4E-59-MC Phantom, 73-1195, seen at Alconbury in July 1979 on delivery to the 52d TFW* (Starliner Aviation Press, Neg No CS548).

In February 1973, however, the first of 178 F-4Ns flew at the Naval Air Rework Facility, North Island NAS, San Diego, California. These were F-4Js rebuilt with newly inserted structural components to extend fatigue life, but also incorporated J79-GE-10 engines with power approach compensation, an AN/AWG-10 missile control system and dogfight computer, AJB-7 bombing system, helmet-sight Visual Target Acquisition System (VTAS), ASW-25 one-way data-link, miniaturised CNI, fin-top radar warning system, 30-kVA alternators and a GVR-10 vertical reference.

The larger 30 × 11.5-inch mainwheels were now adopted, as was the slotted stabilator and fixed inboard wing leading edge. An additional No 7 fuel cell was added in the rear fuselage.

For the US Marine Corps an Air Combat (AC) version of the F-4N was also developed, incorporating the highly successful manoeuvring wing slats (then being introduced on later F-4Es for the USAF) as well as a digital version of the AWG-10 weapon control system—the Navy version was analog.

Both Navy and Marine Corps versions introduced the Sidewinder Expanded Acquisition Mode (SEAM) to allow for the improved acquisition capabilities of the latest Side-winders. The F-4J served on Navy Fighter Squadrons VF-21, -154, -171, -201, -202 and --301, and on Marine Fighter-Attack Squadrons VMFA-3, -314, -321, -323 and -531, Marine Attack Squadron VMA-112, and Marine Fighter-Attack Training Squadron VMFAT-101.

The latest version of the Navy's Phantom is the F-4S, a yet further life-extended rework of the F-4J/F-4N to a common standard which includes the slatted wing on *all* aircraft. In

Above *RF-4C-38-MC, 68-0654/AR, with smooth-contour camera fairing and blue fin tip, identifying the aircraft as belonging to the 1st Tactical Reconnaissance Squadron, 10th Tactical Reconnaissance Wing, based at RAF Alconbury, England, in July 1981* (Starliner Aviation Press, Neg No CS526).

Opposite page *Marine Corps F-4Ns.* **Top** *F-4N, 152252/EC-04 (previously an F-4B-22-MC) of VMFA-531 at El Toro MCAS, California, in October 1978; the fin was blue with grey skull, yellow lightning flash and white letters and stars* (Neg No CS562). **Centre** *F-4N, 150485/SH-42 (previously F-4B-14-MC) of VMFAT-101 at Yuma MCAS, Arizona, in October 1978; this unit undertook all Phantom fighter attack crew training for the Marine Corps* (Neg No CS557). **Bottom** *Smart F-4N, 152975/VW-4 (previously F-4B-25-MC) of VMFA-314 at El Toro MCAS, California, in October 1978; the fin was black with white letters* (Neg No CS563. All photographs, Starlilner Aviation Press).

addition to the Navy and Marine Corps squadrons just mentioned, the F-4S has also served with VF-74, -102, -103, -121, -161 and -302, VX-4, VMFA-115, -235, -251, -312, -333 and -451. A total of 265 F-4S Phantoms was converted at North Island in a programme known as Project Bee Line, or Conversion In Lieu Of Procurement (CILOP), with deliveries starting in 1978.

Target drones

Customarily reserved for near time-expired operational and second-line aircraft, conversion to RPVs (remotely-piloted vehicles) usually signals the end of a military aircraft's Service life yet, as long ago as 1971 the first QF-4B was flown at the Naval Air Development Center (NADC), Warminster, Pennsylvania. This was the first of about 44 F-4Bs converted to the 'target drone' configuration by the NADC, a programme that was later to include conversion of 24 QF-4Bs to QF-4Ns, and later still one QF-4N to a QF-4S.

Although their principal function was to test air-to-air missiles (being remotely flown by 'mother' DB-4Bs), the RPV Phantoms were also employed in basic aerodynamic research, air-combat manoeuvring trials and other hazardous flying and combat exercises in which destruction of the pilotless aircraft was likely.

QF-4Bs, DB-4Bs and QG-4Ns were flown at the Pacific Missile Test Center (PMTC), Point Mugu NAS, California, and the Naval Weapons Center (NWC), China Lake, California, but roughly half are now in storage.

The USAF's Thunderbirds

Above *Using early F-4Es the USAF 'Thunderbird' formation aerobatic demonstration team (the 4510th Air Demonstration Squadron) adopted a striking colour scheme of white aircraft with red, white and blue wing and stabilator tips (red outermost); red, white and blue nose (red foremost) and red and white vertical tail. A panel of world flags appeared on the port air intake and the Thunderbird motif on the starboard side. Unlike the US Navy's 'Blue Angels' the Air Force aicraft did not carry any Sparrow missiles* (Master Sergeant David W. Menard). **Below** *Five aircraft of the Thunderbird team; aircraft assigned to the 4510th ADS included the F-4E-31s 66-0286, -0289 and -0294; the F-4E-32s 66-0315, -0319, -0321 and -0329; and the F-4E-33s 66-0353 (team trainer) and -0377* (McDonnell Douglas, Neg No 1190-105, dated October 1971). **Above right** *The Thunderbirds give a demonstration at Nellis AFB, Nevada* (US Air Force, via Master Sergeant David W. Menard). **Right** *F-4E-32-MC, 66-0321/No 3, seen here over Saint Louis; this aircraft was written off at Andrews AFB in June 1972, its place being taken by another -32, 66-0315* (McDonnell Douglas, Neg No 414-12).

Two Marine Corps F-4Ns, 152222/WS-01 and 152243/WS-04, of VMFA-323 based at El Toro MCAS, California. WS-04 features the low-visibility star-and-bar insignia; the fin and fuselage bands are black with yellow diamonds superimposed (Starliner Aviation Press, Neg Nos BW1064 and BW1066).

Chapter 9

Foreign Phantoms

Western air forces select the F-4

Great Britain

The origins of the decision by the British Government to purchase Phantoms for the Royal Navy lay in the year 1964. During the early 1960s the Hawker Siddeley Group was engaged in developing an advanced V/STOL aircraft, the P 1154, an aircraft whose design had been to some extent compromised by attempts to satisfy conflicting requirements put forward by the Air Staff (Royal Air Force) for a single-seat strike aircraft, and by the Royal Navy for a two-seat carrier-borne interceptor. Although there is no evidence to suggest that the widely differing aircraft would not have satisfied their respective requirements, the overall cost of the P 1154 programme, as it shifted away from the original aims of commonality, so frightened the newly elected socialist government under Harold Wilson that one of the new administration's first acts was to cancel the entire programme at a stroke.

Clearly no indigenous replacement could possibly be initiated from scratch to reach service within three years, with the predictable result that the Royal Navy opted for the Phantom—an aircraft it was thought likely could be purchased at relatively low cost; indeed, apart from its lack of V/STOL capability, the Phantom's demonstrated performance was not significantly different from that hoped for from the defunct P 1154. The British order was complicated by the Government's insistence that—in order to recover as many of the jobs lost after cancellation of the P 1154—powerplant and many of the subsystems should be of British origin and manufacture.

Choice of powerplant fell on the Rolls-Royce Spey 202/203, a powerful and reliable turbofan which developed over 20,000 lb-thrust with afterburner, and it was perhaps reasonable to anticipate an aircraft of quite outstanding performance; yet the marriage of airframe and engine was far from satisfactory, and even today problems with the installation have not been entirely cured. Compared to the American J79-powered counterpart the British Spey-powered Phantom is significantly inferior in speed, range and ceiling, and has been widely referred to as the most expensive white elephant flown by the British armed forces. In all probability the cause of these shortcomings lay in the indecent haste for development demanded by the British Government. The military Spey had been adapted from a civil airliner powerplant for the subsonic Buccaneer strike aircraft, and in order to suit it for the Phantom the engine had to be re-stressed for supersonic flight and combat manoeuvres, and provided with afterburner with variable nozzle—all within the space of one year; at the same time the Phantom's fuselage had to be widened and new intake ducts provided to cope with the 20 per cent increase in mass flow (204 lb/sec).

Thus it was in 1965 that two Spey-powered YF-4K prototypes and 20 production Phantom FG Mark 1s were ordered from McDonnell; soon afterwards 39 further

Background photograph *First of the Rolls-Royce Spey-powered Phantoms, the first YF-4K, XT595, for the Royal Navy, flying over Saint Louis* (McDonnell Douglas, Neg No 299-10).

Inset left *Another view of* XT595, *here suitably inscribed, taking off at Lambert Field, Saint Louis* (McDonnell Douglas).

Inset right *A Royal Navy Phantom FGA 1 of the Aeroplane and Armament Experimental Establishment, Boscombe Down, prepares to launch from HMS* Eagle; *note the extra-extensible nose gear leg* (Peter R. Marsh, via Richard Ward).

Above *Phantom FGA 1, XT859/VL-725, in landing attitude with hook and flaps extended* (via Richard Ward).

Above right *Royal Navy helicopters fly past as No 892 Squadron prepares to leave RNAS Yeovilton to embark its Phantoms in HMS* Ark Royal *on September 4 1972* (Ministry of Defence). **Right** *A No 892 Squadron Phantom launches from HMS* Ark Royal *with a load of ten 1,000-lb bombs* (via Richard Ward).

Below right *A Phantom FGA 1, XV572, of No 767 Squadron* (Peter R. Marsh, via Richard Ward).

production aircraft were ordered. However, as the British Government insisted on a fixed-cost contract—as distinct from cost-plus—the rising costs associated with power-plant mating reduced the number of Phantoms delivered to the Royal Navy to no more than 52.

The Royal Navy's Phantom FG 1 features AWG-11 fire control system, Elliott auto-pilot and Ferranti electronics, the latter producing the inertial nav/attack systems; and in order to match the smaller decks of British aircraft carriers improved wing slats were included, together with an extra-extensible (from 20 to 40 ins) nosewheel leg to enable the aircraft to maintain altitude after launch at an effectively lower wind-over-deck speed. To meet the size restriction imposed by the small British deck elevators the entire nose, with radar dish and radome, was made to fold through 180 degrees.

In little over one year McDonnell completed the first YF-4K and this aircraft (the 1,449th F-4) was flown in June 1966. Soon joined by the Second YF-4K, the aircraft underwent trials at Edwards AFB and the US Navy's Patuxent River test centre, British pilots taking part in the flight programme. The aircraft were then brought to the United Kingdom where one was delivered to Hawker Siddeley (the British prime contractor) at Holme-on-Spalding-Moor and the other to Rolls-Royce Ltd at Hucknall.

The first three production deliveries were made direct to RNAS Yeovilton on April 29 1968 after a transatlantic flight; these aircraft were delivered to No 700P Squadron, the Phantom training squadron which was formed at Yeovilton the following day, and were joined by three more during the following two months. Training was taken over by No 767 Squadron, formed in January 1969, it being intended that this unit would be the shore-based back-up squadron for those embarked at sea. In the event only one other Royal Navy Phantom squadron, No 892, was formed (on March 31 1969) and this was embarked in HMS *Ark Royal*, serving until November 27 1978.

In the Royal Air Force, with the benefit of greater engineering back-up, the Phantom fared perceptibly better, although the shortcomings of the Spey adaptation and installation, of course, remained. The situation was not made any less complex when the decision was taken to de-commission HMS *Ark Royal*, end a fixed-wing combat commitment by the Royal Navy, and to pass some of the naval Phantom FG 1s to the Royal Air Force. (This decision was to some extent reversed with the commissioning of the new anti-submarine carrier which, as the world now knows, embarked Sea Harriers which performed so well in the Falkland Islands campaign of 1982.)

Reasoning behind the decision to purchase Phantoms for the RAF was much the same as that of the Admiralty, although the future planning was, of course, somewhat different. It was intended that the RAF's Mark 2 Phantom would perform strike and reconnaissance rôles with NATO's Second Tactical Air Force until replaced by the SEPECAT Jaguar, due to arrive in service in 1971, whereupon the Phantom FGR 2 would replace the RAF's old Lightnings in the air defence rôle over Britain. Such planning, involving as it did a

Below *The Royal Air Force's first F-4M Phantom FGR 2, XT852, on an early flight from Saint Louis* (McDonnell Douglas, Neg No 44457, dated April 1967).

Above right *Much-embellished RAF Phantom FRG 2, XV424—one might say an all-embracing anniversary aircraft—displayed at Greenham Common in 1978. Named 'Alcock and Brown' on the fin, and inscribed '1919 First Non-stop Transatlantic Flight' on the wing drop tanks, the aircraft carried the inscription '1919 Rolls-Royce Eagle, 1979 Rolls-Royce Spey' on the nose. Painted along the fuselage spine were the 14 flags of NATO members and the inscription 'NATO Thirtieth Anniversary'. Crew members, whose names were painted on the canopy sills, were Squadron Leader A.J.N. Alcock, MBE, and Flight Lieutenant W.N. Browne!* (Starliner Aviation Press, Neg No CS581).

Right *Bearing the Squadron's 45-year-old zig-zag flash is this Phantom FGR 2, XV475, of No 17 (Fighter) Squadron based at Bruggen, Germany* (RAF Bruggen, Neg No 7213G/5A, dated January 12 1970).

Below right *A Phantom FGR 2 of the RAF's No 43 (Fighter) Squadron—'The Fighting Cocks'—leads a pair of USAF F-4Es of the 525th TFS, 36th TFW, over Germany* (Ministry of Defence, Neg No TN6611/35, dated 1969).

reversal of the customary 'interceptor-then-ground attack' pattern, obviously ran a considerable risk of inducing fatigue life limitations during the punishing low-level phase of the Phantom's career, such that it might arrive in service in the air defence rôle with fatigue-induced airframe limitations.

The British Government ordered two prototype YF-4Ms and 150 production Phantom FGR Mark 2s in 1965-6, and the first prototype (*XT852*) was first flown at Holloman AFB on February 17 1967. The second aircraft was also flown that year and once again British pilots took part in the initial trials and development, and prepared pilots' notes in draft form. The first production FGR 2 (*XT891*) flew in to Yeovilton on July 18 1968, and two days later moved on to No 23 Maintenance Unit at Aldergrove in Northern Ireland for final Service preparation. (Some of the later naval Phantoms were delivered direct to Aldergrove.)

First RAF unit to fly Phantom 2s was No 228 Operational Conversion Unit at Coningsby which, although formed in February 1968, did not receive its first aircraft until the following August; however, thereafter Phantoms arrived at an increasing rate and by October 29 1969 the RAF's order had been completed. Once again the fixed-cost nature of the British contract reduced the number of Phantoms for the RAF from 150 to 118, but to make up part of the deficiency 14 Royal Navy aircraft were delivered direct to the RAF.

First RAF Phantom squadron was No 6, re-formed at Coningsby on May 7 1969 with crews trained by No 228 OCU. On September 1 No 43 (Fighter) Squadron re-formed at Leuchars as No 54 (Fighter) Squadron re-formed at Coningsby, the former unit being equipped with the naval version to perform the air defence rôle over Britain. The next squadron, No 14, re-formed at Bruggen in Germany on June 30 1970, being joined almost immediately by No 17 (Fighter) Squadron. No 2 Squadron, a tactical reconnaissance unit, formed at Laarbruch on December 14 1970, its Phantoms equipped to carry a centreline pod containing EMI infra-red linescan and sideways-looking radar. Last squadron to equip with Phantoms in Germany during this initial re-equipment phase was No 31 at Bruggen in October 1971.

The SEPECAT Jaguar eventually arrived in the RAF in 1973, and in March the following year No 54 Squadron gave up its Phantoms to take on the Anglo-French aircraft. The Phantoms, now equipped with the conventional armament of four Sparrows and four Sidewinders, were then passed to that most famous of all RAF fighter squadrons, No 111 at Conningsby. Nos 23 and 29 Squadrons also received Phantoms as the Jaguar slowly came into service in Germany.

During the mid-1970s Phantoms underwent limited re-engineering, which included strengthening of the wing (to make good extended fatigue life), and were equipped with a radar warning receiver (RWR) in a fairing at the top of the fin. It was expected that, following the phasing out of the Phantom with the Royal Navy, the Mark 1s would enable the RAF to form another squadron, but in the event No 111 (Fighter) Squadron gradually converted to the naval aircraft, its own Mark 2s being pooled to support the other existing squadrons.

As a postscript to this account of British use of the Phantom, one further episode remains to be told. Following the successful British campaign to recover the Falkland

Above left *Phantom FGR 2, XV437, of No 54 (Fighter) Squadron loaded with wing drop tanks, four rocket launchers, two Sparrow missiles, a centreline reconnaissance pod and two ECM units* (Ministry of Defence, Neg No TN6443/5). **Left** *Phantom FGR 2, XV432, on No 6 (Fighter) Squadron carrying two wing drop tanks, six rocket launchers, three Sparrows and a ventral gun pod* (Ministry of Defence, Neg No TN6443/15).

Top *No 228 Operational Conversion Unit Phantom FGR 2, XV488/R, at Biggin Hill in 1980; the aircraft features a fin-tip RWR antenna fairing* (Neg No BW1057). **Above** *FGR Mark 2, XV401, of No 41 (Fighter) Squadron with centreline drop tank at Coltishall in September 1973* (Neg No CS579). **Below** *XV499/R of No 92 (Fighter) Squadron with four Sparrow missiles at Finningley in 1977* (Neg No CS591). **Bottom** *XV469/A of No 56 (Fighter) Squadron at Wattisham in April 1980* (Neg No CS587. All photographs, Starliner Aviation Press).

Islands from illegal occupation by Argentine forces in 1982, the problem arose of maintaining a medium-term air defence over the islands, a problem involving the creation of an autonomous squadron at the far end of a costly supply route, with no more than limited radar cover and flying aircraft of adequate performance and reliability to ensure defence against the modern aircraft being flown by the Argentine Air Force and Navy. The choice once more fell upon the F-4 and, so as to avoid logistic complications which might arise if the Spey-powered Phantom were deployed, negotiations were started by the British Government to purchase some 15–20 late model ex-US aircraft—probably the F-4s—at a unit fly-away price of around £800,000. At the time of writing no exact details of the order had been announced, nor any date given for delivery of the aircraft.

Israel

Following the 1967 Six-Day War between Israel and her Arab neighbours the United States became the largest overseas supplier of aircraft to the Israeli Air Force (Heyl Ha'Avir), and after an initial order for 48 Douglas A-4Hs and TA-4H trainers had been completed late in 1967, a contract was negotiated for the supply of 50 F-4E Phantoms and six RF-4E reconnaissance aircraft, these aircraft entering service with three squadrons in 1969.

By 1973—the year of the Yom Kippur War—around 180 F-4Es and 12 RF-4Es had been delivered and served with six strike squadrons (their air defence rôle being secondary). In that bitter war Israeli Phantoms were in constant action over Egyptian territory along the Suez Canal, using both unguided and 'smart' bombs against soft targets, but proved disastrously vulnerable to the newly-deployed Soviet SA-6 missiles, 33 aircraft being lost—almost all to these continuous wave-guidance SAMs. In reply to

Below and overleaf *These F-4Es of the Tsvah Haganah le Israel/Heyl Ha'Avir—whose deliveries started in 1969—display the unmistakable signs of hurried obliteration of USAF markings, not to mention the near-paranoic flourishes of an Israeli censor (all squadron markings are systematically painted out).* (McDonnell Douglas; photograph overleaf, Neg No 149-2, dated January 1974).

frantic requests by the Israelis for an antidote to these troublesome weapons the United States began supplying AGM-45A Shrike anti-radiation missiles, but these proved inadequate to counter the disconcerting manoeuvrability of the SA-6 which, once launched, could out-perform even an evading Phantom. It was this experience (as well as that of the Vietnam War, so recently ended for the United States) that caused the USAF to upgrade its whole programme of anti-radiation weaponry.

By 1978 a total of 204 F-4Es had been delivered to the Israeli Air Force, of which around 65 had been lost in accidents, air combat and to SAMs. The Israelis had, however, adopted the use of decoy flares to counter heat-seeking SAMs, and it has been reported that equipment updating has included the installation of the indigenous Elta EL/M-2021 radar, multi-mode equipment capable of terrain-following/avoidance, automatic target acquisition, air-to-ground weapon delivery, search and mapping. It is also said that the Israeli F-4E has been made compatible with the indigenous Luz stand-off weapon. At least six of the RF-4Es were still in service in 1980, serving alongside the F-4Es on seven squadrons.

West Germany

The West German Luftwaffe regained its major status among world air forces during the early 1960s with its controversial choice of the Lockheed F-104G 'Super Starfighter', aircraft which, within the structure of NATO, were assigned to the strike rôle, with 30 aircraft assuming the quick-reaction nuclear strike task. Two Geschwader were also assigned to the air defence rôle, and it was to replace their F-104Gs that West Germany decided on the McDonnell F-4EF at the end of the 1960s.

Originally conceived as a single-seat, simplified development of the F-4E, the EF was a contender in the US International Fighter Competition of 1969–71, intended to produce an aircraft suited to the relatively limited funding available among foreign air forces; it was to incorporate an internal gun, reduced fuel capacity, a simplified APQ-120 radar and simplified electronics, and lacked flight refuelling capability.

In due course the German Air Force opted to return to the two-seat configuration, and the German F-4F, ultimately purchased, was in effect a less simplified version of the F-4E. Most of the classified items of American electronics—not being available for export—were omitted, while wings, rear fuselage, tail unit and engines were manufactured in West Germany and shipped to Saint Louis for assembly. A total of 175 F-4Fs was purchased at a cost of around £400 m. First flight was in May 1975 and production deliveries took place between June that year and April 1976.

The F-4F entered service with the Luftwaffe's JG 71 *Richthofen* at Wittmundhafen and JG 74 *Mölders* at Neuberg in the interception rôle (30 aircraft on each unit), and in the fighter-strike rôle with JaboG 35 and 36 at Pferdsfeld and Rheine-Hopsten respectively (with 36 aircraft on each unit).

Assuming a numerically greater importance in the Luftwaffe than in other air forces, the reconnaissance RF-4E replaced the RF-104G and served with Aufklärungsgeschwader 51 *Immelmann* at Bremgarten and AG 52 at Leck (both Geschwader with 30 aircraft). Four other RF-4Es were assigned to special operations and the remainder held in reserve storage. A total of 88 aircraft was ordered in 1968 and once more external costs were to a large extent offset by indigenous component and equipment manufacture. Their equip-

A slatted F-4F of the German Luftwaffe (McDonnell Douglas, Neg No 2545-12, dated May 1973).

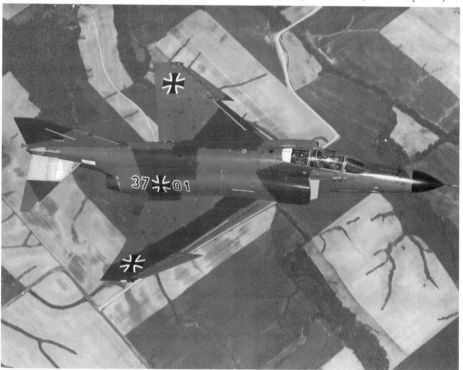

Above *Two RF-4Es (35 + 12 and 35 + 34) of Aufklärungsgeschwader 51 « Immelmann »* (Top, Starliner Aviation Press, Neg No CS574; bottom, Archiv Redemann, via Richard Ward).

Below *The first RF-4E-43-MC destined for the Luftwaffe in flight over the Mississippi River* (McDonnell Douglas).

ment included Goodyear sideways-looking radar and a real-time data link for ground processing of reconnaissance information.

Incidentally German manufacturers have been able to underbid American companies for numerous components of the Phantom, and have pursued a lucrative sub-contract programme for many foreign users. Ultimately the RF-4E and F-4F will be replaced by the multi-rôle Panavia Tornado in the Luftwaffe.

Australia

In 1963 the Australian Government announced its decision to purchase 24 General Dynamics F-111 variable-geometry strike and reconnaissance aircraft at a cost of $146 m, their delivery being planned for 1968. However, owing to the onset of fatigue problems with this aircraft, delivery was repeatedly postponed (while overall costs soared to around $345 m), and it was decided to lease 24 F-4E and RF-4E Phantoms as an interim measure pending delivery of the F-111s.

The Phantoms served with the RAAF's Nos 1 and 6 Squadrons at Amberley between 1970 and 1973 (when the F-111s finally arrived); one F-4E crashed at Evans Head in June 1971, and the remainder were flown back to the United States in 1973–74, subsequently to serve with the USAF.

An ex-USAF F-4E being checked out at Saint Louis prior to delivery on loan to the Royal Australian Air Force (McDonnell Douglas, Neg No 748-3, dated September 1970).

Top *F-4Es in service with the RAAF; individual Australian aircraft numbers corresponded to the last two digits of the USAF BuAer Nos* (Royal Australian Air Force, Neg No CNB71-16-2, dated March 25 1971).
Above *RAAF F-4E No 05 taxying at Amberley where the Phantom equipped Nos 1 and 6 Squadrons* (via Richard Ward).

Iran

As evidence of the United States' support for the Shah of Iran in his somewhat precarious stand against revolutionary factions in the oil-rich regions of the Middle East, America undertood a massive programme to modernise the Imperial Iranian Air Force (Nirou Havai Shahanshahiye Iran) in the early 1970s. Cornerstone of the air force's air defence

An F-4D of the Imperial Iranian Air Force's 306th Fighter Squadron at Mehrabad, fitted with a ventral gun pod (McDonnell Douglas, Neg No 461-4, dated August 1969).

and reconnaissance elements was to be the F-4E and RF-4E, the purchase cost of which ran to billions of dollars, supported by massive oil revenues from the fuel-thirsty West.

Initially Iran had ordered 32 F-4Ds in 1966, and these had entered service with two interceptor squadrons based at Mehrabad in 1969. Four years later orders totalling 177 F-4Es and 28 RF-4Es were placed, deliveries being made between 1974 and 1977. The F-4Es, whose normal armament included the M-61 Vulcan 20 mm gun in centreline pod, four Sparrows and four Sidewinders, equipped eight further squadrons based at Mehrabad, Tabriz and Shiraz, and 12 of the RF-4Es served on one squadron (delivery of the remaining 16 RF-4Es was prevented by the revolution that ended the Shah's monarchy, and these aircraft were placed in storage at Davis-Monthan AFB).

Iranian F-4Es carried APR-37 passive warning receivers to detect ground radar emissions and SAM launching, and ALQ-72 active ECM pods could be fitted in the rear pair of Sparrow recesses. To complement the F-4Es' secondary strike rôle, no fewer than 2,850 Hughes Maverick ASMs were purchased by Iran. All Iranian F-4Es and RF-4Es possessed in-flight refuelling facilities, the tanker force comprising 12 Boeing 707-3J9-Cs and eight ex-TWA Boeing 747s.

The presence, however, of Soviet-built MiG-25 Foxbats in neighbouring Arab states in the mid-1970s prompted the purchase of 80 F-14A Tomcats and these were intended to take over the air interception rôle from the F-4Es, the latter assuming a primary strike rôle. Nevertheless, on account of American withdrawal of technical advisers from Iran and the imposition of a military equipment sales ban at the time of the revolution, the serviceability of the F-4Es, RF-4Es and F-14As declined sharply from the opening weeks of the war with Iraq that started in 1981.

Japan

The only Phantoms not built by the parent company at Saint Louis are those manufactured under licence in Japan by Mitsubishi. After the ending of a prohibition of Japanese military forces in 1954 the Japanese Air Self-Defence Force (Koku Jiei Tai) was established almost exclusively with American-built aircraft but, as the nation's manufacturing industries were re-built, greater emphasis came to be laid on licence production of foreign aircraft, and during the Third Defence Build-up Programme (DBP) of 1965–70 it was intended to develop a new indigenous fighter, known then as the F-X, but owing to constant reductions in defence expenditure it was decided to negotiate licence production of the Phantom instead.

Two pattern F-4EJ prototypes were built by McDonnell and delivered in July 1971, and during the Fourth DBP (1971–76) orders were placed for 128 production aircraft with Mitsubishi Heavy Industries at Nagoya, the first of which flew in 1972. These F-4EJs entered service with Nos 301, 302, 303 and 304 Squadrons of the 8th Air Wing based at Hyakuri, Chitose and Tsuiki, and, with ten further aircraft ordered in 1977, No 305 Squadron.

Fourteen photo reconnaissance RF-4EJs were also ordered from the United States to equip No 501 Squadron based at Hyakuri.

The Koku Jiei Tai F-4EJs featured the lengthened gun fairing and slatted stabilator, but not the slatted wing. **Below** *One of the Saint Louis-built pattern aircraft flying in America before delivery* (McDonnell Douglas, Neg No 862-6, dated January 10 1971). **Right** *F-4EJs (built by Mitsubishi) first entered service with Japan's No 301 Squadron at Hyakuri in 1973* (McDonnell Douglas, Neg No 117597-5, dated June 1977).

Below right *First RF-4EJ (all of which were produced by the parent company) flying in America; as the reconnaissance version of the Phantom has no Sparrow recesses, the EROS collision avoidance pod is mounted on the centreline* (McDonnell Douglas, Neg No 3723-20, dated October 1974).

RF-4EJs equipped No 501 Squadron at Hyakuri; they were of the late production standard with smooth-contour camera fairing. The aircraft in the lower photograph features a three-tone camouflage—stone, olive-drab and dark blue-green (McDonnell Douglas, Neg Nos 5605-2, dated June 1977, and 118173-15, dated June 1973).

Spain

Although Spain remained outside the North Atlantic Treaty Organisation until several years after the end of the Franco régime (per se), the United States had entered into a number of periodically-renewable defence agreements linking the supply of military equipment in consideration of the use of a number of bases in Spain. In particular the large base at Torrejon, 15 miles north-east of Madrid, was built following the conclusion of a mutual defence pact between the two nations in 1953, opening up as a joint USAF/EdA (Ejercito del Aire, Spanish Air Force) some six years later.

After initial supplies of North American F-86F Sabres, 18 F-104G and three TF-104G Super Starfighters were delivered through Mutual Weapons Assistance Programme funding between March 1965 and January 1966, the aircraft serving with Escuadrón 161 (later Esc 194) of Ala de Caza 16.

In 1971 the EdA selected the F-4 to replace the F-104G and, as it was proposed to phase out the latter fairly quickly, the choice of replacement fell upon the F-4C as being readily available from the USAF in Europe. Accordingly in 1972 36 F-4Cs of the 81st Tactical Fighter Wing (some of which had already served in combat operations over Vietnam) were handed over to the EdA and, after thorough overhaul at the CASA plant at Getafe, were delivered to the newly commissioned Escuadrón 121 at Torrejon, and later Esc 122 (after disbanding Esc 104).

Designated the C.12 in Spanish service, the Phantoms continued to serve on Ala 12's

Ex-USAF McDonnell Douglas F-4Cs destined for the Ejercito del Aire. Owing to the excellent servicing facilities available in Spain, these elderly aeroplanes (designated the C.12) have given excellent service (McDonnell Douglas, Neg No 90013, dated January 1972).

Displaying the famous black cat insignia on its fin, this Spanish C.12 (C12-40) served on EdA/Ala 12 at Torrejon (Starliner Aviation Press, Neg No CS576).

two squadrons at Torrejon throughout the 1970s, four aircraft being lost in accidents and being joined by four further ex-USAF F-4Cs (from the 35th TFW and 58th TTW) late in 1978, and flew more than 50,000 hours. Four RF-4Cs (designated CR.12s) were also acquired, and each Escuadrón flies two. Normal weapon load of the C.12s comprises four AIM-9J Sidewinders, four AIM-7E Sparrows and the SUU-16/A gun pod.

Although EdA's Mirage F 1s now undertake the majority of alert interceptions, it is not intended to phase out the Phantom until 1985–86 when the McDonnell Douglas F-18 Hornet will be delivered.

Greece

The Hellenic Air Force (Helleniki Aeroporia) is almost entirely equipped with American-supplied aircraft, having for years been a strange amalgam of strength and weakness within the NATO structure; on the one hand Greece occupies a position of strategic importance on Europe's southern flank facing the Soviet Union, yet enjoys strained relations with her neighbouring NATO partner, Turkey—for centuries a traditional enemy.

In the early 1970s an initial batch of 38 standard export F-4Es was supplied by the United States to Greece, and these entered service with two mire (squadrons) of the 117ª Pterigha (Wing), assigned to the 28th Tactical Air Command, USAFE and based at Andravidha. Two aircraft were lost in accidents but made good by a pair of replacements in about 1975, followed soon afterwards by eight RF-4Es. In 1977 President Carter approved the sale of 18 further F-4Es for delivery in 1978–79.

Slatted, late-standard F-4E in the markings of the Helleniki Aeroporia; note the long-barrel gun fairing and combat camera (McDonnell Douglas, Neg No 3345-2).

Turkey

At roughly the same time as Greece was introducing the F-4E into her air force, Turkey received the first of two batches of F-4Es, each of 20 aircraft, for the Türk Hava Kuvvetleri (Turkish Air Force) within NATO's 6th Allied Tactical Air Force, to perform the fighter-strike rôle. They equipped 113 Filo (squadron) of Turkey's 1st Tactical Air Force (Birinci Taktik Hava Kuvveti) based at Eskisehir, and 162 Filo at Bandirma; and in 1977 the supply of 32 further F-4Es and eight RF-4Es was approved by the US Government, these probably replacing the aged F-100s of 131 and 132 Filo at Konya. Turkish F-F-4Es are compatible with the Hughes Maverick air-to-surface missile.

South Korea

Ever since the end of the Korean War in 1953 relations between the north and south have remained volatile, with the result that the United States has continued to assist in the strengthening of the Republic of Korea Air Force (ROKAF)—at least until 1978 when President Carter threatened to withdraw American assistance. 112 F-86F Sabres, supplied in 1956-7, were followed by F-5S Freedom Fighters in the 1960s, together with 50 ex-USAF F-86Ds.

In 1969 18 F-4D Phantoms began to replace the F-86Ds with the ROKAF's 1st Fighter Wing, and in 1972—after South Korean F-5s were transferred to South Vietnam—a further batch of 18 F-4Ds was supplied to ROKAF; in the mid-1970s 37 F-4Es, together with 341 AIM-7E Sparrow missiles, were delivered to complete the equipping of four squadrons.

Above *F-4E for Turkey. Although essentially dual-rôle aircraft the slatted Phantoms of the Türk Hava Kuvvetleri were primarily tasked with ground attack duties as part of NATO's 6th ATAF* (McDonnell Douglas, Neg No 3532-9, dated July 1974).

Below *South Korea has been a relatively large user of the Phantom. The photograph shows an early delivery, one of the first batch of ex-USAF F-4Ds* (McDonnell Douglas). **Above right** *A late-standard F-4E, delivered to the ROKAF in the mid-1970s* (McDonnell Douglas, Neg No 111040, dated February 1974).

Reports of orders for 16 ex-USAF RF-4Es have not been confirmed, although it was said that the requirement might be filled by the Iranian aircraft whose delivery was suspended in 1978.

Egypt

Most recent recipient of the F-4E Phantom was Egypt which, as the result of improving relations with the West in the late 1970s (as much as deteriorating relations with neighbouring Libya), was supplied with 35 ex-USAF aircraft in 1980. The aircraft, however, were early production examples and had already seen considerable service and, with only limited servicing facilities available, the Egyptian 222nd Tactical Fighter Brigade (with which the two Phantom squadrons served at Cairo West), soon expressed growing dissatisfaction with the aircraft's serviceability, and all were flown back to America with temporary US markings in May 1982 for major overhaul. Meanwhile the Egyptian government was considering discarding the aircraft altogether and selling them to Turkey.

However, although Egypt's plans to acquire 120 F-16 Fighting Falcons and 120 F-5G Tigersharks were well advanced at that time, it was decided to retain the F-4Es (at least for a further year), and by January 1983 they had been flown back to Cairo West.

*   *   *

Although it is likely that the Phantom will continue to enjoy further 'second-hand' sales for years to come, the last newly-built aircraft at Saint Louis—the 5,057th—was rolled out some years ago to make way for McDonnell Douglas' new F-18 fighter. Total production over 20 years, including the 138 aircraft produced in Japan, thereby reached 5,195, representing a programme of some 20 billion dollars in first-time sales.

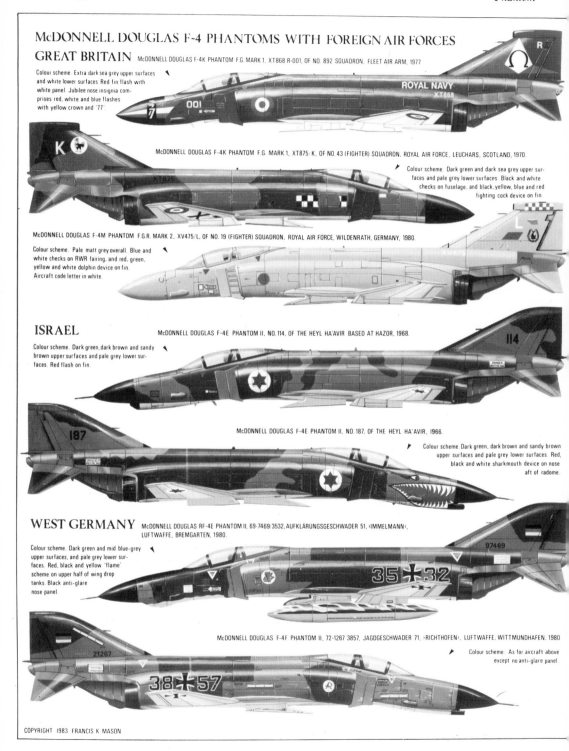

McDONNELL DOUGLAS F-4 PHANTOMS WITH FOREIGN AIR FORCES

GREAT BRITAIN McDONNELL DOUGLAS F-4K PHANTOM F.G. MARK 1, XT868 R-001, OF NO. 892 SQUADRON, FLEET AIR ARM, 1977

Colour scheme. Extra dark sea grey upper surfaces
and white lower surfaces. Red fin flash with
white panel. Jubilee nose insignia comprises red, white and blue flashes
with yellow crown and '77'.

ROYAL NAVY
XT868
001

McDONNELL DOUGLAS F-4K PHANTOM F.G. MARK 1, XT875/K, OF NO. 43 (FIGHTER) SQUADRON, ROYAL AIR FORCE, LEUCHARS, SCOTLAND, 1970.

Colour scheme. Dark green and dark sea grey upper surfaces and pale grey lower surfaces. Black and white
checks on fuselage, and black, yellow, blue and red
fighting cock device on fin.

McDONNELL DOUGLAS F-4M PHANTOM F.G.R. MARK 2, XV475/L, OF NO. 19 (FIGHTER) SQUADRON, ROYAL AIR FORCE, WILDENRATH, GERMANY, 1980.

Colour scheme. Pale matt grey overall. Blue and
white checks on RWR fairing, and red, green,
yellow and white dolphin device on fin.
Aircraft code letter in white.

ISRAEL McDONNELL DOUGLAS F-4E PHANTOM II, NO. 114, OF THE HEYL HA'AVIR BASED AT HAZOR, 1968.

Colour scheme. Dark green, dark brown and sandy
brown upper surfaces and pale grey lower surfaces. Red flash on fin.

114

McDONNELL DOUGLAS F-4E PHANTOM II, NO. 187, OF THE HEYL HA'AVIR, 1966.

187

Colour scheme. Dark green, dark brown and sandy brown
upper surfaces and pale grey lower surfaces. Red,
black and white sharkmouth device on nose
aft of radome.

WEST GERMANY McDONNELL DOUGLAS RF-4E PHANTOM II, 69-7469/3532, AUFKLÄRUNGSGESCHWADER 51, ›IMMELMANN‹, LUFTWAFFE, BREMGARTEN, 1980.

Colour scheme. Dark green and mid blue-grey
upper surfaces, and pale grey lower surfaces. Red, black and yellow 'flame'
scheme on upper half of wing drop
tanks. Black anti-glare
nose panel.

97469
35✠32

McDONNELL DOUGLAS F-4F PHANTOM II, 72-1267 3857, JAGDGESCHWADER 71, ›RICHTHOFEN‹, LUFTWAFFE, WITTMUNDHAFEN, 1980

Colour scheme. As for aircraft above
except no anti-glare panel.

21267
38✠57

McDONNELL DOUGLAS F-4 PHANTOMS WITH FOREIGN AIR FORCES

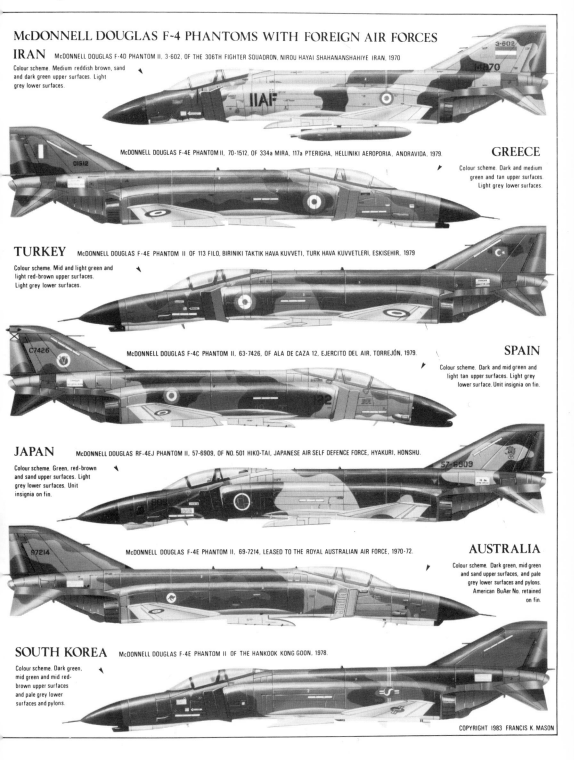

IRAN   McDONNELL DOUGLAS F-4D PHANTOM II, 3-602, OF THE 306TH FIGHTER SQUADRON, NIROU HAVAI SHAHANANSHAHIYE IRAN, 1970

Colour scheme. Medium reddish brown, sand and dark green upper surfaces. Light grey lower surfaces.

McDONNELL DOUGLAS F-4E PHANTOM II, 70-1512, OF 334a MIRA, 117a PTERIGHA, HELLINIKI AEROPORIA, ANDRAVIDA, 1979.

GREECE

Colour scheme. Dark and medium green and tan upper surfaces. Light grey lower surfaces.

TURKEY   McDONNELL DOUGLAS F-4E PHANTOM II OF 113 FILO, BIRINIKI TAKTIK HAVA KUVVETI, TURK HAVA KUVVETLERI, ESKISEHIR, 1979

Colour scheme. Mid and light green and light red-brown upper surfaces. Light grey lower surfaces.

McDONNELL DOUGLAS F-4C PHANTOM II, 63-7426, OF ALA DE CAZA 12, EJERCITO DEL AIR, TORREJÓN, 1979.

SPAIN

Colour scheme. Dark and mid green and light tan upper surfaces. Light grey lower surface. Unit insignia on fin.

JAPAN   McDONNELL DOUGLAS RF-4EJ PHANTOM II, 57-6909, OF NO. 501 HIKO-TAI, JAPANESE AIR SELF DEFENCE FORCE, HYAKURI, HONSHU.

Colour scheme. Green, red-brown and sand upper surfaces. Light grey lower surfaces. Unit insignia on fin.

McDONNELL DOUGLAS F-4E PHANTOM II, 69-7214, LEASED TO THE ROYAL AUSTRALIAN AIR FORCE, 1970-72.

AUSTRALIA

Colour scheme. Dark green, mid green and sand upper surfaces, and pale grey lower surfaces and pylons. American BuAer No. retained on fin.

SOUTH KOREA   McDONNELL DOUGLAS F-4E PHANTOM II OF THE HANKOOK KONG GOON, 1978.

Colour scheme. Dark green, mid green and mid red-brown upper surfaces and pale grey lower surfaces and pylons.

Appendices

1 Glossary of abbreviations

AAC Alaskan Air Command.
A&AEE Aircraft & Armament Experimental Establishment (UK).
AAG/S/W Aeromedical Airlift Group/Squadron/Wing.
AB Air Base.
ABW Air Base Wing.
ACCS/W Air Command & Control Squadron.
AD Air Division.
ADCOM Aerospace Defense Command.
ADTC Armament Development & Test Center.
ADWC Air Defense Weapons Center.
AF Air Force.
AFAF Air Force Auxiliary Field.
AFB Air Force Base.
AFCS Air Force Communications Service.
AFFTC Air Force Flight Test Center.
AFM Air Force Museum.
AFRES Air Force Reserve.
AFSC Air Force Systems Command.
AIM Airborne Interception Missile.
AK (Ak) Alaska.
AL (Al) Alabama.
AMCS Airborne Missile Control System.
ANG Air National Guard.
ANGB Air National Guard Base.
ARDC Air Research & Development Center.
ARPS Aerospace Research Pilots' School.
ARS/G/W Airborne Refuelling Squadron/Group/Wing.
ASD Aeronautical Systems Division.
ASM Air-to-surface missile.
ASPJ Advanced, self-protection jammer.
ASW Air-to-surface warfare.
ATC/W Air Training Command/Wing.
ATTW Aircrew Training & Test Wing.
AW/CW (also **AWaCS/W**) Airborne Early Warning and Control Squadron/Wing.
AZ (Az) Arizona.
BG/S/W Bombardment Group/Squadron/Wing.
BIS (US Navy) Board of Inspection and Survey.
BLCS Boundary Layer Control System.
BuAer Bureau of Aeronautics.
CA (Ca) California.
CADC Central Air Data Computer.
CAF Canadian Armed Forces.
CAP Combat Air Patrol.
CBU Cluster bomb unit.
CCRS Combat Crew Replacement Squadron.
CCTW Combat Crew Training Wing.
CFE Central Fighter Establishment (UK).
CILOP Conversion in Lieu of Procurement.
CNI Communications/Navigation/Identification (System).
CNO Chief of Naval Operations.
CO (Co) Colorado.
CORDS Coherent-On-Receive Doppler System.
CS/W Composite Squadron/Wing.
CSG/W Combat Support Group/Wing.
CST Carrier Suitability Trials.
CT (Ct) Connecticutt.
CVA(N) Aircraft Carrier (Heavier-than-Air), Attack Category (Nuclear powered).
CW Centimetric wavelength.
CZ (Cz) Canal Zone.
DC District of Columbia.
DE (De) Delaware.
Det Detachment.
DFC Dogfight Computer.
DLC Direct-Lift Control.
DSARC Defense Systems Acquisition Review Council

DSES Defense Systems Evaluation Squadron.
DWCS Digital Weapon Control System.
ECM Electronic Countermeasures.
ECS Electronic Countermeasures Squadron.
EENG Extra-extendible nose gear.
ELINT Electronic Intelligence.
EO Electro-optics.
EP/B Eclipse Pioneer/Bendix.
ERASE Electromagnetic Radiation Source Elimination.
EROS Eliminate Range-Zero System.
EW Electronic Warfare.
FAA Fleet Air Arm (UK).
FAI Fédération Aéronautique Internationale.
FCLP Field Carrier Landing Practice.
FCS Facility Checking Squadron (also Fire Control System).
FDS Flight Demonstration Squadron (Blue Angels).
FGR Fighter, general reconnaissance.
FIS/G Fighter Interceptor Squadron/Group.
FITS Fighter Interceptor Training Squadron.
FLIR Forward-looking infra-red.
FTS/W Flying Training Squadron/Wing.
FWS Fighter Weapons School.
GA (Ga) Georgia.
GBU Guided bomb unit.
GE General Electric.
HAC Hellenic Air Force.
HF High Frequency.
HI (Hi) Hawaii.
HUD Head-up Display.
IA (Ia) Iowa.
ID (Id) Idaho.
IDF/AF Israeli Defence Force/Air Force.
IFF Indentification, friend or foe.
IFR In-flight refuelling.
IIAF Imperial Iranian Air Force.
IL (Il) Illinois.
IN (In) Indiana.
INS Inertial Navigation System.
IR Infra-red.
JASDF Japan Air Self-Defence Force.
KS (Ks) Kansas.
KY (Ky) Kentucky.
LA (La) Louisiana.
LCG Lead-computing Gunsight.
LGB Laser-guided bomb.
LLLTV Low-light-level television.
LORAN Long-range Navigation (System).
LTV Ling-Temco-Vought.
MA (Ma) Massachusetts.
MAAG Military Air Advisory Group.
MAC McDonnell Aircraft Company.
MCAS Marine Corps Air Station.

MASDC Military Aircraft Storage & Disposition Center.
MDC McDonnell Douglas Corporation.
MD (Md) Maryland.
ME (Me) Maine.
MER Multiple ejector rack.
MI (Mi) Michigan.
MN (Mn) Minnesota.
MO (Mo) Missouri.
MS (Ms) Mississippi.
MT (Mt) Montana.
NADC Naval Air Development Center.
NAF Naval Air Facility.
NARF Naval Air Rework Facility.
NAS Naval Air Station.
NASA National Aeronautical & Space Administration.
NATC/F Naval Air Test Center/Facility.
NB (Nb) Nebraska.
NC (Nc) North Carolina.
ND (Nd) North Dakota.
NFWS Navy Fighter Weapons School.
NH (Nh) New Hampshire.
NJ (Nj) New Jersey.
NM (Nm) New Mexico.
NRL Naval Research Laboratory.
NTPS Naval Test Pilots' School.
NV (Nv) Nevada.
NWC Naval Weapons Center.
NWEF Naval Weapons Evaluation Facility.
NY (Ny) New York.
OH (Oh) Ohio.
OK (Ok) Oklahoma.
OR (Or) Oregon.
PA (Pa) Pennsylvania.
PACAF Pacific Air Forces.
PMTC Pacific Missile Test Center.
PR (Pr) Puerto Rico.
RC Raytheon Corporation.
RHAWS Radar Homing and Warning System.
RI (Ri) Rhode Island.
RIO Radar Intercept Officer (Operator).
RTAF/B Royal Thai Air Force (Base).
RW Reconnaissance Wing.
SAM Surface-to-Air missile.
SC (Sc) South Carolina.
SD (Sd) South Dakota.
SEAM Sidewinder Expanded Acquisition Mode.
SLAR Side-looking Aircraft Radar.
Sqn Squadron.
SV(N)AF South Vietnam Air Force.
TAC Tactical Air Command (also Tactical Airlift Command).
TASS Tactical Air Support Squadron.

TFS/W Tactical Fighter Squadron/Wing.
TFTAS Tactical Fighter Training &
Aggressor Squadron.
TFTS Tactical Fighter Training Squadron.
TISEO Target Identification System, Electro-
optical (AN/ASX-1).
TN (Tn) Tennessee.
TRS/W Tactical Reconnaissance
Squadron/Wing.
TS/G Test Squadron/Group.
TTC Tactical Training Center.
TTW Tactical Training Wing.
TX (Tx) Texas.
UHF Ultra-high frequency.
USAFA United States Air Force Academy.
UT (Ut) Utah.
V (In US Navy and Marine Corps units)
Heavier-than-Air.
VA Navy Attack Squadron (also Va, Virginia).
VC Navy Composite Squadron.
VF Navy Fighter Squadron.
VFA Navy Fighter Attack Squadron.

VFP Navy Photographic Reconnaissance
Squadron.
VMA Marine Corps Attack Squadron.
VMA(AW) Marine Corps All-weather Attack
Squadron.
VMAT Marine Corps Attack Training
Squadron.
VMFA Marine Corps Fighter Attack
Squadron.
VMFAT Marine Corps Fighter Attack
Training Squadron.
VMFP Marine Corps Photographic
Reconnaissance Squadron.
VX Navy Air Test and Valuation Squadron.
VT (Vt) Vermont.
VTAS Visual Target Acquisition System.
WA (Wa) Washington.
WI (Wi) Wisconsin.
WRC Weapons Release Computer.
WSO Weapons Systems Operator.
WV (Wv) West Virginia.
WY (Wy) Wyoming.

2   Specifications
Geometric data
McDonnell F4H-1/F-4B Phantom II
(Basic design configuration)
General: Wing span (spread), 38 ft 4.9 in; wing
span (folded), 27 ft 7 in; tailplane span, 16 ft
5.1 in; overall length (flight configuration), 58 ft
3 in; overall height (aircraft on ground with full
internal fuel, no missiles), 16 ft 5.4 in; undercarriage wheel base (between wheel centres),
23 ft 3 in; undercarriage track, 17 ft 11 in;
height of fuselage above ground (mid-fuselage),
4 ft 6 in; minimum fuselage ground clearance
(below infra-red seeker fairing), 3 ft 10 in;
height of wing tip above ground (spread), 6 ft
1.5 in; height of wing tip above ground
(folded), 11 ft 5.5 in; ground clearance below
centreline drop tank (600 US gallons), 1 ft 1 in;
ground clearance beneath wing drop tanks, 1 ft
9 in; radius of arrester hook movement, 6 ft 11 in;
height of fuselage top contour above ground
(mid fuselage), 10 ft 8.5 in.
Wing data: Wing incidence, 1 degree; dihedral
(inner sections), nil; dihedral (outer sections),
12 degrees; quarter-chord sweepback, 45
degrees; wing area, 530 sq ft; aspect ratio, 2.82;
wing sections: root, NACA 0006.4–64 (modified); at fold, NACA 0004–64 (modified); tip,
NACA 0003–64 (modified).

McDonnell RF-4B Phantom II
As above, but overall length, 63 ft 5 in.
McDonnell F-4C and F-4D Phantom II
As for F-4B, but ground clearance below centre-
line drop tank, 6 in.
McDonnell RF-4C Phantom II
As RF-4C, but overall length 62 ft 9 in.
McDonnell F-4E and F-4G (Wild Weasel) Phantom II
As for F-4B, but overall length, 62 ft 11.8 in.

Equipment standards of preparation
McDonnell F4H-1/F-4A Phantom II
Powerplant: Two General Electric J79-GE-2
engines each rated at 10,350 lb-thrust (dry),
and 16,150 lb-thrust with afterburner selected.
Engine weight, 3,630 lb each. Power/weight
ratios, 2.851:1 (dry), 4.449:1 (in afterburner).
Equipment standard: Westinghouse APQ-72
with 24-inch (32-inch from aircraft No 19) diameter scanner dish; ASA-32 autopilot; AJB-3
bombing system computer; AAA-4 infra-red
seeker; 5-degree engine intake fixed ramp/10-
degree variable ramp; ASQ-19 communications/
navigation/identification pack (CNI); A/A-24G

Central Air Data Computer (CADC). Main-wheels 30 × 7.7-inch. In-flight refuelling probe.

McDonnell F-4B Phantom II
Powerplant: Two General Electric J79-GE-8 engines each rated at 10,900 lb-thrust (dry), and 17,000 lb-thrust with afterburner selected. Engine weight, 3,633 lb each. Power/weight ratios, 3.000:1 (dry), 4,679:1 (in afterburner).
Equipment standard: As for F-4A but 32-inch diameter scanner dish on all aircraft; 10-degree engine intake fixed ramp/14-degree variable ramp.

McDonnell RF-4B Phantom II
Powerplant: Two General Electric J79-GE-8 engines each rated at 10,900 lb-thrust (dry), and 17,000 lb-thrust with afterburner selected. Engine weight, 3,633 lb each. Power/weight ratios, 3.000:1 (dry), 4,679:1 (in afterburner).
Equipment standard: Missile control system removed. Three rotatable camera mounts in nose. Flight controls in front cockpit only. CNI and CADC retained. Main landing gear wheels, 30 × 7.7-inch. In-flight refuelling probe.

McDonnell F-4C Phantom II
Powerplant: Two General Electric J79-GE-15 (Spec No E-2027) engines each rated at 10,900 lb-thrust (military) and 17,000 lb-thrust with afterburner selected. Engine weight, 3,627 lb each. Power/weight ratios, 3.005:1 (military), 4.687:1 (in afterburner).
Fuel and oil: Fuselage fuel tanks, six bladder-type, total capacity, 1,118 Imp gallons (1,342 US gallons); wing integral tanks, capacity, 525 Imp gallons (630 US gallons); fuselage centre-line drop tank, capacity, 500 Imp gallons (600 US gallons); two underwing drop tanks, capacity (each, 308.5 Imp gallons (370 US gallons). Total fuel capacity (internal and external), 2,760 Imp gallons (3,312 US gallons). Fuel grade, JP-4; specification, MIL-J-5624. Oil, two integral tanks, total capacity, 8.58 Imp gallons (10.3 US gallons). Oil specification, MIL-L-7808.
Equipment standard: CADC, A/A-24G; CNI, AN/ASQ-19; Automatic Flight Control Subsystem (AFCS), AN/ASA-32; Inertial navigation subsystem, AN/ASN-48; navigation computer, AN/ASN-46; altimeter, AN/APN-155. Fire Control System: Radar and optical sight, AN-APQ-100; Radar Set Group, AN/APA-157; air-to-ground missile (AGM-12) control system, AN/ARW-77; all-altitude bombing system, AN/AJB-7. Sequential timer, TD-709/AJB-7. RHAWS, AN/APR-25, -26.

McDonnell RF-4C Phantom II
Powerplant: As for F-4C.
Fuel and oil: Fuselage fuel tanks, six bladder-type, total capacity, 1,049 Imp gallons (1,259 US gallons); wing integral tanks, capacity, 525 Imp gallons (630 US gallons); fuselage centre-line drop tank, capacity, 500 Imp gallons (600 US gallons); two underwing drop tanks, capacity (each), 308.5 Imp gallons (370 US gallons). Total fuel capacity (internal and external), 2,691 Imp gallons (3,229 US gallons). Fuel grade, JP-4; specification, MIL-J-5624. Oil, two integral tanks, total capacity, 8.58 Imp gallons (10.3 US gallons). Oil specification, MIL-L-7808.
Equipment standard (electronics): CNI, AN/ASQ-88B; HF radio, AN/ARC-105; sound recorder, RO-254/ASQ; navigation computer, AN/ASN-46A; AFCS, AN/ASA-32J; infra-red detecting set, AN/AAS-18A; altitude-heading reference equipment, AN/ASN-55; inertial navigation system, AN/ASN-56; radar mapping set, AN/APQ-102; radar set, AN/APQ-99; radar altimeter, AN/APN-159. Data display set, AN/ASQ-90; data recording camera set, KS-74A; aircraft camera mount set, LS-58A; aircraft camera parameter control, LA-311A; photoflash camera control detector, LA-285A. Countermeasures receiving set, AN/ALR-17; homing and warning subsystem, AN/APR-25; warning set, AN/APR-26. Electronic counter-measures pods, AN/ALQ-71, AN/ALQ-72 and AN/ALQ-87. Interference blanker, MX-7933/A.

McDonnell F-4D Phantom II
Powerplant: As for F-4C.
Fuel and oil: As for F-4C.
Equipment standard: CADC, A/A-24G; CNI, AN/ASQ-15; AFCS, AN/ASA-32; inertial navigation system, AN/ASN-63; navigation computer, AN/ASN-46A; altimeter, AN/APN-155. Fire control system: radar set, AN/APQ-109A; radar set group, AN/APA-165. Computing sight, AN/ASG-22; air-to-ground missile (AGM-12) control system, AN/ARW-77; all-altitude bombing system, AN/AJB-7. Sequential timer, TD-709/AJB-7. Weapons release system AN/ASQ-91; radar homing and warning system (RHAWS), AN/APS-107A.

McDonnell F-4E Phantom II
Powerplant: Two General Electric J79-GE-17 (Spec No E-2029) engines each rated at 11,870 lb-thrust (military) and 17,900 lb-thrust with afterburner selected. Engine weight, 3,835 lb

each. Power/weight ratios, 3.095:1 (dry), 4.668:1 (military).

Fuel and oil: Fuselage fuel tanks, seven bladder-type, total capacity, 1,021 Imp gallons (1,225 US gallons); wing integral tanks, capacity, 525 Imp gallons (630 US gallons); fuselage centre-line drop tank, capacity, 500 Imp gallons (600 US gallons); two underwing drop tanks, capacity (each), 308.5 Imp gallons (370 US gallons). Total fuel capacity (internal and external), 2,663 Imp gallons (3,195 US gallons). Fuel grade, JP-4; specification, MIL-J-5624. Oil, two integral tanks, total capacity, 8.58 Imp gallons (10.3 US gallons). Oil specification, MIL-L-7808.

Equipment standard (electronics): CADC, A/A-24G; CNI, AN/ASQ-15A; AFCS, AN/ASA-32; inertial navigation system, AN/ASN-63; navigation computer, AN/ASN-46A; altimeter, AN/APN-155. Fire control system: radar, AN/APQ-120. Computing sight, AN/ASG-26 (modified); air-to-ground missile (AGM-12) control system, AN/ARW-77; all-altitude bombing system, AN/AJB-7. Sequential timer, TD-709/AJB-7. Weapons release system, AN/ASQ-91 (modified); RHAWS, AN/APR-36, -37. Target Identification, Electro-Optical (TISEO), AN/ASX-1 (fitted from aircraft BuAer No *71-237* onwards).

McDonnell F-4G Phantom II (Wild Weasel)

Powerplant: As for F-4E.
Fuel and oil: As for F-4E.
Equipment standard (electronics): As for F-4E except: Optical sight, AN/APQ-30; no AN/ASX-1 fitted; radar receiving set, AN/APR-38.

External store carriage

Explanation of store positions (stations). The Phantom features nine store positions as follows: *Station 1:* Underwing pylon, outboard, port wing (inboard of fold). *2:* Underwing pylon, inboard, port wing. *3:* Recessed in rear fuselage, port side. *4:* Recessed in front fuselage, port side. *5:* Fuselage centreline pylon/attachment. *6:* Recessed in front fuselage, starboard side. *7:* Recessed in rear fuselage, starboard side. *8:* Underwing pylon, inboard, starboard

wing. *9:* Underwing pylon, outboard, starboard wing (inboard of fold).

McDonnell F-4A/F-4B Phantom II

Stores cleared for carriage/discharge/jettisoning:
Wing fuel drop tank (308.5 Imp gallon, 370 US gallons). Weight empty, 234 lb. One carried on stations 1 and 9.
Centreline fuel drop tank (500 Imp gallon, 600 US gallon). Weight empty, 235 lb. One carried on station 5.
Sidewinder 1A air-to-air missile. Weight, 155 lb. Two carried on each of stations 2 and 8.
Sidewinder 1C air-to-air missile. Weight, 204 lb. Two carried on each of stations 2 and 8.
AIM-4D Falcon air-to-air missile. Weight, 134 lb. Two carried on each of stations 2 and 8.
AIM-7D/E Sparrow III air-to-air missile. Weight, 402/455 lb. One carried on each of stations 2, 3, 4, 6, 7 and 8.
AGM-45A Shrike air-to-ground missile. Weight, 400 lb. One carried on each of stations 1, 2, 8 and 9.
AGM-12B Bullpup air-to-ground missile. Weight, 580 lb. One carried on each of stations 1 and 9.
AGM-12C Bullpup air-to-ground missile. Weight, 1,778 lb. One carried on each of stations 1 and 9.
LAU-32A/A rocket launcher. Weight, 173 lb. Three carried on each of stations 1, 2, 5, 8 and 9.
LAU-3A/A rocket launcher. Weight, 427 lb. Three carried on each of stations 1, 2, 5, 8 and 9.
LAU-10/A rocket launcher. Weight, 533 lb. Three carried on each of stations 1, 2, 5, 8 and 9.
SUU-16/A M61 20 mm gun pod. Weight, 1,775 lb. One carried on each of stations 1, 5 and 9.
MK-4 20 mm gun pod. Weight, 1,348 lb. One carried on station 1.
SUU-11/A 7 62 mm gun pod. Weight, 325 lb. Three carried on each of stations 1, 2, 5, 8 and 9.
MK-81 general purpose bomb. Weight, 260 lb. Six carried on each of stations 1, 5 and 9; and three carried on each of stations 2 and 8.
MK-82 general purpose bomb. Weight, 531 lb.

Right *Impressive array of ordnance and stores applicable to the USAF Phantom, including (from the foreground) 24 260-lb MK-81 GP bombs; 15 660-lb MLU-10/B land mines; 24 531-lb MK-82 GP bombs; 15 985-lb MK-83 GP bombs **and four** Sidewinders; 15 SUU-11/A 7.62 mm gun pods and six Sparrows; 13 533-lb LAU-10/A rocket **launchers**, seven M-116A2 napalm bombs and four AGM-12B Bullpup missiles; 15 LAU-32A rocket launchers and 11 BLU-1 napalm bombs; groups of 18 1,000-lb bombs of various types; centreline and wing drop tanks.*

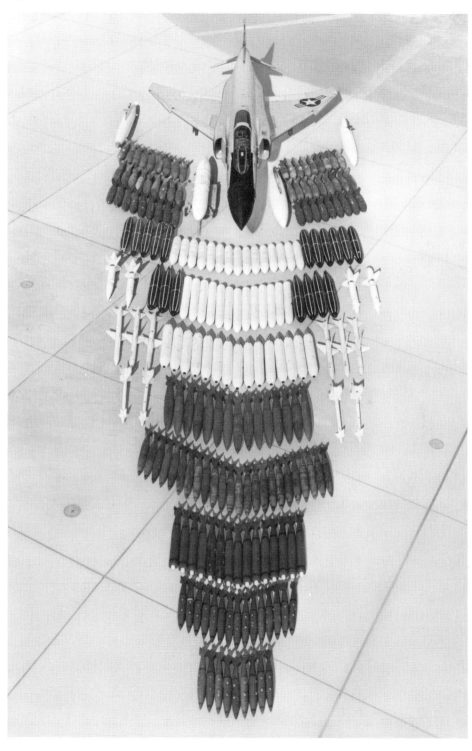

Six carried on each of stations 1, 5 and 9; and three carried on each of stations 2 and 8.

MK-83 general purpose bomb. Weight, 985 lb. Two carried on each of stations 1, 2, 8 and 9; and three carried on station 5.

MK-81 Snakeye retarded bomb. Weight, 295 lb. Six carried on each of stations 1, 5 and 9; and three carried on each of stations 2 and 8.

MK-82 Snakeye retarded bomb. Weight, 560 lb. Six carried on each of stations 1, 5 and 9; and three carried on each of stations 2 and 8.

SUU-20 practice bomb and rocket dispenser. Weight, 451 lb. One carried on each of stations 1, 2, 5, 8 and 9.

SUU-21/A practice bomb dispenser. Weight, 622 lb. One carried on station 5.

Sadeye weapon. Weight 750 lb. Three carried on each of stations 1, 5 and 9; and two carried on each of stations 2 and 8.

MC-1 chemical bomb. Weight, 720 lb. Three carried on each of stations 2 and 8; and five carried on station 5.

Weteye store. Weight 530 lb. Six carried on each of stations 1, 5 and 9; and three carried on each of stations 2 and 8.

M-129E1 leaflet bomb. Weight, 220 lb. Three carried on each of stations 1, 2, 8 and 9; and six carried on station 5.

MK-28 MOD 1 FF nuclear weapon. Weight, 2,040 lb. One carried on station 5.

MK-43 MOD 0 nuclear weapon. Weight, 2,060 lb. One carried on station 5.

MK-57 nuclear weapon. Weight, 500 lb. One carried on station 5.

AB45-Y1 spray tank. Weight, 776 lb. One carried on each of stations 1 and 8.

MK-12 Smoke Tank 220. Weight, 560 lb. Three carried on each of stations 1, 2, 5, 8 and 9.

M-117 general purpose bomb. Weight, 820 lb. Three carried on each of stations 2 and 8; and five carried on station 5.

MLU-10/B land mine. Weight, 660 lb. Three carried on each of stations 1, 2, 5, 8 and 9.

BLU-1/B napalm bomb (91.6 Imp gallon, 110 US gallon). Weight (full), 694 lb. Two carried on each of stations 1, 2, 8 and 9, and three on station 5.

M-116A2 napalm bomb (91.6 Imp gallon, 110 US gallon). Weight (full), 685 lb. Two carried on each of stations 1, 2, 8 and 9, and three on station 5.

MK-77 napalm bomb. Weight, 520 lb. Six carried on each of stations 1, 5 and 9; and three on each of stations 2 and 8.

MK-79 napalm bomb. Weight, 912 lb. Three carried on each of stations 1, 5 and 9; and two on each of stations 2 and 8.

Fireye napalm bomb. Weight, 225 lb. Six carried on each of stations 1, 5 and 9; and two on each of stations 2 and 8.

CBU-1A/A cluster bomblets. Weight, 749 lb. Two carried on each of stations 1 and 9; and one carried on each of stations 2, 5 and 8.

CBU-2A/A cluster bomblets. Weight, 830 lb. Two carried on each of stations 1 and 9; and one carried on each of stations 2, 5 and 8.

CBU-7/A cluster bomblets. Weight, 795 lb. Four carried on each of stations 1 and 9; three carried on each of stations 2 and 8; and five carried on station 5.

Practice Multiple Bomb Rack A/A37B-3. Weight, 87 lb. One carried on each of stations 1, 2, 5, 8 and 9.

QRC-160 electronic countermeasures pod. Weight, 180 lb. One carried on station 9.

Note The Sparrow air-to-air missiles are normally carried on all sorties on stations 3, 4, 6 and 7, and combinations of all the other stores may be carried in the positions shown up to a maximum take-off weight of 59,689 lb (subsonic manoeuvres and load factor of 5.3).

McDonnell F-4E Phantom II

Note All the stores cleared for the F-4A/F-4B are assumed cleared for the F-4E, although in many cases they had been declared obsolete and superseded. The following are additional. Stores cleared for carriage/discharge/operating/jettisoning:

AIM-7E-2 Sparrow III air-to-air missile. Weight, 435 lb. One carried in each of stations 3, 4, 6 and 7.

M36E2 incendiary bomb. Weight, 930 lb. Two carried on each of stations 2 and 8; and four carried on station 5.

M117D destruction weapon and M117RE retarded bomb Weight, 880 lb. Four carried on each of stations 1, 5 and 9; and two carried on each of stations 2 and 8.

M118 general purpose bomb. Weight, 3,020 lb. One carried on station 5.

MC-1 gas bomb. Weight 720 lb. Three carried on each of stations 1, 2, 8 and 9; and five carried on station 5.

BLU-1/B and -1B/B unfinned fire bomb. Weight, 865 lb. Two carried on each of stations 1, 2, 8 and 9; three carried on station 5.

BLU-27B and -27A/B unfinned fire bomb. Weight, 850 lb. Two carried on each of stations 1, 2, 8 and 9; three carried on station 5.

BLU-27B and -27A/B finned fire bomb. Weight, 868 lb. One carried on each of stations 1 and 9; and two carried on station 5.

BLU-52/B finned fire bomb. Weight, 800 lb. One carried on each of stations 1 and 9; and two carried on station 5.

BLU-76 fire bomb. Weight, 2,600 lb. One carried on each of stations 2, 5 and 8.

MLU-32/B99 (Briteye) flare dispenser. Weight, 152 lb. Two carried on each of stations 1 and 9; and six carried on station 5.

QRC-160A-1/ALQ-71 ECM pod. Weight 203 lb. One carried on each of stations 2, 4, 6 and 8.

QRC-160A-2/ALQ-72 ECM pod. Weight, 185 lb. One carried on each of stations 2, 4, 6 and 8.

QRC-160A-8/ALQ-87 ECM pod. Weight, 269 lb. One carried on each of stations 2, 4, 6 and 8.

QRC-335A(V)-3/ALQ-101 ECM pod. Weight, 393 lb. One carried on each of stations 2, 4, 6 and 8.

QRC-335A(V)-4/ALQ-101 ECM pod. Weight, 468 lb. One carried on each of stations 2, 4, 6 and 8.

TMU-28B or PAU-7/A spray tank. Weight, 1,923 lb. One carried on each of stations 1 and 9.

A/A 37U-15 tow target. Weight, 1,500 lb. One carried on station 9.

RMU-8/A tow target. One carried on station 5.

PAVE KNIFE pod. One carried on each of stations 5 and 8.

AAVS IV camera pod. One carried on each of stations 1, 2, 5, 8 and 9.

KMU-351/B (MK-84LGB) guided bomb. Weight, 2,052 lb. One carried on each of stations 1, 2, 8 and 9.

KMU-353A/B (MK-84EO) guided bomb. Weight, 2,288 lb. One carried on each of stations 1, 2, 8 and 9.

KMU-359/B (MK-84IR) guided bomb. Weight, 2,123 lb. One carried on each of stations 1, 2, 8 and 9.

KMU-370A/B (MK-118LGB) guided bomb. Weight, 3,020 lb. One carried on each of stations 2 and 8.

KMU-390/B (MK-118EO) guided bomb. Weight, 3,450 lb. One carried on each of stations 2 and 8.

Camera reconnaissance equipment, McDonnell RF-4C Phantom II

Optical sensors, including framing, panoramic and mapping cameras, are located in three camera stations in the nose of the aircraft. Electronic sensors include forward-looking radar, sideways-looking radar and an infra-red reconnaissance set. Associated reconnaissance facilities include photoflash ejection (from upper rear fuselage) for night photography, a photographic control set, a data annotation set for recording on reconnaissance film aircraft data parameters, an HF communications set for extended communications range, a voice recorder set for recording pilot or radar observer comments, a photoflash detector, and vertical stabilised camera mounts.

Standard basic configuration

1 Forward location. 6-inch KS-87 camera; forward/oblique/vertical cover for low-level day or night missions.

2 Centre location. 3-inch KA-56 camera; vertical panoramic cover for low-level daylight missions.

3 Rear location. 12-inch KA-55 camera in stabilised mounting; vertical panoramic cover for high-level daylight missions.

Additional/alternative camera installation

4 Forward location. 3-inch KS-87 camera; forward/oblique/vertical cover for low-level day or night missions.

5 Centre location. 6-inch/3-inch/6-inch three-camera fan of KS-87s for low-level daylight missions.

6 Centre location. 18-inch KS-87 camera; side oblique cover for high or low-level daylight missions.

7 Centre location. 12-inch KS-87 camera; side oblique cover for high or low-level daylight missions.

8 Centre location. 3-inch KS-87 camera; vertical cover for low-level day or night missions.

9 Rear location. 18-inch KS-87 camera; vertical cover for high-level daylight missions. Requires stabilised mounting.

10 Rear location. 6-inch KS-87 camera; split vertical cover for low-level day or night missions.

11 Rear location. 18-inch KS-87 camera; split vertical cover for high-level daylight missions.

12 Rear location. 6-inch T-11 camera; vertical mapping cover for high-level daylight missions.

Performance

McDonnell F-4B and F-4C Phantom II
1. Ground Attack Sortie

Configuration: 500 Imp gallon centreline drop tank, two underwing 308.5 Imp gallon drop

Cockpits of slatted F-4E. **Above** *Front cockpit.* **Below** *Rear cockpit* (McDonnell Douglas, Neg Nos 8089-51, -53, -54 and -55, dated June 1979).

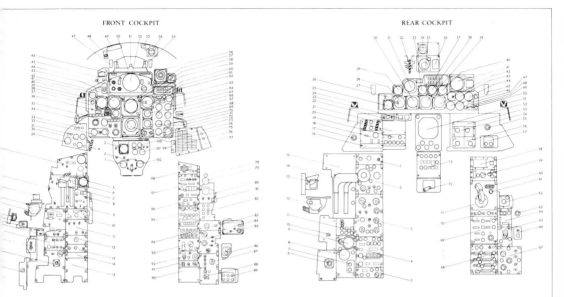

FRONT COCKPIT   REAR COCKPIT

MCDONNELL DOUGLAS F-4E PHANTOM II
COCKPIT INSTRUMENTATION AND SYSTEM CONTROLS
(Representative Aircraft)

HT 1983 FRANCIS K. MASON

Key to front cockpit drawing

1 Rounds remaining indicator
2 Rudder pedal adjustment crank
3 Accelerometer
4 Emergency brake control
5 AGM control handle
6 Throttles
7 Throttle friction adjustment
8 Inboard engine control panel (engine master and starter switches); also rudder trim switch
9 Drag chute control handle
10 VOR/ILS control panel
11 Automatic flight control system control panel
12 Boarding steps position indicator
13 Intercom system control panel
14 Spare panel
15 Spare panel
16 Armament safety override switch
17 Anti-g suit control valve
18 Slats override switch
19 AN/ALE-40 programmer with chaff/flare interval selectors
20 AN/ALE-40 control panel
21 Gun camera switch
22 Extra picture switch
23 Canopy selector control
24 Flaps/slats control panel
25 Fuel control panel (including air refuelling receptacle control switch)
26 Eject light switch
27 Outboard engine control panel (including anti-icing switch)
28 Utility panel with oxygen controls and anti-skid switch
29 Stabilator trim indicator
30 Booster pump pressure indicators
31 Slats/flaps indicators
32 Automatic weapons release unit
33 Landing gear indicators
34 Landing gear control handle
35 Multiple weapons selector, LABS weapon release programmer and weapon arming switches
36 Angle of attack indicator
37 Radar altimeter
38 Flight instruments light control
39 Canopy emergency jettison handle
40 Airspeed indicator and Machmeter

41 True airspeed indicator
42 UHF remote channel indicator
43 Reference system selector switch
44 Head-up display switches
45 Range indicator
46 Landing gear warning light
47 Angle of attack indexer (left)
48 LABS pull-up light
49 Air refuelling indicator panel
50 Optical sight camera
51 Optical sight unit
52 Radar scope (AN/APQ-120 display)
53 Air refuelling lights
54 Standby magnetic compass
55 Angle of attack indexer (right)
56 CRT azimuth and azimuth/elevation indicators
57 Attitude director indicator
58 Marker beacon light
59 Threat display panel
60 Master caution light
61 Altimeter
62 Internal fuel contents gauge
63 Fire/overheat warning lights
64 Canopy manual unlock handle
65 Fuel flow indicators (2)
66 Rate of climb/descent indicator
67 Engine tachometers (2)
68 Feed tank check switch
69 Arrester hook control handle
70 Exhaust temperature indicators (2)
71 Standby attitude idicator
72 Exhaust nozzle position (duel) indicator
73 Eight-day clock
74 Horizontal situation indicator
75 Navigation function selector switch
76 Right indicator light sub-panel
77 Instrument lights intensity circuit breakers
78 CNI equipment cooling reset button
79 Emergency vent handle
80 Cabin conditioning, pilot heater and rain removal switch panel
81 Demist/foot heat control handle
82 Control switch circuit breaker panel
83 Temperature control panel
84 Emergency floodlights panel
85 Cockpit lights control panel

86 Standby attitude circuit breaker and intensity control panel
87 Formation lights control switch
88 Exterior light control panel
89 Instrument lights intensity control panel
90 Spare panel
91 KY-28 control panel
92 Compass control panel
93 DCU-94A bomb control panel
94 DCU-94A station selector panel and indicators
95 IFF control panel
96 Navigation control panel
97 Communication control panel
98 Generator control panel
99 KY-28 mode light panel
100 Engine oil pressure indicators (2)
101 Hydraulic pressure indicators (2)
102 Pneumatic pressure indicator

Key to rear cockpit drawing

1 Intercom control panel
2 Control monitor panel
3 Radar (AN/APQ-120) control panel
4 Communication control panel
5 Navigation control panel
6 Anti-g suit control valve
7 Marker beacon VOR/ILS audio control
8 Oxygen contents gauge
9 Cabin altimeter
10 Pull-up tone cut-out switch
11 AN/ALE-40 programmer panel
12 Emergency flap control panel
13 Canopy selector
14 Throttles
15 Spare panel
16 Spare panel
17 Cockpit air vent
18 Oxygen control panel
19 Landing gear/flap indicator panel
20 Spare panel
21 Emergency landing gear and brake control handles
22 Gun camera and contrast switches
23 Air-to-air and video selectors
24 Canopy emergency jettison handle
25 Rate of climb/descent indicator

26 UHF channel remote indicator
27 Angle of attack indexer (left)
28 Altimeter
29 Angle of attack indicator
30 Attitude indicator
31 Eight-day clock
32 Command selector valve
33 Eight-day clock
34 Standby magnetic compass
35 Course indicator
36 KY-28 mode light panel
37 Threat display panel
38 Accelerometer
39 Airspeed indicator and Machmeter
40 Turn and slip indicator
41 CRT azimuth indicator
42 Bearing-distance-heading-indicator
43 Ground speed indicator
44 True airspeed indicator
45 Angle of attack indexer (right)
46 Engine tachometers (2)
47 Canopy unlocked warning light
48 Inertial navigator out warning light
49 Radar-CNI cooling reset button
50 Radar-CNI cool off warning light
51 Canopy manual unlock handle
52 Radar scope (AN/APQ-120 display)
53 Spare panel
54 ECM control panel
55 Cockpit air vent
56 LABS release angle control panel
57 Bombing timer controls
58 Laser coder control
59 Inertial navigator control panel
60 Antenna range strobe
61 Boresight adjuster
62 Stall warning tone control panel
63 Extra picture switch
64 Cursor control panel
65 Nuclear store consent switch
66 SST-181X pulse selector switch
67 Cockpit light control panel
68 Navigation system control panel
69 Weapons release computer control panel
70 Weapon delivery panel
71 Antenna control panel
72 Rudder pedal ajustment crank
73 Target designator panel

tanks, four AIM-7 Sparrow air-to-air missiles and six M-117 general purpose bombs. Fuel load, 12,818 lb. Weapon load, 6,758 lb.

Take-off weight, 59,453 lb. Wing loading, 112.2 lb/sq ft. Stalling speed, power off, 154.5 knots. Take-off ground run at sea level, afterburners lit, 4,260 ft; distance to 50 ft, afterburners lit, 5,200 ft. Rate of climb at sea level, military rating, 5,900 ft/min. Rate of climb (one engine out, afterburner lit on other) at sea level, 4,810 ft/min. Time from sea level to 20,000 ft, military rating, 5.61 minutes; time from sea level to 30,000 ft, military rating, 12.85 minutes. Service ceiling (military rating in this configuration), 26,800 ft. Service ceiling (one engine out, military rating on the other), 25,500 ft. Combat radius (see sortie definition below), 468 nautical miles. Average cruising speed, 492 knots. Initial cruising altitude 25,950 ft. Final cruising altitude, 38,000 ft. Total mission time, 2.18 hours.

Combat weight, 40,591 lb. Combat altitude, sea level. Combat speed, afterburners lit, 741 knots; combat speed, military rating, 622 knots. Maximum speed at 40,000 ft, 1,112 knots. Landing weight, 34,878 lb. Ground run, no parachute, 3,205 ft; with parachute, 2,505 ft. Total distance from 50 ft, no parachute, 4,290 ft; with parachute, 3,600 ft.

Sortie profile: Take-off with afterburners, climb on course at military rating to optimum cruise altitude, cruise-climb at best range speed; descend to sea level; search for target for five minutes at military rating; discharge stores. Climb on course at military rating to optimum cruise altitude, cruise-climb at best range speed. Range allowances include five minutes at normal thrust for starting and taxying, one minute in afterburner for take-off, and reserve of 20 minutes' fuel for loiter at maximum endurance speed awaiting turn to land and return to dispersal.

2. CAP (Combat Air Patrol) Sortie

Configuration: 500 Imp gallon centreline drop tank, two underwing 308.5 Imp gallon drop tanks, four AIM-7 Sparrow air-to-air missiles. Fuel load, 12,818 lb. Weapon load, 1,820 lb.

Take-off weight, 53,797 lb. Wing loading, 101.5 lb/sq ft. Stalling speed, power off, 146.7 knots. Take-off ground run at sea level, afterburners lit, 3,380 ft; distance to 50 ft, afterburners lit, 4,130 ft. Rate of climb at sea level, military rating, 8,210 ft/min. Rate of climb (one engine out, afterburner lit on other) at sea level, 7,470 ft/min. Time from sea level to

20,000 ft, military rating, 3.60 minutes; time from sea level to 30,000, military rating, 7.05 minutes. Service ceiling (military rating at this configuration), 33,050 ft. Service ceiling, one engine out (military rating on the other), 32,900 ft. Combat radius (see sortie definition below), 250 miles. Average cruising speed, 502 knots. Initial cruising altitude, 30,400 ft. Final cruising altitude, 39,700 ft. Total mission time, 2.48 hours. CAP time, 1.39 hours.

Combat weight, 36,140 lb. Combat altitude, 40,000 ft. Combat speed, 1,178 knots at maximum power. Maximum speed at 40,000 ft, 1,188 knots. Basic speed at 35,000 ft, 1,183 knots. Landing weight, 32,192 lb. Ground run, no parachute, 2,975 ft; with parachute, 2,320 ft. Total distance from 50 ft, no parachute, 4,000 ft; with parachute, 3,350 ft.

Sortie profile: Take-off with afterburners, climb on course at military rating to optimum cruise altitude, cruise-climb at best range speed; patrol at maximum endurance altitude; climb with afterburners to acceleration altitude (40,000 ft), accelerate at maximum thrust to Mach 1.5 and remain at this speed and altitude for two minutes, discharge missiles, cruise back at best range speed. Range allowances include five minutes at normal thrust for starting and taxying, and reserve of 20 minutes' fuel for loiter at maximum endurance speed awaiting turn to land and return to dispersal.

McDonnell RF-4C Phantom II
1. High altitude reconnaissance sortie

Configuration: 500 Imp gallon centreline drop tank, two underwing 308.5 Imp gallon drop tanks. No other stores. Fuel load, 17,490 lb.

Take-off weight, 52,823 lb. Wing loading, 99.7 lb/sq ft. Stalling speed, approach power, BLC on, 148 knots. Take-off ground run at sea level, afterburners lit, 3,220 ft; distance to 50 ft, afterburners lit, 3,990 ft. Rate of climb at sea level, military rating, 8,700 ft/min. Rate of climb (one engine out, afterburner lit on other) at sea level, 8,010 ft/min. Time from sea level to 20,000 ft, military rating, 3.14 minutes; time from sea level to 30,000 ft, military rating, 6.02 minutes. Service ceiling (military rating in this configuration), 34,000 ft; service ceiling (one engine out, military rating on the other), 34,000 ft. Combat radius (see sortie definition below), 673 nautical miles. Average cruising speed, 499 knots. Initial cruising altitude, 30,900 ft. Final cruising altitude, 38,800 ft. Target altitude, 40,050 ft. Target speed, 533 knots. Total mission time, 2.71 hours.

Combat weight, 40,267 lb. Combat altitude, 40,050 ft. Combat speed, 1,204 knots. Combat climb with afterburners lit, 12,850 ft/min. Maximum rate of climb at sea level with afterburners lit, 44,800 ft/min. Maximum speed at 40,000 ft, 1,204 knots. Landing weight, 33,598 lb. Ground run, no parachute, 3,100 ft; with parachute, 2,430 ft. Total distance from 50 ft, no parachute, 4,150 ft; with parachute, 3,490 ft. *Sortie profile:* Take-off with afterburners, climb on course at military rating to optimum cruise altitude, cruise climb at best range speed; 15-minute normal thrust reconnaissance run-in to target, two minutes' evasion at normal thrust, eight minutes' escape at normal thrust; cruise-climb back at best range speed. Range allowances include five minutes at normal thrust for starting and taxying; one minute in afterburner for take-off, and reserve for 20 minutes' fuel for loiter at maximum endurance speed, plus five per cent of initial fuel load.

2. Nuclear strike sortie

Configuration: Two underwing 308.5 Imp gallon drop tanks. One B28 nuclear store on station 5. Fuel load, 17,088 lb. Weapon load, 2,040 lb.

Take-off weight, 50,763 lb. Wing loading, 95.8 lb/sq ft. Stalling speed, approach power, BLC on, 145 knots. Take-off ground run at sea level, afterburners lit, 2,970 ft; distance to 50 ft, afterburners lit, 3,620 ft. Rate of climb at sea level, military rating, 9,500 ft/min. Rate of climb (one engine out, afterburner lit on other) at sea level, 8,850 ft/min. Time from sea level to 20,000 ft, military rating, 2.82 minutes; time from sea level to 30,000 ft, military rating, 5.34 minutes. Service ceiling (military rating in this configuration), 35,250 ft; service ceiling (one engine out, military rating on the other), 35,250 ft. Combat radius (see sortie definition below), 414 nautical miles. Average cruising speed, 499 knots. Initial cruising altitude, 31,750 ft. Final cruising altitude, 38,850 ft. Target altitude, sea level. Total mission time, 1.75 hours.

Combat weight, 37,992 lb. Combat altitude, sea level. Combat speed, 787 knots. Combat climb with afterburners lit, 47,600 ft/min. Maximum speed at 40,000 ft, 1,205 knots. Landing weight, 33,510 lb. Ground run, no parachute, 3,090 ft; with parachute, 2,410 ft. Total distance from 50 ft, no parachute, 4,140 ft; with parachute, 3,475 ft. *Sortie profile:* Take-off with afterburners, climb on course at military rating to optimum cruise altitude; cruise-climb at best range speed; descend to sea level; search for target at military rating, expend store, and climb on return course at military rating to optimum cruise altitude, and cruise-climb back at best range speed. Range allowances include five minutes at normal thrust for starting and taxying, one minute in afterburner for take-off, reserve of 20 minutes' fuel for loiter at maximum endurance speed awaiting clearance to land, plus five per cent of initial fuel load.

McDonnell F-4E Phantom II
1. Ground attack sortie

Configuration: 500 Imp gallon centreline drop tank, two underwing 308.5 Imp gallon drop tanks, four AIM-7E Sparrow air-to-air missiles and six M-117 general purpose bombs. Fuel load, 20,768 lb. Weapon load, 6,740 lb.

Take-off weight, 61,629 lb. Wing loading, 116.3 lb/sq ft. Stalling speed, approach power, BLC on, 158.4 knots. Take-off ground run at sea level, afterburners lit, 4,360 ft; distance to 50 ft, afterburners lit, 5,840 ft. Rate of climb at sea level, military rating, 6,570 ft/min. Rate of climb (one engine out, afterburner lit on other engine), 3,830 ft/min. Time from sea level to 20,000 ft, military rating, 4.47 minutes; time from sea level to 30,000 ft, military rating, 12.08 minutes. Service ceiling (military rating in this configuration), 29,750 ft; service ceiling (one engine out, military rating on the other), 23,150 ft. Combat radius (see sortie definition below), 439 nautical miles. Average cruising speed, 502 knots. Initial cruising altitude, 29,050 ft. Final cruising altitude, 38,750 ft. Total mission time, 2.02 hours.

Combat weight, 43,384 lb. Combat altitude, sea level. Combat speed, afterburners lit, 723 knots; combat speed, military rating, 622 knots. Maximum speed at 40,000 ft, 1,159 knots. Landing weight, 37,821 lb. Ground run, no parachute, 3,760 ft; with parachute, 3,110 ft. Total distance from 50 ft, no parachute, 5,670 ft; with parachute, 5,020 ft.

Sortie profile: Take-off with afterburners, climb on course at military rating to optimum altitude, cruise-climb at best range speed; descend to sea level; search for target for five minutes at military rating; discharge stores. Climb on course at military rating to optimum cruise altitude, cruise-climb at best range speed. Range allowances include five minutes at normal thrust for starting and taxying, one minute in afterburner for take-off, and loiter reserve of 20 minutes' fuel at best endurance speed.

2. CAP Sortie

Configuration: 500 Imp gallon centreline drop tank, two underwing 308.5 Imp gallon drop tanks, four AIM-7E Sparrow air-to-air missiles. Fuel load, 20,768 lb. Weapon load, 1,820 lb. Take-off weight, 55,991 lb. Wing loading, 105.6 lb/sq ft. Stalling speed, approach power, BLC on, 151 knots. Take-off ground run at sea level, afterburners lit, 3,490 ft; distance to 50 ft, afterburners lit, 4,850 ft. Rate of climb at sea level, military rating, 8,600 ft/min. Rate of climb (one engine out, afterburner lit on other) at sea level, 5,220 ft/min. Time from sea level to 20,000 ft, military rating, 3.03 minutes; time from sea level to 30,000 ft, military rating, 6.07 minutes. Service ceiling (military rating in this configuration), 34,850 ft; service ceiling, one engine out, military rating on the other, 30,650 ft. Combat radius (see sortie definition below), 250 miles. Average cruising speed, 506 knots. Initial cruising altitude, 31,950 ft. Final cruising altitude, 40,400 ft. Total mission time, 2.21 hours. CAP time, 1.13 hours.

Combat weight, 39,188 lb. Combat altitude, 40,000 ft. Combat speed, 1,211 knots at maximum power. Maximum speed at 40,000 ft, 1,223 knots. Basic speed at 35,000 ft, 1,222 knots. Landing weight, 35,134 lb. Ground run, no parachute, 3,520 ft; with parachute, 2,910 ft. Total distance from 50 ft, no parachute, 5,430 ft; with parachute, 4,820 ft.

Sortie profile: Take-off with afterburners, climb on course at military rating to optimum cruise altitude, cruise-climb at best range speed; patrol at maximum endurance altitude; climb with afterburners to acceleration altitude (40,000 ft), accelerate at maximum thrust to Mach 1.5 and remain at this speed and altitude for two minutes, discharge missiles, cruise back at best range speed. Range allowances include five minutes at normal thrust for starting and taxying, reserve of 20 minutes' fuel for loiter at maximum endurance speed before landing and return to dispersal, plus five per cent of initial fuel load.

General Electric J79 leading particulars and power ratings

Model	Overall length (in)	Maximum diameter (in)	Maximum power/RPM (lb/RPM)[1]	Military rating/RPM (lb/RPM)[2]	Normal power/RPM (lb/RPM)[3]
J79-GE-2	207.96	38.37	16,150/7,721	10,350/7,721	9,700/7,460
J79-GE-8	207.96	38.37	17,000/7,658	10,900/7,685	10,300/7,385
J79-GE-15 Spec E-2027	208.45	38.3	17,000/7,685	10.900/7,685	10,300/7,385
J70-GE-17 Spec E-2029	208.7	39.1	17,900/7,460	11,870/7,460	11,110/7,435

1. With afterburner lit (max 3,600°F); 30 minutes maximum below 30,000 ft; 2 hours limit above 30,000 ft.

2. 30 minutes limit below 30,000 ft; 2 hours limit above 30,000 ft.

3. Continuous (no limit).

General description: The General Electric J79 is a variable-stator axial flow turbojet with 17-stage compressor, three-stage turbine and fully-variable afterburner. Annular intake with central bullet fairing; -8 and -15 engines have anti-icing on first-stage stator. First six stator stages and inlet guide vanes have variable-incidence vanes adjusted by dual actuators moved by engine fuel to obtain optimum airflow angles for each stage at all engine speeds. Twin-bearing rotor is constructed in Lapelloy, B5F5 and titanium; total of 403 stainless steel blades. Pressure ratio, 12.4/13.1; air mass flow range 160–172 lb/sec. Cannular-type combustion chamber with ten combustion cans. Outer casing of Chromolloy, flame tubes of Hastelloy. Three-stage nozzle guide vanes, first with 58 vanes of R41, second with 62 vanes of Hastelloy R235 and R41, and third with 44 vanes of A286. Three-stage turbine, of which first stage has 148 blades of Udimet 500, second has 114 blades of M252, and third has 84 blades of M252. All blades attached by fir-tree roots. Engine has three bearings, roller front, ball main thrust, and roller rear. Afterburner has 'petal-type' fully-variable nozzle actuated by hydraulic rams using engine lubricating oil; core annulus burning with radial spray bars. Two gearboxes on the bottom of the engine drive all engine controls, accessories, aircraft hydraulic pumps, alternators and constant-speed drives. Lubrication of dry sump type, with vane-type pumps with sump

pressure provided from compressor. J79-GE-2 and -8 have turbine air impingement starter; -15 has combination cartridge/pneumatic starter on transfer gearbox.

3 Phantom production and representative aircraft allocation

Note In the interests of space Fleet Carrier/type classification numbers are used instead of ship names; these are as follows:

CVA-14 USS *Ticonderoga*
CVA-19 USS *Hancock*
CVA-31 USS *Bonne Homme Richard*
CVA-34 USS *Oriskany*
CVA-38 USS *Shangri-La*
CVA-41 USS *Midway*
CVA-42 USS *Franklin D. Roosevelt*
CVA-43 USS *Coral Sea*
CVA-59 USS *Forrestal*
CVA-60 USS *Saratoga*
CVA-61 USS *Ranger*
CVA-62 USS *Independence*
CVA-63 USS *Kitty Hawk*
CVA-64 USS *Constellation*
CVAN-65 USS *Enterprise*
CVA-66 USS *America*
CVA-67 USS *John F. Kennedy*

MCDONNELL F4H-1 (XF4H-1) Two prototype aircraft, BuAer Nos *142259* and *142260*. Production Block 1a. General Electric J79-GE-3A engines replaced by -2 engines before first flight by *142259* on May 27 1958. Letter contract signed October 18 1954; configuration definition, July 19 1955; mock-up agreed, November 1955.

142259 trials with MAC: aerodynamic and powerplant systems; demonstrations, 5-58 to 10-59; Project Top Flight, altitude record, 6-12-59. *142260* trials with MAC: development of powerplant systems, 10-58 to 2-65; Project Skyburner, 15/25 km World Speed Record, 22-11-61.

MCDONNELL F4H-1F (F-4A) PHANTOM II 45 research and development aircraft. BuAer Nos *143388–143392* (Block 1a); *145307–145317* (Block 2b); *146817–146821* (Block 3c); *148252–148261* (Block 4d); *148262–148275* (Block 5e). J79-GE-2 engines rated at 10,350 lb dry thrust and 16,150 lb-thrust with afterburners. Contract signed for five Block 1a aircraft, September 1955; Blocks 2b and 3c contracted, June 1957.

143388 trials with MAC: equipment evaluation, 12-58 to 9-60. *143389* trials with MAC: armament development, primary missile system, 1-59 to 2-61. *143390* trials with Raytheon: primary missile system, 6-59 to 8-59. *143391* trials with MAC: carrier suitability, 3-59 to 16-60. *143392* trials with MAC: aerodynamic development and demonstrations, 5-59 to 8-61.

145307 trials with MAC: structural demonstration, 6-59 to 11-61; VF-101/Detachment A, Project Sageburner, World 3 km Speed Record. *145308* trials with MAC: aerodynamic and equipment development, 7-59 to 11-61. *145309* trials with Raytheon: primary missile system at NATC, Patuxent River, 2-60 to 5-60. *145310* trials with MAC: primary and secondary (Sidewinder) armament system evaluation, 8-59 to 8-61. *145311* trials with MAC: aircraft and engine performance measurement, 2-60 to 6-61. *145312* trials with General Electric: engine development at Edwards AFB, 2-60 to 3-60. *145313* trials at NMC: BIS (Raytheon) evaluation, 4-60 to 7-60. *145314* trials at NATC: BIS stability and control, Patuxent River, 3-60 to 7-60. *145315* trials at NATC: BIS, Patuxent River, 3-60 to 6-60. *145316* trials at NATC/NASWF: BIS and TED programmes, 5-60 to 7-60. *145317* trials at NMC: Project Wire, 5-60 to 1-61; trials at MAC, chase and target, 7-63 to 6-65.

146817 Trials with MAC: primary missile system evaluation; carrier suitability and structural demonstration, 5-60 to 10-61. *146818* trials at NATC: BIS evaluation, 5-60 to 7-60. *146819* trials at NATC: BIS evaluation, 5-60 to 11-60. *146820* trials at NMC: pressure suit and Data Link, 5-60 to 7-60. *146821* trials at NMC: Data Link, 3-61 to 8-61.

148252 trials at NMC: Data Link, 3-61 to 7-61. *148253* trials at NMC: Data Link, 4-61 to 9-61. *148254* trials at MAC: Prototype Data Link evaluation, 2-61 to 12-61. *148263* trials at MAC: dual control evaluation, 11-60 to 1-61.

MCDONNELL F4H-1/F-4B PHANTOM II 48 production aircraft built as F4H-1 but re-designated F4B in September 1962. General Electric J79-GE-8 engines rated at 10,900 lb dry thrust and 17,000 lb-thrust with afterburners. APQ-72 radar dish of 32-inch diameter and raised canopy. BuAer Nos *148363–148386* (Block 6f) and *148387–148410* (Block 7g).

148365 Converted to QF-4B, NMC, Point Mugu, 1980. *148396* 'AF-106', VF-106, 1962. *148402* 'AF-105', VF-102, 1962. *148408* 'TL-110', VF-22L1 Reserve, 1969.

MCDONNELL F-4B-8-MC PHANTOM II 24 aircraft. BuAer Nos *148411–148434* (Block 8h).

148416 'NJ-OJT2', VF-121/FRAMP.

MCDONNELL F-4B-9-MC PHANTOM II 24 aircraft, BuAer Nos *149403–149426* (Block 9i).

149409 '42' Converted to QF-4B, NMC, Point Mugu, 1980. *149421* 'SB-00', VMFAT-101.

MCDONNELL F-4B-10-MC PHANTOM II 24 aircraft. BuAer Nos *149427–149450* (Block 10j).

149433 'AG-110', VF-41.

MCDONNELL F-4B-11-MC PHANTOM II 24 aircraft. BuAer Nos *149451–149474* (Block 11k).

149453 'VW-2', VMF(AW)-314, 1962. *149457* 'VW-1', VMF(AW)-314, 1962; 'AB-214', VF-32, 1972; 'NL-113', VF-51, 1972; shot down MiG-17, 11-6-72, Vietnam *149459* 'AB-214', VF-32, 1972.

MCDONNELL F-4B-12-MC PHANTOM II 30 aircraft. BuAer Nos *150406–150435* (Block 121).

150412 'DC-16', VMFA-122.

MCDONNELL F-4B-13-MC PHANTOM II 44 aircraft. BuAer Nos *150436–150479* (Block 13m).

150456 'NL-100', VF-51; shot down MiG-17, 6-5-72, Vietnam. *150468* 'SH-31', VMFAT-101. *150472* 'NL-206', VF-111, 1963. *150479* 'AB-207', VF-32, 1973.

MCDONNELL F-4B-14-MC/F4G/YRF4C PHANTOM II 44 aircraft (MACAIR Nos 266 to 309). BuAer Nos *150480–150493* and *150624–150651* (Block 14n).

The following were loaned to the USAF for Service trials and given temporary AF numbers (they retained F-4B designation): No 267 (became *62-12170*), No 274 (*62-12171*), 281 (*62-12172*), 288 (*62-12173*), 292 (*62-12174*) and 301 (*62-12175*).

The following were F-4G: No 269 (*150481*), 272 (*150484*), 275 (*150487*), 277 (*150489*), 280 (*150492*), 283 (*150625*), 287 (*150629*), 291

(*150633*), 294 (*150636*), 297 (*150639*), 300 (*150642*) and 303 (*150645*).

The following aircraft were modified to become YRF-4C with the USAF: No 266 (became *62-12200*) and 268 (*62-12201*).

150480 (as F-4N) 'WS-00', VMFA-323, El Toro, 1981. *150485* 'SH-42'. VMFAT-101. *150487* 'XF-3', VX-4, 1967-70; became F-4G. *150490* (as F-4N) 'WS-03', VMFA-323, El Toro, 1981. *150492* 'XF-2', VX-4.

MCDONNELL F-4B-15-MC PHANTOM II 33 aircraft. BuAer Nos *150652–150653, 150993–151021* and *151397–152398* (Block 15). From this Block 19 F-4Bs were allotted to the USAF and BuAer Nos *62-12178* to *62-12195*, but after deliveries of F-4Cs had started these were returned to MAC for delivery to USN and USMC squadrons.

151007 'EC-05', VMFA-531. *151398* 'NL-110', VF-51, 1972; shot down MiG-17, 10-5-72, Vietnam.

MCDONNELL F-4B-16-MC PHANTOM II 28 aircraft. BuAer Nos *151399–151426* (Block 16).

151400 'AB-206'. VF-32, 1973.

MCDONNELL F-4B-17-MC PHANTOM II 21 aircraft. BuAer Nos *151427–151447* (Block 17).

151438 'NG-607', VF-95. *151442* 'DR-3', VMFA-312.

MCDONNELL F-4B-18-MC PHANTOM II 25 aircraft. BuAer Nos *151448–151472* (Block 18).

151469 'A-103', VF-11, CVA-59, 1972.

MCDONNELL F-4B-19-MC PHANTOM II 25 aircraft. BuAer Nos *151473–151497*. (Block 19).

151477 'EC-13', VMFA-531. *151497* NATF, Lakehurst.

MCDONNELL F-4B-20-MC PHANTOM II 21 aircraft. BuAer Nos *151498–151519* and *152207–152215* (Block 20).

151499 'NG-206', VF-92. *151510* 'NM-204', VF-111.

MCDONNELL F-4B-21-MC PHANTOM II 28 aircraft. BuAer Nos *152216–152243* (Block 21).

152217 'EC-07', VMFA-531. *152222* (as F-4N) 'WS-01', VMFA-323, E1 Toro, 1981. *152232* 'WH-4', VMFA-542. *152243* (as F-4N) 'WS-04', VMFA-323, El Toro, 1981.

MCDONNELL F-4B-22-MC PHANTOM II 29 aircraft. BuAer Nos *152244–152272* (Block 22).

152247 'NK-202' VF-142; shot down MiG-21,

The 1,000th Phantom, an F-4B-23-MC, 152276 (McDonnell Douglas, Neg No 29340, dated July 1965).

10-8-67, Vietnam. *152252* 'EC-04', VMFA-531. *155258* 'WS-6', VMFA-323, 1966.

MCDONNELL F-4B-23-MC PHANTOM II 32 aircraft. BuAer Nos *152273–152304* (Block 23).

MCDONNELL F-4B-24-MC PHANTOM II 27 aircraft. BuAer Nos *152305–152331* (Block 24).
152306 'DR-5', VMFA-212, Beaufort MCAS, 1970. *152307* 'AA-101', VF-11. *152310* 'NM-110', VF-51. *152315* 'AC-213', CVA-60. *152318* (as F-4N) 'WS-02', VMFA-323, El Toro, 1981. *152321* 'SH-25', VMFAT-101. *152327* 'DW-3', VMFA-251, Beaufort MCAS, 1970.

MCDONNELL F-4B-25-MC PHANTOM II 30 aircraft. BuAer Nos *152965–152994* (Block 25).
152975 'VW-4', VMFA-314. *152980* 'AA-104', VF-11. *152992* 'EC-02', VMFA-531.

MCDONNELL F-4B-26-MC PHANTOM II 35 aircraft. BuAer Nos *152995–153029* (Block 26).
153006 'NE-401', VF-154, CVA-61, 1968; 'SH-24', VMFAT-101. *153009* 'NL-100', VF-51, 1972. *153011* 'NH-104', VF-213, CVA-63, 1968. *153012* 'NM-200', CVA-42. *153014* 'NE-103', VF-21, CVA-61, 1967. *153017* 'NH-107', VF-213, CVA-63, 1969,. *153018* 'NH-205', VF-114, 1972. *153019* 'NL-201', VF-111; shot down MiG-17, 6-3-72, Vietnam. *153020* 'NF-100', VF-161; shot down two MiG-17s, 23-5-72, Vietnam. *153022* 'NH-215', VF-144; shot down An-2, 20-12-66, Vietnam. *153024* 'AA-111', VF-11, CVA-59, 1972. *153027* VF-144; shot down MiG-17, 24-4-67, Vietnam; 'NL-103', VF-51, 1972.

MCDONNELL F-4B-27-MC PHANTOM II 27 aircraft BuAer Nos *153030–153056* (Block 27)
153036 'VE-00', VMFA-115, Iwakuni, 1971. *153045* 'NH-211', VF-114, CVA-63, 1968.

MCDONNELL F-4B-28-MC PHANTOM II 18 aircraft. BuAer Nos *153057–153070* and *153912–153915* (Block 28).
153068 'NH-115', VF-213, CVA-63, 1969; 'NF-110', VF-161; shot down MiG-19, 18-5-72, Vietnam. *153070* 'GD-9', VAQ-33. *153915* 'NJ-113', VF-121; 'NF-105', VF-161; shot down MiG-19, 18-5-72, Vietnam.

MCDONNELL RF-4B PHANTOM II 46 reconnaissance aircraft for the US Marine Corps. BuAer Nos *151975–151977* (Block 20); *151978–151979* (Block 21); *151980–151981* (Block 22); *151982–151984* (Block 23); *153089–153094* (Block 24); *153095–153100* (Block 25); *153101–153107* (Block 26); *153108–153115* (Block 27); *157342–157346* (Block 41); *157347–157351* (Block 43).
153095 'TN-6', VMCJ-3 (RF-4B-25-MC). *153098* 'CY-5', VMCJ-2; 'TN-8', VMCJ-3, 1971 (RF-4B-25-MC). *153101* 'RF-10',

VMFP-3; 'RM-600', VMCJ-1, 1976 (RF-4B-26-MC). *153105* 'RM-603', VMCJ-1, 1976 (RF-4B-26-MC). *157345* 'RF-21', VMPF-3, 1978 (RF-4B-41-MC).

MCDONNELL F-4C-15-MC PHANTOM II One pre-production aircraft, BuAer No *62-12199*, ordered for US Air Force. Evaluation at Edwards AFB, and with 4453d Combat Crew Training Wing, McDill AFB. First flight May 27 1963. General Electric J79-GE-15 engines rated at 10,900 lb dry thrust, and 17,000 lb-thrust with afterburners. Design take-off weight 58,000 lb.

MCDONNELL F-4C-15-MC PHANTOM II Trials and training batch of 14 aircraft, as above, BuAer Nos *63-7407* to *63-7420* (Block 15).
63-7407 Air Force Systems Command, 1976. *63-7410* 4453d CCTW, Davis-Monthan AFB, 1964. *63-7413* 559th TFS, 12th TFW ('Blue Avenger'). *63-7415* 4453d CCTW, Davis-Monthan AFB, 1964.

MCDONNELL F-4C-16-MC PHANTOM II 22 aircraft. BuAer Nos *63-7421* to *63-7442* (Block 16).
63-7436 57th FIS, 1976. *63-7439* 58th TFW.

MCDONNELL F-4C-17-MC PHANTOM II 26 aircraft. BuAer Nos *63-7443* to *63-7468* (Block 17).
63-7443 52d TFW. *63-7460* 57th FIS, 1976. *63-7467* 81st TFW, 52d TFW.

MCDONNELL F-4C-18-MC PHANTOM II 58 aircraft. BuAer Nos *63-7469* to *63-7526* (Block 18).
63-7470 67th TFS, 18th TFW, Kadena, AB, Okinawa ('Rub-a-Dub-Dub, two men in a tub'). *63-7497* 58th TFW.

MCDONNELL F-4C-19-MC PHANTOM II 71 aircraft. BuAer Nos *62-7527* to *63-7597* (Block 19).
63-7529 Michigan ANG. *63-7534* Michigan ANG ('Defiance II'). *63-7550* 58th TFW. *63-7566* 58th TFW. *63-7576* Commander's aircraft, Air Defense Weapons Center. *63-7584* Commander's aircraft, 58th TFW. *63-7589* Michigan ANG.

Production of the USAF's F-4C in 1963 (McDonnell Douglas, Neg No 15720, dated October 1963).

MCDONNELL F-4C-MC PHANTOM II
Two 17,000 lb-thrust General Electric J79-GE-15

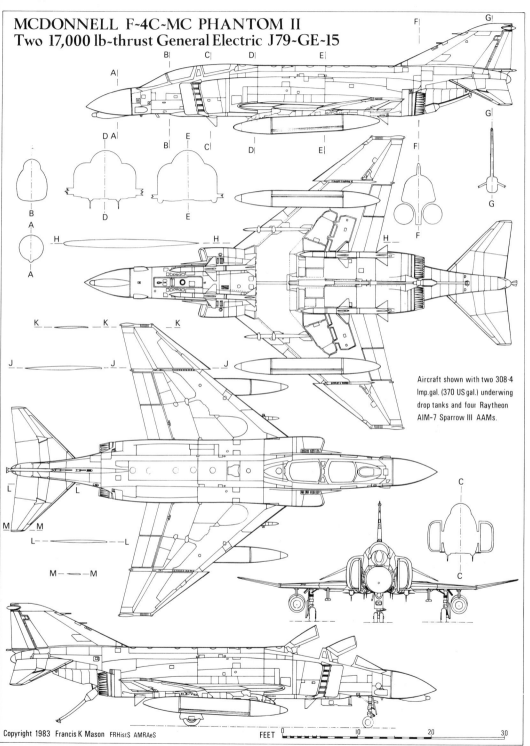

Aircraft shown with two 308·4 Imp.gal. (370 US gal.) underwing drop tanks and four Raytheon AIM-7 Sparrow III AAMs.

FEET   0   10   20   30

**MCDONNELL F-4C-20-MC PHANTOM
II** 65 aircraft. BuAer Nos *63-7598* to *63-7662*
(Block 20).
63-7604 559th TFS, 12th TFW ('Sugar Foot
III'). *63-7618* 57th FIS, Air Defense Command. *63-7626* Michigan ANG. *63-7647* 555th
TFS, 8th TFW, Thailand; Captain Dick
Pascoe shot down MiG-17, 5-6-67, Vietnam.
63-7654 Weapons and performance test air-
craft, Edwards AFB.
**MCDONNELL F-4C-21-MC PHANTOM
II** 70 aircraft. BuAer Nos *63-7663* to *63-7713*,
and *64-0654* to *64-0672* (Block 21).
63-7663 555th TFS, 8th TFW, Thailand
(flown by Colonel Robin Olds). *63-7665* 57th
FIS, 1976. *63-7666* 171st FIS, Michigan ANG,
1980. *63-7670* 58th TFW. *63-7676* 58th TFW.
63-7680 555th TFS, 8th TFW, Thailand;
Colonel Robin Olds shot down MiG-21, 4-5-67,
Vietnam. *63-7685* 57th FIS, 1976. *63-7686*
58th TFW. *63-7693* 58th TFW. *64-0660* 58th
TFW, 1979. *64-0665* 557th TFS, 12th TFW
('Hell's Angel').
**MCDONNELL F-4C-22-MC PHANTOM
II** 65 aircraft. BuAer Nos *64-0873* to *64-0737*
(Block 22).
*MCDONNELL F-4C-23-MC PHANTOM
II* 80 aircraft BuAer Nos *64-0738* to *64-0817*
(Block 23).
64-0785 Hawaii ANG. *64-0803* 480th TFS,
366th TFW. *64-0806* 480th TFS, 366th TFW.
64-0807 432d TRS, Thailand ('Hillbilly Slick').
64-0813 Sold to Spain; fatal crash, 7-5-79.
**MCDONNELL F-4C-24-MC PHANTOM
II** 73 aircraft. BuAer Nos *64-0818* to *64-0881*,
and *64-0929* to *64-0937* (Block 24).
64-0829 555th TFS, 8th TFW, Thailand
('Scat'; flown by Colonel Robin Olds, shot
down two MiG-17s, 20-5-67, Vietnam). *64-
0839* 555th TFS, 8th TFW, Thailand; Captain
Dick Pascoe shot down MiG-21, 6-1-67,
Vietnam. *64-0879* 81st TFW, Bentwaters. *64-
0937* North Dakota ANG ('The Happy
Hooligans'). The following sold to Spain:
*-0820, -0844, -0846, -0850, -0853, -0854,
-0855, -0856, -0857, -0858, -0859, -0861,
-0862, -0864, -0866, -0867, -0868, -0870, -
-0871, -0872, -0877, -0878, -0880* and *-0881*.
(*64-0857* destroyed in fatal crash, 14-10-77;
64-0881 destroyed in fatal crash, 14-2-75.)
**MCDONNELL F-4C-25-MC PHANTOM
II** 73 aircraft. BuAer Nos *64-0882* to *64-0928*,
and *64-0938* to *64-0963* (Block 25).
64-0888 401st TFW, Torrejon, Spain. The
following sold to Spain: *-0882, -0886, -0887,*

*-0894, -0895, -0896, -0900, -0903, -0906,
-0907, -0909, -0920, -0924* and *-0925*.
(*64-0906* destroyed in fatal crash when landing
at Torrejon, 26-11-73.)
**MCDONNELL F-4C-26-MC PHANTOM
II** 17 aircraft. BuAer Nos *64-0964* to *64-0980*
(Block 26). Production of F-4Cs completed in
May 1966.
64-0964 35th TFS, 347th TFW, Yokota AB,
1969.

MCDONNELL RF-4C PHANTOM II
Developed to Specific Operational Requirement
(SOR) 196, a total of 503 reconnaissance aircraft,
with nuclear delivery capability, produced for
USAF. General Electric J79-GE-15 engines
(rated as in F-4C). Design take-off weight
58,000 lb. First flight (by a converted F-4B,
BuAer No *12200*, purchased from the US Navy),
August 8 1963; first flight by production RF-
4C-16-MC, *63-7740*, May 18 1964. (*12200* later
employed for 'Fly-by-Wire' [Survivable Flight
Control System] trials, Air Force Systems
Command).
**MCDONNELL RF-4C-16-MC PHANTOM
II** 2 aircraft. BuAer Nos *63-7740, 63-7741*
(Block 16).
**MCDONNELL RF-4C-17-MC PHANTOM
II** 1 aircraft. BuAer No *63-7742* (Block 17).
**MCDONNELL RF-4C-18-MC PHANTOM
II** 7 aircraft. BuAer Nos *63-7743* to *63-7749*
(Block 18).
**MCDONNELL RF-4C-19-MC PHANTOM
II** 14 aircraft. BuAer Nos *63-7750* to *63-7763*
(Block 19).
63-7760 1st TRS, 10th TRW.
**MCDONNELL RF-4C-20-MC PHANTOM
II** 21 aircraft. BuAer Nos *64-0997* to *64-1017*
(Block 20).
**MCDONNELL RF-4C-21-MC PHANTOM
II** 20 aircraft. BuAer Nos *64-1018* to *64-1037*
(Block 21).
64-1021 106th TRS, Nevada ANG. *64-1033*
11th TRS, 432d TRW, Udorn RTAFB,
Thailand ('Ol' Bullet').
**MCDONNELL RF-4C-22-MC PHANTOM
II** 24 aircraft. BuAer Nos *64-1038* to *64-1061*
(Block 22).
64-1050 4416th Tactical Electronic Warfare
Squadron, 363d TRW, Saint Louis.
**MCDONNELL RF-4C-23-MC PHANTOM
II** 16 aircraft. BuAer Nos *64-1062* to *64-1077*
(Block 23).
64-1066 Minnesota ANG. *64-1073* 10th
TRW, Alconbury, 1966.

MCDONNELL RF-4C-24-MC PHANTOM II 24 aircraft. BuAer Nos *64-1078* to *64-1085*, and *65-0818* to *65-0838* (Block 24).

MCDONNELL RF-4C-25-MC PHANTOM II 26 aircraft. BuAer Nos *65-0839* to *65-0864* (Block 25).

65-0854 106th TRS, Nevada ANG.

MCDONNELL RF-4C-26-MC PHANTOM II 37 aircraft. BuAer Nos *65-0865* to *65-0901* (Block 26).

65-0881 192d TRS, Nevada ANG, 1976.

MCDONNELL RF-4C-27-MC PHANTOM II 31 aircraft. BuAer Nos *65-0902* to *65-0932* (Block 27).

65-0921 67 TRW.

MCDONNELL RF-4C-28-MC PHANTOM II 18 aircraft. BuAer Nos *65-0933* to *65-0945*, *66-0383* to *66-0386*, and *66-0388* (Block 28).

Sold to Spain: *65-0936*, *65-0937*, *65-0942* and *65-0943*.

MCDONNELL RF-4C-29-MC PHANTOM II 19 aircraft. BuAer Nos *66-0387*, and *66-0389* to *66-0406* (Block 29).

MCDONNELL RF-4C-30-MC PHANTOM II 22 aircraft. BuAer Nos *66-0407* to *66-0428* (Block 30).

66-0413 1st TRS, 10th TRW, Alconbury, 1980.

MCDONNELL RF-4C-31-MC PHANTOM II 22 aircraft. BuAer Nos *66-0429* to *66-0450* (Block 31).

MCDONNELL RF-4C-32-MC PHANTOM II 22 aircraft. BuAer Nos *66-0451* to *66-0472* (Block 32).

MCDONNELL RF-4C-33-MC PHANTOM II 21 aircraft. BuAer Nos *66-0473* to *66-0478*, and *67-0428* to *67-0442* (Block 33).

MCDONNELL RF-4C-34-MC PHANTOM II 11 aircraft. BuAer Nos *67-0443* to *67-0453* (Block 34).

67-0444 4th TRS, 75th TRW, Bergsrom AFB.

MCDONNELL RF-4C-35-MC PHANTOM II 8 aircraft. BuAer Nos *67-0454* to *67-9461* (Block 35).

MCDONNELL RF-4C-36-MC PHANTOM **II** 8 aircraft. BuAer Nos *67-0462* to *67-0469* (Block 36).

MCDONNELL RF-4C-37-MC PHANTOM II 14 aircraft. BuAer Nos *68-0548* to *68-0561* (Block 37).

68-0555 1st TRS, 10th TRW.

MCDONNELL RF-4C-38-MC PHANTOM II 15 aircraft. BuAer Nos *68-0562* to *68-0576* (Block 38).

68-0564 1st TRS, 10th TRW, Alconbury,

1980. *68-0568* 1st TRS, 10th TRW, Alconbury 1980.

MCDONNELL RF-4C-39-MC PHANTOM II 17 aircraft. BuAer Nos *68-0577* to *68-0593* (Block 39).

MCDONNELL RF-4C-40-MC PHANTOM II 18 aircraft. BuAer Nos *68-0594* to *68-0611* (Block 40).

MCDONNELL RF-4C-41-MC PHANTOM II 9 aircraft. BuAer Nos *69-0349* to *69-0357* (Block 41).

69-0349 14th TRS, Udorn RTAFB, Thailand, 1973.

MCDONNELL RF-4C-42-MC PHANTOM II 9 aircraft. BuAer Nos *69-0358* to *69-0366* (Block 42).

MCDONNELL RF-4C-43-MC PHANTOM II 9 aircraft. BuAer Nos *69-0367* to *69-0375* (Block 43).

69-0369 1st TRS, 10th TRW, Alconbury, 1980.

MCDONNELL RF-4C-44-MC PHANTOM II 9 aircraft. BuAer Nos *69-0376* to *69-0384* (Block 44). Film ejector deleted henceforth.

MCDONNELL RF-4C-48-MC PHANTOM II 5 aircraft. BuAer Nos *71-0248* to *71-0252* (Block 48).

MCDONNELL RF-4C-49-MC PHANTOM II 7 aircraft. BuAer Nos *71-0253* to *71-0259* (Block 49).

MCDONNELL RF-4C-51-MC PHANTOM II 4 aircraft. BuAer Nos *72-0145* to *72-0148* (Block 51).

MCDONNELL RF-4C-52-MC PHANTOM II 4 aircraft. BuAer Nos *72-0149* to *72-0152* (Block 52).

72-0150 67th TRW.

MCDONNELL RF-4C-53-MC PHANTOM II 4 aircraft. BuAer Nos *72-0153* to *72-0156* (Block 53).

MCDONNELL F-4D PHANTOM II 741 production aircraft. Block 26 to 33. Letter Contract received, March 1962; mock-up approved, April 1962; first flight and delivery to Tactical Air Command, November 1963; production completed, May 1966. Two General Electric J79-GE-15 (Spec E-2027) engines each rated at 10.900 lb dry thrust, and 17,000 lb-thrust with afterburners. Design take-off weight, 58,000 lb.

MCDONNELL F-4D-26-MC PHANTOM II 32 aircraft. BuAer Nos *65-0580* to *65-0611* (Block 26).

65-0580 36th TFW, 3-67. *65-0581* 49th TFW, 10-75; 388th TFW, 8-77; 56th TFW, 11-78.

The 2,000th Phantom, a USAF F-4D (McDonnell Douglas, Neg No 118173-16, dated 1966).

65-085 49th TFW, 10-77; 56th TFW, 11-78. **65-088** 49th TFW, 10-75; 56th TFW, 11-78; 18th TFW, 9-79. **65-0590** 49th TFW, 8-72; 388th TFW, 10-78; 127th TFTS, Kansas ANG, 9- 79. **65-0595** 49th TFW, 10-75; 388th TFW, 10-78. **65-0597** 18th TFW, 11-76; 388th TFW, 10-78. **65-0601** 36th TFW, 9-67. **65-0603** 49th TFW; written off, Wurstberg, 7-10-75. **65-0609** 18th TFW, 11-76; 388th TFW, 10-78; 129th TFTS, Kansas ANG, 9-79. **65-0611** 49th TFW, 10-76; 56th TFW, 10-78; 31st TFW, 11-79. Following aircraft supplied to Republic of Korea Air Force: *-0582, -0589, -0591, -0592, -0605, -0610.*

MCDONNELL F-4D-27-MC PHANTOM II 54 aircraft. BuAer Nos *65-0612* to *65-0665* (Block 27).

65-0612 18th TFW, 11-76; 388th TFW, 8-77. **65-0614** 474th TFW, 10-77; 56th TFW, 11-78. **65-0617** 49th TFW, 10-75; 56th TFW, 11-78.

65-0620 56th TFW, 9-67. **65-0622** 36th TFW, 9-67. **65-0625** 49th TFW, 10-75; 388th TFW, 10-78; 31st TFW, 11-79. **65-0627** 49th TFW, 10-75. **65-0630** 36th TFW, 9-67. **65-0635** 474th TFW, 10-77; 56th TFW, 11-78. **65-0639** 49th TFW, 10-73; 388th TFW, 9-77; 56th TFW, 11-78; 31st TFW, 11-79. **65-0641** 35th TFW, 7-76; 388th TFW, 10-78. **65-0644** 474th TFW. **65-0646** 48th TFW, 11-76; 11-78. **65-0648** 48th TFW, 1-77; 388th TFW, 10-78. **65-0652** 49th TFW, 10-75; 388th TFW, 9-77; 56th TFW, 11-78. **65-0654** 49th TFW, 10-76; 388th TFW, 10-78; 31st TFW, 11-79. **65-0659** 48th TFW, 1-77; 388th TFW, 10-78; 31st TFW, 11-79. **65-0660** 49th TFW, 9-77; 56th TFW, 11-78. **65-0662** 81st TFW; written off at Aviano Air Base, 14-3-74. **65-0665** 35th TFW, 7-76; 388th TFW, 10-78. Following aircraft supplied to Republic of Korea Air Force: *-0620, -0622, -0623, -0630, -0640, -0650.*

Production of F-4Ds and RF-4Cs in 1966 (McDonnell Douglas, Neg No 36084, dated May 12 1966).

MCDONNELL F-4D-28-MC PHANTOM
II 105 aircraft. BuAer Nos *65-0666* to *65-0770*. (Block 28).

65-0666 18th TFW, 1-79. *65-0669* 50th TFW, 12-66; scrapped 1967. *65-0670* Air Defense Test Center, Air Force Systems Command, 10-78. *65-0671* 49th TFW, 10-76; 388th TFW, 10-78; 31st TFW, 11-79. *65-0673* 81st TFW; written off in Spain, 9-5-72. *65-0676* 48th TFW, 2-77; 388th TFW, 10-77. *65-0681* 81st TFW, 7-78; 52d TFW, 12-78. *65-0685* 18th TFW, 5-77; 56th TFW, 11-78. *65-0687* 81st TFW, 1-78; 401st TFW, 9-79. *65-0690* 48th TFW, 2-77; 388th TFW, 10-78. *65-0696* 474th TFW, 10-77; 56th TFW, 9-78. *65-0697* 49th TFW, 10-76; 388th TFW, 10-77; written off, Hill AFB, 28-8-78. *65-0698* Air Defense Test Center, Air Force Systems Command, 7-79. *65-0700* 49th TFW, 10-75; 474th TFW, 10-77; 56th TFW, 10-78. *65-0702* 81st TFW, 11-78;

401st TFW, 9-79. *65-0710* 81st TFW, 11-78; 401st TFW, 9-79. *65-0711* 81st TFW, 3-79; 401st TFW, 4-79. *65-0713* became McDonnell YF-4E; Air Force Test Center, 11-78. *65-0716* 49th TFW, 3-74; 81st TFW, 3-79; 401st TFW, 4-79; 388th TFW, 9-79. *65-0717* 49th TFW, 10-76; 388th TFW, written off, Hill AFB, 5-2-79. *65-0721* 48th TFW, 1-77; 388th TFW, 10-78. *65-0729* 35th TFW, 10-75; 388th TFW, 10-78. *65-0733* 50th TFW, 9-67. *65-0736* 81st TFW, 3-79; 401st TFW, 9-79. *65-0741* 48th TFW, 2-77; 388th TFW, 10-78; 474th TFW, 9-79. *65-0743* 49th TFW, 10-75; 388th TFW, 8-77; 474th TFW, 11-78. *65-0746* 49th TFW, 10-75; 388th TFW, 10-78; 31st TFW, 11-79. *65-0749* 81st TFW, 11-78; 401st TFW, 9-79. *65-0751* 36th TFW, 9-67. *65-0755* 405th TFW, 6-47; 388th TFW, 10-79. *65-0765* 474th TFW, 10-77; 56th TFW, 11-78. *65-0770* 388th TFW, 10-77; 56th TFW, 11-78. Following supplied to Republic of Korea Air Force: *-0678, -0691, -0709, -0715* (written off at Seoul, 25-9-78), *-0732, -0762.*

MCDONNELL F-4D-29-MC PHANTOM II 139 aircraft. BuAer Nos *65-0771* to *65-0801, 66-0226* to *66-0283*, and *66-7455* to *66-7504* (Block 29).
65-0772 81st TFW, 11-78; 401st TFW, 9-79. *65-0776* 81st TFW; written off, Nuremburg, 9-7-74. *65-0782* 18th TFW, 2-79. *65-0785* 18th TFW, 12-76. *65-0790* 49th TFW, 10-76; damaged by fire, Ramstein AB, 13-9-77. *65-0798* 18th TFW, 11-76. *65-0799* 432d TRW; written off, Vietnam, 18-2-72. *66-0226* 49th TFW, 10-76; 56th TFW, 10-78. *66-0227* 48th TFW, 2-77; 388th TFW; written off at Nellis ranges, 7-3-79. *66-0229* 81st TFW, 9-78; 401st TFW, 9-79. *66-0234* 81st TFW, 3-79; 401st TFW, 4-79. *66-0235* 48th TFW; written off in Spain, 16-1-75. *66-0237* 432d TRW; written off in Vietnam, 18-2-72. *66-0241* 432d TRW; written off in Vietnam, 18-1-72. *66-0249* 48th TFW, 3-77; 474th 11-78. *66-0256* 48th TFW; written off in North Sea, 22-11-75. *66-0261* 81st TFW, 3-79; 401st TFW, 9-79. *66-0269* 35th TFW, 10-75; 18th TFW, 12-76. *66-0274* 388th TFW, 10-78; 8th TFW, 3-79. *66-0280* 48th TFW, 3-77; 474th TFW, 11-78. *66-0282* 474th TFW, 10-77; Air Defense Test Center, Air Force Systems Command, 9-78. *66-7458* 4485th Test Squadron, 10-75; Air Defense Test Center, Air Force Systems Command, 1978. *66-7465* 49th TFW, 10-76; 56th TFW; crashed in sea off Florida, 28-6-78. *66-7474* 474th TFW, 9-77. *66-7480* 48th TFW; written off at Lakenheath, 24-8-76. *66-7483* Air Defense Center, Air Force Systems Command, 10-78.

MCDONNELL F-4D-30-MC PHANTOM II 146 aircraft. BuAer Nos *66-7505* to *66-7650* (Block 30).
66-7505 18th TFW, 12-79. *66-7508* 52d TFW, 12-77. *66-7512* 4485th Test Squadron, 10-76; Air Defense Test Center, Air Force Systems Command, 7-79. *66-7514* 52d TFW, 6-78. *66-7526* 49th TFW, 10-75. *66-7529* 49th TFW, 10-75; 474th TFW, 10-78; 8th TFW, 11-78. *66-7538* 18th TFW, 2-79; 8th TFW, 3-79. *66-7548* On loan to Republic of Korea Air Force, c 1973; 8th TFW, 3-79 *66-7554* 474th TFW, 10-78; 8th TFW, 3-79. *66-7558* 81st TFW, 11-78; 52d TFW, 9-78. *66-7560* 81st TFW, 11-78; 401st TFW; 3-79. *66-7566* 81st TFW, 9-78; 401st TFW, 9-79. *66-7572* 52d TFW, written off, Jöllenbeck, Germany,

7-10-74. *66-7581* 474th TFW, 9-77. *66-7584* 57th FWW, 10-73. *66-7585* 52d TFW, written off, Incirlik, Turkey, 17-11-68. *66-7596* 18th TFW, 2-79. *66-7606* 405th TFW, written off, Taiwan Straits, 14-8-73. *66-7608* 4485th Test Squadron, 10-75; 49th TFW, 10-76; 474th TFW, 10-78; 8th TFW, 3-79. *66-7625* 18th TFW, 2-77. *66-7629* 81st TFW, 11-78. *66-7635* General Dynamics chase aircraft, 10-75. *66-7642* 18th TFW, 2-79. *66-7644* 52d TFW, 6-6-78. *66-7648* 49th TFW, 10-76; 474th TFW, 11-78. *66-7650* 49th TFW, 10-75; 474th TFW, 11-78.

MCDONNELL F-4D-31-MC PHANTOM II 138 aircraft. BuAer Nos *66-7651* to *66-7774* and *66-8685* to *66-8698* (Block 31).
66-7651 36th TFW, written off in Spain, 14-3-72. *66-7657* 52d TFW, written off at Rheinfeld, Germany, 4-4-78. *66-7662* 52d TFW, 6-78. *66-7666* 18th TFW, 11-76. *66-7674* 49th TFW, 10-76; 474th TFW, 11-78. *66-7685* 49th TFW, 10-75; 474th TFW, 10-78; 8th TFW, 3-79. *66-7690* 49th TFW, 10-75; 18th TFW, 12-76. *66-7694* 81st TFW, 9-78. *66-7698* 50th TFW, 8-74; 18th TFW, 2-79. *66-7700* ADTC, AFSC, 9-78. *77-7708* 81st TFW, 11-78; 401st TFW, 4-79. *66-7713* 50th TFW; written off near Hahn AB, 5-74. *66-7716* ADTC, AFSC, 10-78. *66-7726* 49th TFW, 10-75; 474th TFW, 10-78; 8th TFW, 3-79. *66-7733* 52d TFW, 3-79. *66-7738* 405th TFW, 8-73; 52d TFW, 2-79. *66-7741* ADTC, AFSC, 10-78. *66-7743* 18th TFW; written off, Kadena AB, 1-11-77. *66-7744* 4453d Combat Crew Training Wing; written off, Tucson, Arizona, 18-12-67. *66-7758* 52d TFW, 9-78. *66-7768* 81st TFW, 9-78; 401st TFW, 9-78; 401st TFW, 4-79. *66-8698* ADTC, AFSC, 10-78.

MCDONNELL F-4D-32-MC PHANTOM II 88 aircraft. BuAer Nos *66-8699* to *66-8786* (Block 32).
66-8699 ADTC, AFSC, 10-78. *66-8710* 52d TFW, 12-78. *66-8713* 8th TFW, 12-75. *66-8715* 50th TFW, 7-76; 52d TFW, 6-78. *66-8723* 4485th Test Squadron, 10-76; ADTC, AFSC, 10-78. *66-8726* ADTC, AFSC, 8-70. *66-8728* ADTC, AFSC, 7-79. *66-8738* 474th TFW, 10-77. *66-8753* 52d TFW, 3-79. *66-8759* 4485 Test Squadron, 10-75; ADTC, AFSC, 10-76; 52d TFW, 10-78. *66-8761* 8th TFW; written off, Osan AB, 23-1-70. *66-8765* 4485th Test Squadron, 9-72; 52d TFW, 6-78. *66-8769* 405th TFW, 3-70. *66-8779* 52d TFW, written off near Stuttgart, 20-9-78. *66-8781* 52d TFW, crashed in North Sea, 6-7-77. *66-8783* 4485th

Test Squadron, 10-74; 8th TFW, 3-79. *66-8786* 8th TFW, 4-79. Following aircraft modified with LORAN: *66-8708* to *66-8714*, *66-8719*, *66-8722*, *66-8726* to *66-8728*, *66-8730* to *66-8735*, *66-8737* to *66-8739*, *66-8741*, *66-8742*, *66-8744*, *66-8745*, *66-8747* to *66-8750*, *66-8755*, *66-8756*, *66-8758* to *66-8762*, *66-8765*, *66-8768* to *66-8770*, *66-8772*, *66-8774*, *66-8776* to *66-8786*.

MCDONNELL F-4D-33-MC PHANTOM II 39 aircraft. BuAer Nos *66-8787* to *66-8825* (Block 33).
66-8787 8th TFW, 11-76. *66-8790* 52d TFW, crashed near Stuttgart, 20-9-72. *66-8793* 52d TFW; written off, 16-11-76. *66-8798* 4485th Test Squadron, 9-72; 52d TFW, 2-79. *66-8800* Air Force Special Weapons Center, AFSC, 10-10-75; ADTC, AFSC, 7-79. *66-8803* 8th TFW, 4-79. *66-8812* 18th TFW, 11-76; 8th TFW, 4-79. *66-8815*, 18th TFW, 2-79. *66-8819* 49th TFW, 10-75; 18th TFW, 12-76; 8th TFW, 3-79. *66-8825* 52d TFW. Following aircraft modified with LORAN: *66-8787* to *66-8799*, *66-8802* to *66-8806*, *66-8810*, *66-8813*, *66-8816*, *66-8818*, *66-8825*.

MCDONNELL F-4E PHANTOM II Total of 1,329 aircraft. Blocks 31 to 67. Letter Contract received, August 1966; first prototype completed, April 1967; first flight, July 1967; first delivery, August 1967; Cat II flight tests started, January 1968. Two General Electric J79-GE-17 (Spec E-2029) engines each rated at 11,870 lb dry thrust and 17,900 lb-thrust with afterburner.

MCDONNELL F-4E-31-MC PHANTOM II 14 aircraft. BuAer Nos *66-0284* to *66-0297* (Block 31).
66-0284 ADTC, AFSC, 10-78. *66-0286* 'Thunderbirds', 10-73; 57th TTW, 11-71; ADTC, AFSC, 11-78. *66-0289* 57th TTW, 5-74; 31st TFW, 8-76; 56th TFW, 9-77; Air Force Flight Test Center, AFSC, 9-78. *66-0290* 'Thunderbirds' No 8; crashed 20-1-71, but repaired. *66-0292* 56th TFW, 10-75; 4485th Test Squadron, 9-77; ADTC, AFSC, 7-79. *66-0294* 'Thunderbirds', 10-73, 35th TFW, 9-77; AFFTC, AFSC, 11-78. *66-0297* 388th TFW, 3-73; 31st TFW, 9-77; 21st CW, 5-79; 4th TFW, 10-79.

MCDONNELL F-4E-32-MC PHANTOM II 41 aircraft. BuAer Nos *66-0298* to *66-0338* (Block 32).
66-0298 57th FWW, 10-73; 31st TFW, 9-77; 21st CW, 10-78; 35th TFW, 10-79. *66-0299*

1st TFW, 11-70. *66-0300* 56th TFW, 9-77; 57th FIS, 3-79. *66-0301* AFFTC, AFSC, 5-69; 4485th Test Squadron, 10-76; ADTC, AFSC, 10-78. *66-0302* 1st TFW, 10-75; preserved at McDill AFB, 10-78. *66-0303* 57th FWW, 10-73; 35th TFW, 9-77; 21st CW, 10-78. *66-0304* AFFTC, AFSC, 9-74; 57th FWW, 10-75; 33d TFW, 10-76; 31st TFW, 9-77; 57th FIS, 3-79. *66-0309* 388th TFW, 3-72; 3d TFW, 9-77; 31st TFW, 2-79. *66-0310* 1st TFW, 11-70. *66-0314* 57th FWW, 10-73; 31st TFW, 10-77; 57th FIS, 3-79. *66-0315* 'Thunderbirds', No 3, 9-72; 57th FWW, 10-75; AFFTC, AFSC, 11-78. *66-0319* 'Thunderbirds', No 5, 9-72; 4th TFW, 10-75; AFFTC, AFSC, 11-78. *66-0321* 'Thunderbirds', No 3, written off, Andrews AFB, 6-72. *66-0324* 33d TFW, 10-76; 56th TFW, 9-77. *66-0328* 31st TFW, 9-77; 57th FIS, 9-78. *66-0329* 'Thunderbirds', No 7, 9-72; 35th TFW, 9-77; AFFTC, AFSC, 11-78. *66-0331* 57th FWW, 10-72. *66-0337* 1st TFW, 10-74; 56th TFW, 10-76; 31st TFW, 11-78; supplied to Egyptian Air Force.

MCDONNELL F-4E-33-MC PHANTOM II 56 aircraft. BuAer Nos *66-0339* to *66-0382*, and *67-0208* to *67-0219* (Block 19).
66-0339 1st TFW, 10-74; 56th TFW, 9-77; 21st CW, 10-78. *66-0344* 57th FWW, 10-72; 31st TFW, 9-77; 57th FIS, 9-78. *66-0353* 'Thunderbirds', trainer, 2-73; 31st TFW, 11-78. *66-0358* 51st CW; 31st TFW, 9-78. *66-0359* 57th FWW, 10-73; 56th TFW, 9-77; 21st CW, 10-78; 4th TFW, 9-79. *66-0364* 31st TFW, 11-78. *66-0368* AAFTC, AFSC, 11-78. *66-0377* 'Thunderbirds', 10-73; 4th TFW, 9-77; AAFTS, AFSC, 10-78. *66-0379* 1st TFW, 10-74; 56th TFW, 9-77; 21st CW, 10-78. *66-0382* 31st TFW, 9-77; 57th FIS, 3-79. *67-0208* 388th TFW, 1970; 3d TFW, 11-76; 21st CW, 5-79; 4th TFW, 9-79. *67-0215* 31st TFW, 2-79. *67-0218* 1st TFW, 10-74; 56th TFW, 10-76; 31st TFW, 2-79. Following aircraft supplied to Egyptian Air Force: *66-0340*, *-0341*, *-0343*, *-0349*, *-0353*, *-0358*, *-0360*, *-0362*, *-0364*, *-0366*, *-0375*; *67-0211*, *-0212*, *-0213*.

MCDONNELL F-4E-34-MC PHANTOM II 63 aircraft. BuAer Nos *67-0220* to *67-0282* (Block 34).
67-0220 57th FWW, 10-75; 56th TFW, 9-77; 31st TFW, 2-79. *67-0226* 31st TFW, 11-78. *67-0232* 31st TFW, 2-79. *67-0237* 3d TFW, 11-76; 21st CW, 10-78. *67-0244* 1st TFW, 10-74; 56th TFW, 1976. *67-0251* 21st CW, 10-78. *67-0261* 388th TFW, 2-72. *67-0265*

The 4,000th Phantom, a late-standard F-4E (McDonnell Douglas, Neg No 79025, dated February 1971).

ADTC, AFSC, 7-79. *67-0273* 3d TFW, 11-76; 21st CW, 10-78. *67-0277* 388th TFW, 1972. Following aircraft supplied to Egyptian Air Force: *67-0220, -0231, -0236, -0238, -0239, -0242, -0264, -0278.*

MCDONNELL F-4E-35-MC PHANTOM II 59 aircraft. BuAer Nos *67-0282* to *67-0341* (Block 35).

67-0283 388th TFW, 4-74; 3d TFW, 11-76; 21st CW, 5-79. *67-0287* 388th TFW, 4-74. *67-0292* 31st TFW, 6-76. *67-0300* 388th TFW, 11-70. *67-0306* 388th TFW, 4-74; 56th CW, 1975. *67-0317* 31st TFW, 2-79. *67-0323* 1st TFW, 10-74. *67-0332* 31st TFW, 2-79. *67-0334* 388th TFW, 4-74; 8th TFW, 1976; 21st CW, 4-79. *67-0341* 1st TFW, 10-74; 56th TFW, 10-77; 31st TFW, 11-78. Following aircraft supplied to Egyptian Air Force: *67-0289, -0305, -0307, -0309, -0313, -0317, -0322, --0341.*

MCDONNELL F-4E-36-MC PHANTOM II 57 aircraft. BuAer Nos *67-0342* to *67-0398* (Block 36).

67-0342 388th TFW, 4-74; 3d TFW, 11-76; 21st CW, 10-78. *67-0345* 1st TFW, 4—74;

56th TFW, 9-77; 347th TFW, 9-79. *67-0347* 347th TFW, 3-79; 51st CW, 9-79. *67-0349* 56th TFW, 10-76; 33d TFW, 9-78; 347th TFW,9-79. *67-0359* 388th TFW, 11-70. *67-0366* 388th TFW, 11-70; 31st TFW, 10-76; 50th TFW, 12-78. *67-0370* 31st TFW, 9-77; 57th TTW, 11-78. *67-0384* 56th TFW, 10-75; 33d TFW, 9-77; 347th TFW, 3-79. *67-0393* 432d TRW; written off, Thailand, 12-11-74. *67-0397* 479th TFW, written off, Rosamond, California, 9-72. *67-0398* 33d TFW, 9-77; 347th TFW, 9-79. Following aircraft supplied to Egyptian Air Force: *67-0355, -0371, -0373, -0388.*

MCDONNELL F-4E-37-MC PHANTOM II 63 aircraft. BuAer Nos *68-0303* to *68-0365* (Block 37).

68-0303 57th TTW, 11-77. *68-0304* AAFTC, AFSC, 11-78. *68-0308* 35th TFW, 10-73; 33d TFW, 9-77; 347th TFW, 9-79. *68-0317* 33d TFW; 347th TFW, 9-79. *68-0321* 32d TFS, 2-72; 36th TFW, 8-77; 50th TFW, 6-78. *68-0337* 57th TTW, 11-78. *68-0339* 51st CW, 12-75. *68-0347* 3d TFW, 1-79. *68-0365* 31st TFW, 10-76; 51st CW, 9-79.

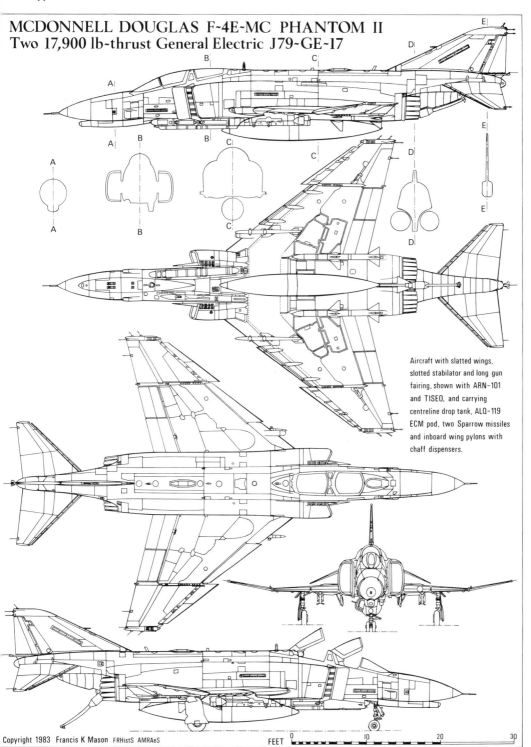

MCDONNELL DOUGLAS F-4E-MC PHANTOM II
Two 17,900 lb-thrust General Electric J79-GE-17

Aircraft with slatted wings, slotted stabilator and long gun fairing, shown with ARN-101 and TISEO, and carrying centreline drop tank, ALQ-119 ECM pod, two Sparrow missiles and inboard wing pylons with chaff dispensers.

FEET 0   10   20   30

MCDONNELL F-4E-38-MC PHANTOM II 43 aircraft. BuAer Nos *68-0366* to *68-0409* (Block 38).

68-0366 33d TFW, 9-77; 347th TFW, 9-79. *68-0371* 3d TFW, 12-79. *68-0378* 36th TFW, 10-75; 86th TFW, 11-78. *68-0385* 35th TFW, 10-73; 33d TFW, 8-77; 347th TFW, 9-79. *68-0388* 32d TFS; 50th TFW, 6-75; 36th TFW, 5-76. *68-0393* 50th TFW, 5-74; 36th TFW, 1-75; 86th TFW, 11-78. *68-0395* 4th TFW, 10-75; 33d TFW, 10-78; 347th TFW, 11-79. *68-0401* 32d TFS, 6-73; 86th TFW, 11-78. *68-0403*, 401st TFW, 4-72; 86th TFW, 12-78. *68-0407* 21st CW, 1971; 51st CW, 4-79. *68-0409* 21st CW, 11-76; 3d TFW, 1-79. Following aircraft supplied to Israeli Air Force: *68-0396* to *68-0399*.

MCDONNELL F-4E-39-MC PHANTOM II 42 aircraft. BuAer Nos *68-0410* to *68-0451* (Block 39).

68-0410 21st CW, 6-70; 3d TFW, 1-79. *68-0413* 32d TFS, 9-74; 36th TFW, 1-76; 86th TFW, 9-78. *68-0422* 32d TFS, written off in sea off Italy, 19-1-70. *68-0425* 21st CW, 1971. *68-0430* 51st CW, 9-79. *68-0433* 32d TFS, written off in Holland, 21-6-71. *68-0443* 32d TFS, 11-74; 36th TFW, 12-76; 50th TFW, 6-78. *68-0446* 32d TFS, 5-73; 86th TFW, 11-78. *68-0451* 33d TFW, 10-75; written off at Nellis AFB, 2-3-78. Following aircraft supplied to Israeli Air Force: *68-0414* to *68-0417*, and *68-0434* to *68-0437*.

MCDONNELL F-4E-40-MC PHANTOM II 43 aircraft. BuAer Nos *68-0452* to *68-0494* (Block 40).

68-0452 32d TFS, 6-73; 86th TFW, 1-77. *68-0461* 31st TFW, 2-79; 347th TFW, 11-79. *68-0468* 3d TFW, 9-78. *68-0477* 4th TFW, 10-74. *68-0489* 36th TFW, 10-73; written off, 20-9-74. *68-0493* 388th TFW, 10-72; 3d TFW, 10-78. Following aircraft supplied to Israeli Air Force: *68-0454* to *68-0457*, *68-0469* to *68-0472*, and *68-0484* to *68-0487*.

MCDONNELL F-4E-41-MC PHANTOM II 53 aircraft. BuAer Nos *68-0495* to *68-0547* (Block 41).

68-0495 36th TFW, 1-74; 50th TFW, 3-79. *68-0503* 50th TFW, 8-77. *68-0508* 36th TFW, 10-73; 50th TFW, 6-78. *68-0514* 50th TFW, 7-78. *68-0518* 35th TFW, 10-75; 33d TFW, written off at Nellis AFB, 2-9-77. *68-0532* 50th TFW, 6-78; 86th TFW, 8-79. *68-0538* 32d TFS, 1-75; 36th TFW, 12-76; 50th TFW, 3-79. Aircraft supplied to Israeli Air Force: *68-0499*

to *68-0502*, *68-0519* to *68-0525*, and *68-0539* to *68-0547*.

MCDONNELL F-4E-42-MC PHANTOM II 68 aircraft. BuAer Nos *69-0236* to *69-0303* (Block 42).

69-0236 36th TFW, 4-76; 50th TFW, 12-77. *69-0243* 50th TFW, 9-75; 35th TFW, 7-78; trials with MAC. *69-0256* 36th TFW, 7-76. *69-0262* 86th TFW, written off in Spain, 10-73 *69-0268* 36th TFW, 10-76; 50th TTW, 8-78; written off, 18-8-79. *69-0277* Loaned to Imperial Iranian Air Force, 1973; 50th TFW, 11-77; 35th TFW, 8-79. *69-0289* 33d TFW, written off in Vietnam, 3-7-72. *69-0300* 347th TFW, 11-77. Following aircraft modified as *F-4G 'Wild Weasel'*: *69-0236* to *69-0243*, *69-0245* to *69-0248*, *69-0250* to *69-0255*, *69-0257* to *69-0259*, *69-0261*, *69-0263*, *69-0265*, *69-0267*, *69-0269* to *69-0275*, *69-0277*, *69-0279* to *69-0281*, *69-0283* to *69-0286*, *69-0292*, *69-0293*, *69-0297* (total of 43 aircraft).

MCDONNELL F-4E-43-MC PHANTOM II 64 aircraft. BuAer Nos *69-0304* to *69-0307*, and *69-7201* to *69-7260* (Block 43).

69-0304 to *69-0307* loaned to Royal Australian Air Force; returned to USAF, c 1974. *69-0304* AFFTC, AFSC, 10-77; 35th TFW, 10-78. *69-0305* 4th TFW, 9-75; 57th TTW, 11-78. *69-0306* 347th TFW, 3-79; 3d TFW, 12-79. *69-0307* 57th TTW, 11-78. *69-7201* to *69-7217*, *69-7219*, *69-7220*, *69-7234* loaned to Royal Australian Air Force; *69-7203* written off, Evans Head, Australia, 6-6-71. Remainder returned to USAF, c 1974. *62-7209* 347th TFW, 9-77; 35th TFW, 11-78. *69-7228* 36th TFW, 7-76; 347th TFW, 11-78; 4th TFW, 7-79. *69-7248* supplied to Israeli Air Force, and remains displayed in Cairo. *69-7252* 401st TFW, 5-72; 51st CW, 1975. *69-7254* Prototype F-4G. AFFTC, AFSC, 10-78; 35th TFW, 8-79. *69-7260* 347th TFW, 9-78; 35th TFW, 10-78; 52d TFW, 6-79. Following aircraft modified as *F-4G 'Wild Weasel'*: *69-0304*, *69-0306*, *69-7201*, *69-7202*, *69-7204* to *69-7220*, *69-7223*, *69-7228*, *69-7231* to *69-7236*, *69-7251*, *69-7253*, *69-7254*, *69-7256* to *69-7260* (total of 37 aircraft).

Note: Unofficial reports state that *69-7237* to *69-7250* were shipped to Israel.

MCDONNELL F-4E-44-MC PHANTOM II 64 aircraft. BuAer Nos *69-7261* to *69-7273*, *69-7286* to *69-7303*, and *69-7546* to *69-7578* (Block 44).

69-7264 86th TFW, 3-74; 36th TFW, 10-74. *69-7265* 4th TFW, 9-75. *69-7272* 33d TFW,

10-74; 347th TFW, 9-77; 35th TFW, 9-79. **69-7290** 35th TFW, 8-79. **69-7294** 51st CW, 9-79. **69-7301** 35th TFW,. 8-79. **69-7546** 33d TFW, 10-76; 35th TFW, 11-78. **69-7551** 388th TFW, 4-74; 51st CW, 8-75. **69-7555** 3d TFW, 1-79. **69-7574** 347th TFW, 9-78; 35th TFW, 11-78. Following aircraft modified as **F-4G 'Wild Weasel':** **69-7261, 69-7263, 69-7270, 69-7272, 69-7286** to **69-7291, 69-7293, 69-7295, 69-7298, 69-7300** to **69-7303, 69-7546, 69-7550, 69-7556, 69-7558, 69-7560, 69-7561, 69-7566, 69-7571, 69-7572, 69-7574** (total of 36 aircraft).

MCDONNELL F-4E-45-MC PHANTOM II 11 aircraft. BuAer Nos *69-7579* to *69-7589* (Block 45).
69-7579 33d TFW, 10-75; 347th TFW, 9-78; 52d TFW, 6-79. **69-7585** 31st TFW, 11-78. **69-7589** 33d TFW, 9-77; ADTC, AFSC, 10-78. All aircraft, except **69-7585** and **69-7589**, modified as **F-4G 'Wild Weasel'** (total of nine aircraft).

MCDONNELL F-4E-46-MC PHANTOM II 16 aircraft. BuAer Nos *69-7711* to *69-7726* (Block 46). All aircraft supplied to Imperial Iranian Air Force.

MCDONNELL F-4E-47-MC PHANTOM II 16 aircraft. BuAer Nos *69-7727* to *69-7742* (Block 47). All aircraft supplied to Imperial Iranian Air Force.

MCDONNELL F-4E-48-MC PHANTOM II 24 aircraft. BuAer Nos *71-0224* to *71-0247* (Block 48).
71-0237 3d TFW, 1-79. **71-0241** crashed, 28-12.74. **71-0243** 4th TFW, 7-79. **71-0244** crashed, 7-1-76. **71-0247** 4th TFW, 9-78; 52d TFW, 5-79. Supplied to Israeli Air Force: **71-0224** to **71-0236, 71-0246.**

MCDONNELL-DOUGLAS F-4E-49-MC PHANTOM II 24 aircraft. BuAer Nos *71-1070* to *71-1093* (Block 49).
71-1070 57th FWW, 5-74; ADTC, AFSC, 10-76; crashed 25-4-77. **71-1075** 3d TFW, 1-79. **71-1091** crashed, 7-1-76. Supplied to Israeli Air Force: **71-1071, 71-1074, 71-1078, 71-1080, 71-1082, 71-1090, 71-1093.**

MCDONNELL-DOUGLAS F-4E-50-MC PHANTOM II 30 aircraft. BuAer Nos *71-1391* to *71-1402,* and *72-0121* to *72-0138* (Block 50).
71-1391 3d TFW, 1-79. **71-1397** 4th TFW, 7-79. **72-0122** 57th FWW, 10-75; 4th TFW, 9-78; 52d TFW, 9-79. **72-0125** 4th TFW; crashed Raleigh, North Carolina, 13-4-78. Supplied to Israeli Air Force: **71-1393** to **71-1396, 71-1398** to **71-1402, 72-0121, 72-0123,** **72-0127, 72-0129** to **72-0133, 72-0137** to **72-0138.**

MCDONNELL-DOUGLAS F-4E-51-MC PHANTOM II 31 aircraft. BuAer Nos *71-1094* to *71-1109, 71-1779* to *71-1784, 72-0139* to *72-0144,* and *72-0157* to *72-0159* (Block 51).
72-0139 4th TFW, 9-78; 52d TFW, 5-79. **72-0144** 4th TFW, 7-79. Supplied to Israeli Air Force: **71-1094** to **71-1109, 71-1779** to **71-1784.**

MCDONNELL-DOUGLAS F-4E-52-MC PHANTOM II 28 aircraft. BuAer Nos *71-1110* to *71-1125, 71-1785* to *71-1790, 72-0160* to *72-0165* (Block 52).
72-0160 4th TFW, 7-79. **72-0165** 4th TFW, 10-77. Supplied to Imperial Iranian Air Force: **71-1110** to **71-1125.** Supplied to Israeli Air Force: **71-1785** to **71-1790.**

MCDONNELL-DOUGLAS F-4E-53-MC PHANTOM II 26 aircraft. BuAer Nos *71-1126* to *71-1141, 71-1791* to *71-1796, 72-0166* to *72-0168, 72-1407* (Block 53).
72-0166 4th TFW, 9-77. **72-0168** ADTC, AFSC, 10-79. **72-1407** 52d TFW, 6-79. Supplied to Imperial Iranian Air Force, **71-1126** to **71-1141.** Supplied to Israeli Air Force: **71-1791** to **71-1796.**

MCDONNELL-DOUGLAS F-4E-54-MC PHANTOM II 31 aircraft. BuAer Nos *71-1142* to *71-1146, 72-1476* to *72-1489, 72-1500* to *72-1511* (Block 54).
72-1476 crashed, 3-3-81. **72-1478** 4th TFW, 7-79. **72-1489** 4th TFW, 9-77. Supplied to Greece: **72-1500** to **72-1511.** Supplied to Israeli Air Force: **72-1480, 72-1481, 72-1487, 72-1488.**

MCDONNELL-DOUGLAS F-4E-55-MC PHANTOM II 26 aircraft. BuAer Nos *71-1147* to *71-1152, 72-1490* to *72-1497,* and *72-1512* to *72-1523* (Block 55).
72-1490 4th TFW, 7-79. **72-1494** 57th TTW, 10-79. Supplied to Imperial Iranian Air Force: **71-1147** to **71-1152.** Supplied to Greece: **72-1512** to **72-1523.** Supplied to Israeli Air Force: **72-1491, 72-1492, 72-1495** to **72-1497.**

MCDONNELL-DOUGLAS F-4E-56-MC PHANTOM II 28 aircraft. BuAer Nos *71-1153* to *71-1166, 72-1498, 72-1499, 72-1524* to *72-1535* (Block 56).
Supplied to Israeli Air Force: **72-1498, 72-1499.** Supplied to Imperial Iranian Air Force: **71-1153** to **71-1166** Supplied to Greece: **72-1524** to **72-1535.**

MCDONNELL-DOUGLAS F-4E-57-MC PHANTOM II 39 aircraft. BuAer Nos *73-1028* to *73-1042, 73-1157* to *73-1164, 73-1519* to *73-1534* (Block 57).

73-1160 4th TFW, 9-78; 57th TTW, 2-80. *73-1164* 4th TFW, 9-78; 57th TTW, 2-80. Supplied to Israeli Air Force: *73-1157* to *73-1159, 73-1161, 73-1162*. Supplied to Turkey: *73-1028* to *73-1042*. Supplied to Imperial Iranian Air Force: *73-1519* to *73-1534*.

MCDONNELL-DOUGLAS   F-4E-58-MC PHANTOM II 48 aircraft. BuAer Nos *73-1043* to *73-1055, 73-1165* to *73-1184* and *73-1535* to *73-1549* (Block 58).

73-1165 4th TFW, 7-79. *73-1174* crashed 8-12-81. *73-1177* 4th TFW, crashed Dane County range, North Carolina, 2-4-79. *73-1180* crashed, 23-3-82. Supplied to Turkey: *73-1043* to *73-1055*. Supplied to Imperial Iranian Air Force: *73-1535* to *73-1549*. Supplied to Israeli Air Force: *73-1169, 73-1170, 73-1178, 73-1179*.

MCDONNELL-DOUGLAS   F-4E-59-MC PHANTOM II 25 aircraft. BuAer Nos *73-1185* to *73-1204*, and *73-1550* to *73-1554* (Block 59).

73-1185 33d TFW, 10-76. *73-1192* 4th TFW, written off, Raleigh, North Carolina, 13-4-78. *73-1200* 4th TFW, 7-79; crashed, 3-9-80. Supplied to Imperial Iranian Air Force: *73-1550* to *73-1554*. Supplied to Israeli Air Force: *73-1190, 73-1191, 73-1201, 73-1202*.

MCDONNELL-DOUGLAS   F-4E-60-MC PHANTOM II 34 aircraft. BuAer Nos *74-0643* to *74-0660, 74-1014, 74-1015, 74-1038* to *74-1049, 74-1618, 74-1619* (Block 60).

74-0643 57th TTW, 11-78; 4th TFW, 7-79. *74-0650* 32d TFS, 8-78; 86th TFW, 4-79. *74-0651* crashed, 1-12-78. *74-0658* 57th TTW, 11-78. *74-0660* 52d TFW, crashed, 23-8-81. *74-1046* 32d TFS, 9-77; 86th TFW, crashed 2-3-79. Supplied to Israeli Air Force: *74-1014, 74-1015*. Supplied to Greece: *74-1618, 74-1619*.

MCDONNELL-DOUGLAS   F-4E-61-MC PHANTOM 11 42 aircraft. BuAer Nos *74-0661* to *74-0666, 74-1016* to *74-1021, 74-1050* to *74-1061, 74-1620* to *74-1637* (Block 61).

74-0661 57th TTW, 10-78. *74-0664* 32d TFS, 9-78; 86th TFW, 4-79. *74-1051* 32d TFS; crashed Terschelling, 29-8-77. *74-1058* 50th TFW; crashed Heilbronn, 27-4-77. *74-1620* 50th TFW, 3-79. *74-1637* 86th TFW, 8-79. Supplied to Israeli Air Force: *74-1016* to *74-1021*.

MCDONNELL-DOUGLAS   F-4E-62-MC PHANTOM II 32 aircraft. BuAer Nos *74-1022* to *74-1037*, and *74-1638* to *74-1653* (Block 62).

74-1638 86th TFW, 3-79. *74-1646* 33d TFW; crashed 12-5-81. *74-1653* 86th TFW, 8-79. Supplied to Israeli Air Force: *74-1022* to *74-1037*.

MCDONNELL-DOUGLAS   F-4E-63-MC PHANTOM II 46 aircraft. BuAer Nos *75-0222* to *75-0257*, and *75-0628* to *75-0637* (Block 63). Supplied to Imperial Iranian Air Force: *75-0222* to *75-0257*. Supplied to German *Luftwaffe: 75-0628* to *75-0637*.

MCDONNELL-DOUGLAS   F-4E-64-MC PHANTOM II 37 aircraft. BuAer Nos *75-0638* to *75-0655*, and *76-0493* to *76-0511* (Block 64). Supplied to South Korea: *76-0493* to *75-0511*.

MCDONNELL-DOUGLAS   F-4E-65-MC PHANTOM II 24 aircraft. BuAer Nos *77-0277* to *77-0300* (Block 65).

MCDONNELL-DOUGLAS   F-4E-66-MC PHANTOM II 8 aircraft. BuAer Nos *77-0301* to *77-0308* (Block 66).

MCDONNELL-DOUGLAS   F-4E-67-MC PHANTOM II 18 aircraft. BuAer Nos *78-0727* to *78-0744* (Block 67). All aircraft supplied to South Korea.

MCDONNELL-DOUGLAS   RF-4E-MC PHANTOM II 150 aircraft (reconnaissance versions of F-4E to overseas customers' requirements; powerplant details as for F-4E). 13 production Blocks (43-47, 61-64 and 66-69).

MCDONNELL-DOUGLAS   RF-4E-43-MC PHANTOM II 8 aircraft for Luftwaffe. BuAer Nos *69-7448* to *69-7455* (Block 43).

MCDONNELL-DOUGLAS   RF-4E-44-MC PHANTOM II 7 aircraft for Luftwaffe. BuAer Nos *69-7456* to *69-7462* (Block 44).

MCDONNELL-DOUGLAS   RF-4E-45-MC PHANTOM II 20 aircraft for Luftwaffe. BuAer Nos *69-7463* to *69-7482*; 6 aircraft for Israeli Air Force. BuAer Nos *69-7590* to *69-7595* (Block 45).

MCDONNELL-DOUGLAS   RF-4E-46-MC PHANTOM II 28 aircraft for Luftwaffe. BuAer Nos *69-7483* to *69-7510* (Block 46).

MCDONNELL-DOUGLAS   RF-4E-47-MC PHANTOM II 25 aircraft for Luftwaffe. BuAer Nos *69-7511* to *69-7535* (Block 47).

MCDONNELL-DOUGLAS   RF-4E-61-MC PHANTOM II 4 aircraft for Imperial Iranian Air Force. BuAer Nos *74-1725* to *74-1728* (Block 61).

MCDONNELL-DOUGLAS   RF-4E-62-MC PHANTOM II 8 aircraft for Imperial Iranian Air Force. BuAer Nos *74-1729* to *74-1736* (Block 62).

MCDONNELL-DOUGLAS   RF-4E-63-MC

The 3,000th Phantom, an F-4J for the US Navy (McDonnell Douglas, Neg No 349-12, dated September 1968).

PHANTOM II 6 aircraft for Israeli Air Force. BuAer Nos *75-0418* to *75-0423* (Block 63).
MCDONNELL-DOUGLAS RF-4E-64-MC PHANTOM II 6 aircraft. BuAer Nos *75-0656* to *75-0661* (Block 64).
MCDONNELL-DOUGLAS RF-4E-66-MC PHANTOM II 8 aircraft for Greece. BuAer Nos *77-0309* to *77-0316* (Block 66).
MCDONNELL-DOUGLAS RF-4E-67-MC PHANTOM II 6 aircraft for Greece. BuAer Nos *77-1761* to *77-1766* (Block 67).
MCDONNELL-DOUGLAS RF-4E-68-MC PHANTOM II 6 aircraft for Imperial Iranian Air Force. BuAer Nos *78-0751* to *78-0754, 78-0788, 78-0854*. (Block 68). Not delivered.
MCDONNELL-DOUGLAS RF-4E-69-MC PHANTOM II 10 aircraft for Imperial Iranian Air Force. BuAer Nos *78-0855* to *78-0864* (Block 69). Not delivered.

MCDONNELL-DOUGLAS F-4F-MC PHANTOM II 164 aircraft for *Luftwaffe*. Specification similar to F-4E (slatted). F-4F-51-MC, *72-1111* to *72-1124* (14 aircraft); F-4F-52-MC, *72-1125* to *72-1137* (13 aircraft); F-4F-52-MC, *72-1138* to *72-1150* (13 aircraft); F-4F-54-MC, *72-1151* to *72-1164* (14 aircraft); F-4F-55-MC, *72-1165* to *72-1182* (18 aircraft); F-4F-56-MC, *72-1183* to *72-1206* (23 aircraft); F-4F-57-MC, *72-1207* to *72-1230* (14 aircraft); F-4F-58-MC, *72-1231* to *72-1254* (24 aircraft); F-4F-59-MC, *72-1255* to *72-1285* (31 aircraft). Became Nos *3706* to *3869* in Luftwaffe.
Note BuAer Nos *72-1116* to *72-1123* also flew with the USAF's 35th TFW in 1975; and *72-1118* flew with AFFTC, AFSC, in 1978.
MCDONNELL F-4G PHANTOM II (US Navy Designation) 12 aircraft within F-4B-14-MC production batch: BuAer Nos *150481,*

Two views of the 5,000th Phantom, an F-4E, during manufacture in 1978 (McDonnell Douglas, Neg Nos 6273-29 and -33, dated February 1978).

150484, 150487, 150489, 150492, 150625, 150629, 150633, 150636, 150639, 150642, 150645. Featured RCA AN/ASW-21 two-way digital data link. First flight by *150481*, March 20 1963. All served in turn with Navy Fighter Squadrons VF-96, VF-121 and VF-213 (VF-116). Most subsequently converted to F-4N.

MCDONNELL F-4J PHANTOM II Two prototypes, YF-4J (within F-4B-19-MC Block). BuAer Nos *151496* and *151497*. 522 production aircraft in 22 Blocks (26-47). General Electric J79-GE-10 engines, Westinghouse AN/AWG-10 pulse Doppler fire control system and Lear-Siegler AJB-7 bombing system. First flight by production aircraft (*153071*), May 27 1966.

MCDONNELL F-4J-26-MC PHANTOM II 5 aircraft. BuAer Nos *153071* to *153075* (Block 26).
153071 NATC, SATD. *153072* MAC. *153073* PMTC. *153074* PMTC. *153075* crashed 1969.

MCDONNELL F-4J-27-MC PHANTOM II 13 aircraft. BuAer Nos *153076* to *153088* (Block 27).
153076 Converted to EF-4J; NWC. *153077* NATC. *153078* crashed 1969. *153079* crashed 1973. *153083* crashed 1973. *153084* NATC. *153088* '7T-121', NATC.

MCDONNELL F-4J-28-MC PHANTOM II 12 aircraft. BuAer Nos *153768* to *153779* (Block 28).
153768 NATC. *153773* 'AD-203', VF-171. *153775* crashed 7-11-77. *153776* 'AA-203', VF-74. *153777* 'AA-201', VF-74. *153779* 'DN-101', VMFA-333.

MCDONNELL F-4J-29-MC PHANTOM II 20 aircraft. BuAer Nos *153780* to *153799* (Block 29).
153780 'NJ-213', VF-151. *153783* 'DN-101', VMFA-333. *153785* 'SH-12', VMFAT-101. *153795* '7T-106', NATC. *153796* 'AA-207', VF-74. *153799* crashed 1972.

MCDONNELL F-4J-30-MC PHANTOM II 40 aircraft. BuAer Nos *153800* to *153839* (Block 30).
153812 '7T-103', NATC. *153821* 'DW-10', VMFA-251. *153827* 'NJ-165', VF-121.

MCDONNELL F-4J-31-MC PHANTOM II 37 aircraft. BuAer Nos *153840* to *153876* (Block 31).
153850 'SH-30', VMFAT-101. *153854* Crashed 13-9-72. *153865* Crashed 1970.

MCDONNELL F-5J-32-MC PHANTOM II 40 aircraft. BuAer Nos *153877* to *153911*, and *154781* to *154785* (Block 32).

153885 crashed 23-12-72. *153892* '7T-107', NATC. *154785* 'SH-23', VMFAT-101.

MCDONNELL F-4J-33-MC PHANTOM II 69 aircraft. BuAer Nos *154786* to *154788*, and *155504* to *155569* (Block 33).
155505 'SH-05', VMFAT-101. *155523* VMFAT-312. *155526* Crashed 11-9-71. *155529* 'AD-204', VF-171. *155543* 'VE-104', VMFA-115. *155553* 'AE-212', VF-33, 1968; Lieutenant Roy Cash, USN, shot down MiG-21, 10-7-68, Vietnam. *155556* Crashed, 20-11-79. *155563* '92', PMTC.

MCDONNELL F-4J-34-MC PHANTOM II 65 aircraft. BuAer Nos *155570* to *155580*, and *155731* to *155784* (Block 34).
155737 crashed 1972. *155748* 'AD-200', VF-171. *155761* 'AE-212', VF-33.

MCDONNELL F-4J-35-MC PHANTOM II 59 aircraft. BuAer Nos *155785* to *155843* (Block 35).
155788 crashed 1969. *155800* 'NG-100', VF-96, 1972; Lieutenant Randy Cunningham, USN, shot down three MiG-17s, 10-5-72, Vietnam. *155803* crashed 10-7-72. *155823* 'VE-110', VMFA-115.

MCDONNELL F-4J-36-MC PHANTOM II 23 aircraft. BuAer Nos *155844* to *155866* (Block 36).
155846 'NK-214', VF-142, CVAN-65, 1972; Lieutenant (jg) Scott Davis, USN, shot down MiG-21, 28-12-72, Vietnam., *155852* 'AA-210', VF-74.

MCDONNELL F-4J-37-MC PHANTOM II 8 aircraft. BuAer Nos *155867* to *155874* (Block 37).
155872 'DW-7', VMFA-251. *155873* crashed 1971.

MCDONNELL F-4J-38-MC PHANTOM II 15 aircraft. BuAer Nos *155875* to *155889* (Block 38).
155880 'AD-214', VF-171. *155884* crashed 27-2-71. *155887* 'WT-11', VMFA-232.

MCDONNELL F-4J-39-MC PHANTOM II 13 aircraft. BuAer Nos *155890* to *155902* (Block 39).
155894 'SH-16', VMFAT-101. *155895* crashed 1974. *155898* 'SH-15', VMFAT-101.

MCDONNELL F-4J-40-MC PHANTOM II 19 aircraft. BuAer Nos *157242* to *157260* (Block 40).
157245 'NH-201', VF-114, CVA-63, 1972; Lieutenant Commander Pete Pettigrew, USN, shot down MiG-21, 6-5-72, Vietnam. *157251* 'SH-17', VMFAT-101. *157258* 'SH-30', VMFAT-101.

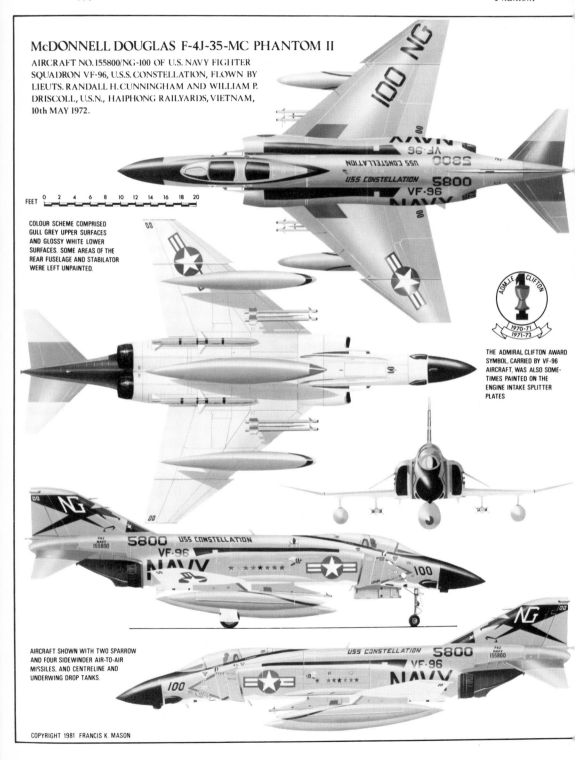

McDONNELL DOUGLAS F-4J-35-MC PHANTOM II

AIRCRAFT NO.155800/NG-100 OF U.S. NAVY FIGHTER
SQUADRON VF-96, U.S.S. CONSTELLATION, FLOWN BY
LIEUTS. RANDALL H. CUNNINGHAM AND WILLIAM P.
DRISCOLL, U.S.N., HAIPHONG RAILYARDS, VIETNAM,
10th MAY 1972.

FEET 0 2 4 6 8 10 12 14 16 18 20

COLOUR SCHEME COMPRISED
GULL GREY UPPER SURFACES
AND GLOSSY WHITE LOWER
SURFACES. SOME AREAS OF THE
REAR FUSELAGE AND STABILATOR
WERE LEFT UNPAINTED.

THE ADMIRAL CLIFTON AWARD
SYMBOL, CARRIED BY VF-96
AIRCRAFT, WAS ALSO SOME-
TIMES PAINTED ON THE
ENGINE INTAKE SPLITTER
PLATES

AIRCRAFT SHOWN WITH TWO SPARROW
AND FOUR SIDEWINDER AIR-TO-AIR
MISSILES, AND CENTRELINE AND
UNDERWING DROP TANKS.

COPYRIGHT 1981 FRANCIS K. MASON

MCDONNELL F-4J-41-MC PHANTOM II
13 aircraft. BuAer Nos *157261* to *157273* (Block 41).
157267 'NG-112', VF-96, CVA-64, 1972; Lieutenant Randy Cunningham, USN, shot down MiG-21 on 19-1-72, and MiG-17 on 8-5-72, Vietnam. *157268* 'SH-06', VMFAT-101. *157271* crashed 18-12-79.

MCDONNELL F-4J-42-MC PHANTOM II
13 aircraft. BuAer Nos *155903*, and *157274* to *157285* (Block 42).
157275 crashed 13-4-80. *157281* VMFAT-101. *157282* 'AD-200', VF-171. *157285* VMFA-312.

MCDONNELL F-4J-43-MC PHANTOM II
12 aircraft. BuAer Nos *157286* to *157297* (Block 43).
157293 'AC-101', VF-31, CVA-60, 1972; Commander Sam Flynn shot down MiG-21, 21-6-72, Vietnam. *157294* VMFAT-101. *157296* 'SH-34', VMFAT-101.

MCDONNELL F-4J-44-MC PHANTOM II
12 aircraft. BuAer Nos *157298* to *157309* (Block 44).
157301 'SH-36', VMFAT-101. *157302* Crashed 8-9-72. *157304* 'SH-33', VMFAT-101. *157305* 'AD-220', VF-171.

MCDONNELL F-4J-45-MC PHANTOM II
9 aircraft. BuAer Nos *158346* to *158354* (Block 45).

MCDONNELL F-4J-46-MC PHANTOM II
11 aircraft. BuAer Nos *158355* to *158365* (Block 46).
158356 'SH-13', VMFAT-101. *158358* 'SH-10', VMFAT-101. *158359* 'SH-22', VMFAT-101.

MCDONNELL F-4J-47-MC PHANTOM II
14 aircraft. BuAer Nos *158366* to *158379* (Block 47).
158369 'SH-04', VMFAT-101. *158371* crashed 7-1-80. *158372* VMFA-333.

MCDONNELL-DOUGLAS F-4K-MC PHANTOM FG MARK 1 Two prototype YF-4K, *XT595* and *XT596* ordered in 1965 by Great Britain, followed by orders for 59 production aircraft, of which 52 were delivered. *XT597, XT598, XT857-XT876*, and *XV565-XV592*. Two Rolls-Royce Spey 202/203 turbofans each of 20,350 lb-thrust with afterburner lit. AWG-11 fire control system. First flight by *XT595*, June 27 1966. Last delivery, 21-11-69. (All following squadrons of the Royal Navy.)
XT597 A&AEE. *XT857* 'U', No 892 Sqn. *XT859* 'VL-725', No 700P Sqn. *XT860* 'VL-726', No 700P Sqn.; 'R-014', No 892 Sqn. *XT861* 'V', No 892 Sqn. *XT864* 'VL-151', No 767 Sqn. *XT865* No 700P Sqn; 'VL-156', No 767 Sqn. *XT866* 'VL-158', No 767 Sqn. *XT867* 'VL-152', No 767 Sqn. *XT868* 'R-001', No 892 Sqn. *XT872* 'R-001', No 892 Sqn. *XV568* and *XV569*, No 892 Sqn.

MCDONNELL-DOUGLAS F-4M-MC PHANTOM FGR MARK 2 Two prototype YF-4M, *XT852* and *XT853*, ordered in 1965 by Great Britain, followed by orders for 150 production aircraft, of which 118 were delivered. *XT891-XT914, XV393-XV442*, and *XV460-XV501*. Powerplant as for F-4K. AWG-12 fire control system. First flight by *XT852*, 17-2-67. (All following Squadrons of the Royal Air Force.) Some Phantom FG Mark 1s also transferred from Royal Navy to Royal Air Force.
XT891 'Z', No 56 Sqn. *XT900* 'E', No 228 OCU. *XT910* 'T', No 2 Sqn. *XT912* 'K', No 23 Sqn. *XV397* 'K', No 23 Sqn. *XV398* No 228 OCU. *XV400* 'A', No 6 Sqn. *XV401* No 228 OCU. *XV403* 'A', No 54 Sqn. *XV408* 'N', No 23 Sqn. *XV411* 'S', No 92 Sqn. *XV417* 'E', No 2 Sqn. *XV418* No 92 Sqn. *XV422* No 14 Sqn. *XV426* 'Q', No 111 Sqn. *XV428* 'E', No 19 Sqn. *XV432* No 6 Sqn. *XV433* 'X', No 29 Sqn. *XV464* 'B', No 56 Sqn. *XV465* 'G', No 41 Sqn. *XV467* 'Q', No 92 Sqn. *XV480* No 31 Sqn. *XV485* 'W', No 2 Sqn. *XV487* No 17 Sqn. *XV492* 'Q', No 6 Sqn. *XV500* 'M', No 111 Sqn.

MCDONNELL-DOUGLAS F-4N-MC PHANTOM II 228 aircraft converted from F-4B (ex-Blocks 12 to 28), becoming F-4N-1-MC to F-4N-46-MC, under Conversion in Lieu of Procurement (CILOP) at the Naval Air Rework Facility, North Island NAS, California (Project Bee Line). 22 aircraft further converted to QF-4N drones (BuAer Nos *150412, 150415, 150489, 151004, 151435, 151455, 151461, 151471, 151475, 152222, 152223, 152229, 152235, 152243, 152253, 152258, 152281, 152303, 152321, 153011, 153053, 153065*).
150407 MASDC. *150442* 'AF-101', VF-201. *150456* 'MG-2', VMFA-321. *150464* 'NK-202', VF-154. *151444* 'NK-206', VF-21' *151449* 'VW-4', VMFA-314. *151463* 'AF-203', VF-202. *151503* 'AF-107', VF-201. *152217* 'EC-01', VMFA-531. *152246* 'MA-6', VMA-112. *152278* 'ND-100', VF-301. *152965* 'AD-253', VF-171.

Top *The 5,000th Phantom, An F-4E-65-MC, 77-0290; colour scheme was predominantly white with medium blue spine and fin leading edge; a pale blue flash extended from air intake to the rudder trailing edge with 11 national flags superimposed; the outer wing panels were striped light blue, white and (outboard) medium blue. The nose inscription was in red* (McDonnell Douglas, Neg No 47-35, dated March 1978).

Above *The last Saint Louis-built Phantom, No 5057, an F-4E* (McDonnell Douglas, Neg No 8522-73, dated October 1979).

MCDONNELL-DOUGLAS F-4S-MC PHANTOM II 265 aircraft converted from F-4J under CILOP. Modified General Electric J79-GE-10B engines. Majority of aircraft delivered to US Marine Corps. First trial conversion was *158360*. First 47 aircraft were without slats on conversion (being retrofitted later); remainder with slats from the outset. Deliveries commenced in 1978.
153780 'NJ-213', VF-151. *153800* 'DC-11', VMFA-122. *153804* 'ND-106', VF-301 *153805* 'DB-05', VMFA-235, *153807* 'VE-101', VMFA-115. *153821* 'DW-10', VMFA-251. *153840* 'NJ-160', VF-121. *153881* 'NF-105', VF-161. *153903* 'DR-1', VMFA-312. *155531* 'ND-213', VF-302. *155539* 'XF-1', VX-4. *155545* 'DN-102', VMFA-333. *155773* 'AA-111', VF-74. *155820* 'VM-07', VMFA-451. *155841* 'SH-27', VMFAT-101. *155901* crashed 23-11-79. *158378* 'WD-13', VMFA-212.

Bibliography

The F-4 Phantom II, G.G. O'Rourke, Arco Publishing Co Inc, USA, 1969.

The F-4 Phantom II, Richard E. Gardner, Almarks Co Inc, USA, 1970.

McDonnell F-4 Phantom II (Parts 1 and 2), R. Ward and R. Francillon, Osprey Publications Ltd, London 1973.

Report MDC A2257 (Phantom II), McDonnell Aircraft Company, Saint Louis, 1973.

. . . And Kill MIGs, L. Drendel, Squadron/Signal Publications, Texas, USA, 1974.

Projectair/Phantom II (parts 1 and 2), J. Dewar Publications, Scotland, 1975.

Configuration Studies, F/RF-4 Phantom, McDonnell Aircraft Company, Saint Louis, 1976.

Phantom II, A Pictorial History, L. Drendel, Squadron/Signal Publications, Texas, USA, 1977.

F-4 Phantom, W.T. Gunston, Ian Allan Ltd, London, 1977.

International Phantoms, McDonnell Aircraft Company, Saint Louis, 1980.

F-4 Phantom II (Parts 1 and 2), B. Kinsey, Aero Publishers, USA/Arms and Armour Press, London, 1981, 1982.

Index